PRAISE FOR *20 SOMETHING, 20 EVERYTHING*

"Timeless and insightful, *20 Something, 20 Everything* is a must-read guide for women in their twenties to create inner balance and take responsibility for their life choices."

— Tracy McWilliams, author of *Dress to Express*

"Christine Hassler, an honest and extremely wise woman, shows us how to transform fear and confusion into courage and solutions. This inspiring guide demonstrates that knowing who you are and believing in yourself enough to go after your dreams are not impossible goals but part of the journey we call life. I highly recommend this wonderful book!"

— Sandy Grason, author of *Journalution: Journaling to Awaken Your Inner Voice, Heal Your Life, and Manifest Your Dreams*

20 SOMETHING
20 EVERYTHING

20 SOMETHING
20 EVERYTHING

A Quarter-Life Woman's Guide
to Balance and Direction

CHRISTINE HASSLER

NEW WORLD LIBRARY
NOVATO, CALIFORNIA

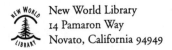 New World Library
14 Pamaron Way
Novato, California 94949

Cover design by Mary Ann Casler and Christina Landers
Text design and typography by Tona Pearce Myers

"Once in a Lifetime" by David Byrne, Chris Frantz, and Tina Weymouth © 1980 WB Music Corp. (ASCAP), Index Music, Inc. (ASCAP), and EG Music Ltd. (PRS). All rights on behalf of itself and Index Music, Inc. administered by WB Music Corp. All rights reserved. Used by permission from Warner Brothers Publications, U.S., Inc., Miami, Florida 33014.

Library of Congress Cataloging-in-Publication Data
Hassler, Christine.
  Twenty something, twenty everything : a quarter-life woman's guide to balance and direction / Christine Hassler.
      p.   cm.
Includes index.
ISBN 1-57731-476-x (pbk. : alk. paper)
  1. Young women—Conduct of life. 2. Young women—Life skills guides. I. Title: 20 something, 20 everything. II. Title.
HQ1229.H287 2005
646.7'0084'22—dc22   2004030827

First printing, May 2005
ISBN 1-57731-476-x
ISBN-13 978-1-57731-476-9

Printed in Canada on partially recycled, acid-free paper

New World Library is dedicated to preserving the earth and its resources. We are now printing 50% of our new titles on 100% chlorine-free postconsumer waste recycled paper. As members of the Green Press Initiative (www.greenpressinitiative.org), our goal is to use 100% recycled paper for all of our titles by 2007.

Distributed to the trade by Publishers Group West

10 9 8 7 6 5 4 3 2 1

*I dedicate this book to each woman who has shared
and continues to share her life with me. Your honesty, humor,
and wisdom are invaluable.*

———⊷⊷⊷———

CONTENTS

PART 3: RELATIONSHIPS AND CAREER DURING YOUR
QUARTER-LIFE

LIST OF EXERCISES

MY STORY

At the age of twenty-eight, let me begin by saying that my twenty-something years definitely have been my twenty-everything years. They simply have not been the type of "everything" that I thought they would be. I know that many other twenty-something women can relate to this feeling. After all, we are young women in a society where an unbelievable amount of attention is focused on doing and having it all — it's only a matter of time before Prozac becomes an impulse buy at Starbucks. Imagine walking into a local coffee shop and saying, "I'll take a grande latte and 50 milligrams of happy pills — oh, and would you add a shot of pheromones so I can attract the man of my dreams, and a crystal ball so I can see if this career I work so hard at will pay off?" If such an order were possible, my coffee habit would have become a serious addiction by now.

You see, I've undergone my own twenty-something crisis. I've always been an overachiever who put a ton of pressure on myself. I graduated from a top-ten university after spending three and a half years stressing myself out to get As, a double major, and a few jobs under my belt. Before the ink on my diploma was dry, I moved to Los Angeles to pursue my dream of working in the entertainment industry. I did not know exactly what I wanted to do, but I assumed that once I got to L.A., things would fall into place. My first job was answering phones at a talent agency for $250 a week. Later I went from job to job in the industry, trying to figure out how I could move from an assistant to an executive position.

At twenty-five, I ended up as a television literary agent at one of the most prestigious entertainment companies in Los Angeles. I had an office with a view, an assistant who answered my phone, an expense account, a real salary, power lunches, industry screenings, clients, and business cards. I dated and attended industry events. From the outside, my life looked great. I appeared successful and well on my way to having it all. There was just one problem: I was absolutely miserable.

Daily I tried to talk myself into liking my job. I had spent four years building my career, not to mention the hundred thousand dollars (yikes!) invested in my education to prepare me for it. I felt obligated to stay on my track, but the long hours, the rude people, the cutthroat competition, the boys'-club environment, and the fact that I hated what I did every day made me sick. I had migraines at least twice a week, the stress threw my hormones completely out of whack, and I was becoming quite a bitch. In order to save myself from a total meltdown, I quit.

Leaving my prestigious career changed most of my circumstances, except one. I was still miserable. Completely burned out and craving a total change of direction, I became a personal trainer. I thought I would love a career in the health business; that it might be my "passion." Wrong again. Working in a gym was boring compared to the fast-paced life I had been living. I was even ashamed to admit to people that I was a trainer and spent my days counting to twelve. I felt as if I had been just floating along ever since I had left my Hollywood gig.

During this time, my boyfriend and I moved in together. We were very much in love, the perfect couple (people even called us Ken and Barbie). Yet our prenuptial cohabitation infuriated my mother to the point of freak-out. She said things I never dreamt she would say to me. We did not speak for a while. This devastated me, as we had always been close. For the first time, I felt that the umbilical cord connecting me to my family had been severed.

When I hit the ripe age of twenty-six, an age by which I had always thought my adult life would really be shaping up, my wonderful boyfriend proposed to me in the most amazing and romantic way. I was in utter bliss (for a while). I was getting married, my mom and I made up, and my future seemed more certain. But then reality set in again: problems with his family; feelings of hesitation about the wedding; ongoing dissatisfaction with myself, my body, my career. By my twenty-seventh birthday, I did not feel much like celebrating. And I felt guilty about my depression because I did have a loving fiancé, a supportive family who would do anything for me, a great opportunity to build a business as a trainer, and terrific friends. Why was I so unhappy?

One month later, the ground completely fell out from under me. In a premarital counseling session, my fiancé told me that he loved me but did not want to marry me. He did not even want to work on our relationship. I fell apart; he was the one thing that I had thought was definite in my life, and in the space of an hour, I lost him. The person I thought was my soul mate was gone just as my ambition and self-confidence had disappeared. I then had to deal with finding a place to live, trying to make more money, and unplanning a wedding. The hurt, embarrassment, and shock of a breakup was something I had never planned on facing. I felt as if I had hit rock bottom — no career, no relationship, no money, and really not much love for myself or my life in general. I lost about twenty pounds, got very depressed, and faced each day with knots in my stomach. In my twenties, I went from having everything I had thought I wanted to having nothing at all. I felt like I was already having a life crisis when my adult life was just beginning.

I had two choices: I could throw in the towel, move home, and try to forget about the life I had failed at; or I could dig in, look at my life, and try to figure out who I really was, what I really wanted, and how I was going to get it. Well, I guess the decision I made is fairly obvious. Let me introduce myself. My name is Christine Hassler, and I am a survivor of a twenty-something crisis.

ACKNOWLEDGMENTS

I feel deeply blessed to know so many people who have touched my life and thus made this book possible. To name just a few: Monika, the best friend I waited my whole life to find; Mona, a wonderful teacher; Jodi; Brett; J.; Janae; Mike; Jan; Noah Lukeman; Georgia Hughes; Marc Hankin, an amazing lawyer and advisor; and my trusted mentor, Karen Gilbert.

I am grateful to my friends and family, who have nurtured me through my journey of lessons, obstacles, and celebrations. I thank each of my clients, the members of the Sirens Society, and everyone from At Your Side for their unconditional support and loyalty. Finally, I would not be who or where I am today without those whose love for me fills my heart and soul daily: Dad, Mom, and Carrie. And I want to express my gratitude to Chris, who is my greatest gift and best partner.

WELCOME TO YOUR TWENTY-SOMETHING CRISIS

If you're reading this book, you probably have experienced challenges and setbacks similar to those I faced. When I started talking honestly about my life, and the frustrations and issues that were driving me crazy, I discovered that most of my girlfriends were in the same situation. We bonded over our shared sense that "nothing is really wrong, but nothing really feels right, either." None of us knew what to do about it, which inspired me to start investigating women's experiences of what has been called a mid-twenties breakdown, an early midlife, or perhaps the most popular label: a quarter-life crisis.

A "quarterlife crisis" is defined by the online dictionary Word Spy as "Feelings of confusion, anxiety, and self-doubt experienced by some people in their twenties, especially after completing their education." This phrase has been around since the early nineties but has really caught on as more and more twenty-somethings began to talk about it. Quarter-lifers feel the pressure to make their twenty-*something* years the time when *everything* needs to be decided from where to live, to what to do for a living, to who to live with. Since I felt like I was having one of my own, the issue of how twenty-something women experience an advanced midlife crisis fascinated me. Consequently, I began interviewing women between the ages of twenty-two and thirty-three about what I simply refer to as the "twenty-something crisis."

I began by just talking to my friends, who then starting talking to their friends, about their twenty-something experiences. So many of us had so much to talk about that I started a discussion and support group for twenty-something women out of my apartment in Los Angeles. We gathered monthly, and each meeting focused on a particular topic, from relationships to money to health. I also formulated a survey focusing on the issues and concerns of twenty-something women that eventually became the backbone of my research for this book. Thanks to Internet technology, the survey went all over the country (and even to a few other countries). Hundreds of women completed the survey, the majority of whom I did not know. Additionally, I polled women of our mothers' generation in a similar way. The twenty-something group, surveys, and additional one-on-one interviews I conducted afforded me a wealth of information about the concerns and experiences of twenty-something women who could relate to feeling like their lives were in crises.

Over the past four years, I have had the amazing opportunity to hear from hundreds of women in various circumstances, cities, and cultures. They were open, honest, and willing to share deep personal thoughts. I am grateful for their contribution to this book, which also guided me through critical moments in my own crisis and inspired me to get to my computer and write. Throughout my research, I immediately felt a connection to other twenty-something women as they shared this time in their lives. Here are two stories typical of those I heard.

At twenty-three, Loren admits that she feels like a complete and total mess. Everything in her life seems out of control, as if she were standing in the middle of a circle with every aspect of her life that she loves (such as her family) and everything she is searching for (such as a career) spinning wildly around her. "I am trying to grab on to anything, but it keeps slipping through my fingers. I know it sounds dramatic, but I can't even answer the question 'Who am I?' because I honestly feel like I have no clue, which only further sets me back." Loren always thought she knew what she wanted, but when faced with having to get it, she feels like a failure because she has only unanswered questions. Loren is unemployed, lives at home, is single, and hates the way she looks. But ever since she was a little girl, she had expected to have a great career and be engaged by age twenty-five. To make matters worse, she is surrounded by peers who brag about working for "Big Five" companies. Her friends are in serious relationships and seem happy with their lives. "Seeing all this has left me feeling so empty and like I am just floating along in life, going through the motions." The fact that she is miles from anything she pictured for herself makes her sick to her stomach. Loren is experiencing the typical symptoms of a twenty-something crisis.

At twenty-six, Clara has everything: a journalism degree from a reputable school, a promising job as a junior publicist at an elite magazine, an eclectic group of savvy, stylish friends, a token "Will" (a gay friend who goes to flea markets with her and actually tells her when she looks fat), a boyfriend named Steve who shares her religion, a gym membership, a cozy apartment full of scented candles, and a closet full of clothes she really can't afford but justifies for the "statements" they make. On the list of things that a twenty-something woman supposedly should have, Clara has each item checked off except one: happiness. "On my twenty-sixth birthday, I did not even want to get out of bed because I was unhappy, confused, and stressed out. I feel like I am doing all the right things, but they just are not clicking." On the outside, Clara has everything going for her, but inside she is haunted by questions such as "Am I climbing the right corporate ladder, and should I keep climbing it? Is Steve the one? Should I get engaged? How will I get far enough in my career that I have time to have babies? Do I even want kids? If so, will I keep working once I have them? Will I ever be content with my body? What is my passion?"

If you relate to Loren and/or Clara, you are experiencing symptoms of a twenty-something crisis, which is a common phenomenon that happens to many young women. Although the word *crisis* sounds rather dismal and drastic, do not fret — you have not been diagnosed with something unique or incurable. Quarter-life women all over the country are trying to do and have everything, but they are plagued by anxiety, confusion, and expectations. They describe their twenties as a time of struggle, saying things such as:

- "All of a sudden I feel lots of pressure from society about what a woman should be."

- "I do not feel like a grown-up because I am still learning about myself."

- "I immediately start pursuing what I think I want for a profession, then change my mind and start over. It is time of dating, living with others, breaking up, and establishing independence from my family."

- "I feel conflicted, knowing I need to break away from the security of my parents but not knowing how to do it and, quite honestly, not really wanting to."

- "This is a time of much needed self-discovery and tough learning experiences."

- "Being independent for the first time is scary, dramatic,

lonely, complicated, and harsh, yet at the same time empowering, educational, and exciting."

- "This is a time when I want to figure out who I am, what I want, and what my purpose is in life, but I seem to spend more time learning how much pressure I can handle."

- "I am still searching, trying to figure out what makes me tick and what my voice is in the world."

- "This is a time of everything at once, with a feeling that there is no room for error."

- "I experience misplaced energy from a weak sense of self. A lot of 'two steps forward, three steps back.'"

While a lot of attention has been paid to the midlife crisis and the changes that menopause bring to women, for the most part the changes that happen in our quarter-life are just recently being talked about. During the time when I was looking for answers and guidance, I searched the self-improvement sections of bookstores but always came up empty-handed. There were books that reported on the challenges we face in our twenties, but few that offered personal explanations or solutions. We are told that the twenties are "the time of our lives," yet many of us admit that we are not having much fun. We tuck away our fears and doubts while we try to figure out who we are and what we want. One twenty-seven-year-old woman describes this decade as "a time when the plans and ideals that you've been dreaming of for years come up against reality. You graduate from college and have to find your way in the real world. You learn that there is no perfect job. There is no perfect relationship. My friends and I have referred to this as a period of becoming jaded. Add to this the challenge of developing strategies to have a family and a career, and you get the special stress of being a twenty-something woman."

With thoughts such as these going through most twenty-somethings' minds, clearly we need to discuss and be conscious of what happens in our twenties — and we need some guidance on how to deal with it all. Our twenties are a turning point in our lives where we feel pressure to do, well, everything. As the security blankets of college and parents are peeled away, we are faced with finding jobs, building careers, perhaps moving to new cities, separating from our old support systems, taking care of our own finances, dating, marriage, thinking about children, starting families, making our first large investments, creating new social lives, watching our parents age, and shaping an identity to last the rest of our adulthood. Whew! That is more responsibility than we have ever been faced with.

So while our parents were showing us how to tie our shoes, teaching us to drive, and shipping us off to college, why didn't they warn us about this time in our lives? Most of us got the sex talk and learned a few family recipes; yet few of us were told about these confusing years, when our entire lives lie in front of us and it seems that any step we take will have momentous, lifelong consequences.

Though many of us would like to, we cannot fault our parents entirely. Their twenty-something experiences were just not the same. The concerns of a twenty-something woman today are unique to both our generation and our gender. We face different issues than our parents, particularly our mothers, faced. Our mothers were among the first generation of women who considered a wider range of life options (even though many of them followed traditional paths, working as secretaries, nurses, or teachers and giving up their careers when they had children). We are the first generation of women to grow up hearing, "You can be anything you want to be" and "You can have it all." We are the first to be raised by so many single parents. We are a generation who made eating disorders an epidemic and antidepressants as common as Advil. We watched MTV and sang along to "Like a Virgin." We were on birth control by the time we were sixteen. We made plastic surgery at a young age acceptable.

The generation gap became even clearer to me as I began to ask women of our mothers' generation to describe their experiences of their own twenties. For the most part, their feedback was very different from that of today's twenty-something women. For instance:

- "I was excited about a new sense of responsibility as I entered the real world."

- "I was happy about being a wife, living with a man for the first time, navigating a relationship, and building a home."

- "It was liberating to move away from home for the first time and to be free from needing permission to do things."

- "It was the happiest decade of my life; all my dreams were coming true."

- "I loved waking up every morning, since I was finding out for sure what I wanted and I believed."

What stands out from this feedback is that no one reported feeling a dramatic sense of pressure and expectation. A few mentioned being scared and challenged, yet the sense of being overwhelmed that I hear from women today was not there. Has the "anything is possible" mentality we grew up with made us feel that twenty-something has to become twenty-everything? Has a limitless number of choices created an inability to pick just one? Perhaps our endless options have made us unable to confidently embark on one path.

Now, you might be wondering, "What about men? Don't they experience this kind of crisis, too?" Generally, the answer is yes. The stress that the twenties dish out is a rite of passage for both sexes, since we all must carve out an identity and make life-changing decisions. However, many variables are unique to the female experience. First, women's roles have changed over the years. We've gone beyond being wives, mothers, and homemakers, while the traditional role of a man as provider has remained fairly consistent. Anyone (especially men) would agree that women differ from men psychologically and emotionally, which affects the way we handle our quarter-life issues. We nitpick, analyze, and scrutinize every aspect of our lives, and we tend to be more sensitive and more dramatic. Whether this is determined by our chromosomes or by our environment is irrelevant; it's just the truth. Additionally, physical alterations in our twenties set us apart from men. Thanks to hormones, our bodies tend to change more than theirs do (usually not in ways we are thrilled about), and we can become more obsessed with our physical appearance. Most men in their twenties can still eat a burger and fries, top it off with a six-pack of beer, and not feel guilty or bloated the next day. Women, on the other hand, struggle with eating disorders, diets, and discontentment with our bodies. And while we are dealing with our physical changes, we may also hear the distinct ticktock of the biological clock, made louder by research that tells us fertility declines with age. Unlike men, who can have children at almost any age, women who want babies feel that they have a deadline.

Differences between the male and female twenty-something experience also extend to the workplace. Things might be changing, but most companies are still run by men. Many of us work in predominantly male environments and face such things as boys' clubs, lack of mentoring, and possibly even sexual harassment. Meanwhile, we may encounter competition and little support from our female coworkers. It is also frustrating for us to witness our male counterparts living free from anxiety about balancing a career and children. They do not share our concern that our careers might backpedal if we have children. Plus, they never have to deal with PMS — it's just not fair.

Also, since we are generally more emotional than men, we might get caught up in feelings that can exacerbate our crisis-like moments. An analogy I often use is that men are like dressers, while women are like hot-air balloons. Like dressers, men have an amazing ability to compartmentalize their lives. When they pull out the "career drawer," they focus on it completely. They do not pull out the "relationship drawer" at the same time, because they know that would make the dresser fall over. Ever notice that when you have a fight with a guy, he can go to work and seem to forget about it? Or that two men can poke fun at each other and compete in the workplace but still go out for a beer and watch the game together? The same is not true for women. As with hot-air balloons, every little fire in our lives fuels our emotions, thoughts, and behaviors. For instance, if we have a terrible day at work, we rarely leave it there. We come home needing to talk about it, and it often affects our overall mood. Since we are less likely to take out one drawer at time, we are more likely to find aspects of our life more overwhelming than men do.

The fact that we are unique as a generation and a gender does not in itself produce the angst we feel during our quarter-life years. Such a crisis has many causes and layers, which I address throughout this book. But perhaps you feel that the word *crisis* doesn't apply to you, that maybe you don't really need to read this book. You might be experiencing angst in your twenties, but does angst really merit being called a crisis? Hearing that word can conjure up images of chaotic or drastic events, such as a natural disaster or the tragedies in country-western songs (losing your love, your dog, your wallet, and your job all on the same day). Let's turn to an expert for clarification. *Webster's* defines *crisis* as "an emotionally significant event or radical change of status in a person's life; the decisive moment; an unstable or crucial time or state of affairs in which a decisive change is impending; *especially* one with the distinct possibility of a highly undesirable outcome; a situation that has reached a critical phase." Well, I'd say that that accurately parallels how most women describe their twenties — but, of course, we use much more colorful language. You see, a crisis does not have to be life-threatening to warrant our attention. Many ordinary twenty-something transitions naturally lend themselves to the word *crisis*.

To determine whether you are experiencing symptoms of a twenty-something crisis, please take the following quiz. Read each question carefully and answer quickly with a simple yes or no:

1. Do you feel a need to "have it all"?

2. Do you feel older for the first time in your life?

3. Do you feel pressure to grow up and get your adult life in order?

4. Do you often feel depressed, overwhelmed, lost, and maybe even a little hopeless?

5. Do you ever feel that time is running out when you try to figure out your career and decide whether you want to get married and/or have children?

6. Are you stressed out by choices that seemingly will affect the rest of your life?

7. Do you feel that you have failed because you don't know what you want to do with your life?

8. Do you overanalyze yourself and your decisions?

9. Do you ever feel guilty for complaining about your life when you've lived only about a quarter of it?

10. Are you embarrassed that you have not figured out or accomplished more? ✓

    Total number of yes answers: **9**

If your total is five or more, welcome to your early midlife crisis! Don't worry; you are in good company. The feminine twenty-something crisis has become a bit of an epidemic; and sorry, ladies, there is no vaccine or antibiotic for this ailment. We are all just sweating it out. But is there a way to make this time in our lives a little more comfortable and a bit less of a crisis? *Yes!* And I can say that with confidence because I experienced my own twenty-something crisis.

This book is a guide to what has become a very difficult decade in a woman's life. I wrote it so that we — the daughters of feminists, hippies, wage earners, and homemakers — could share what we are going through and why it's happening. It is up to our generation of twenty-somethings to challenge the pressurized idea that today's young women must have it all and to champion the concept that the twenties are a time to discover our identity and goals while building a firm foundation for the rest of our lives. Our twenty-something years do not have to be so lonely, confusing, and treacherous. By addressing the questions we ask ourselves in our twenties and by providing ways to answer them, this book will guide you toward the contentment, balance, and direction you crave.

When I initially outlined this book, I was still trying to manage my own issues as I came into my quarter-life by attempting to fix, improve, change, or repair every aspect of my life. I always thought my relationships, career, and physical appearance should or could be different in a way that would make me feel more at peace. Yet no matter what I did, the gnawing feeling that something was not right was always present. My excuses — "I do not like this career because it is not the right fit for me" and "I am not happy in this relationship because he is not the right guy for me" — became tiresome. I was stuck in what I call "once/then" thinking. (I even thought about the process of writing this book in those terms: "*Once* I complete this book, *then* I'll be fulfilled, relieved, and successful.") As I realized that blaming my unhappiness on things outside myself was not working, I panicked. I distinctly remember thinking, "How am I going to write a book about how to get out of a crisis if I cannot even pull out of my own?" I started to look deeper within myself. There I found self-imposed roadblocks, cracks in my foundation, places where I had stepped on myself or tucked a part of myself into a corner, and times when I had twisted my own energy to adapt to someone else or to society. Once I started to free up my judgments about myself and discuss feelings I had in common with other women, an inner peace naturally began to come to me. I finally understood what underlies and precedes the moment(s) when we feel that we are having a life crisis. That understanding is what I am inspired to share with you. You already know how a twenty-something crisis feels. Are you ready to dig in and discover what to do about it?

Your journey through this book is organized into three parts. In part 1, I explain what I call the *twenties triangle*, a trio of concerns that frame most women's quarter-life struggles. Here you'll ask yourself essential questions that perhaps you have not yet been able to answer. In part 2, we investigate how secure your foundation is: how have you built the underpinnings of your life thus far, and how solid are they? Finally, in part 3, which is organized around the questions of the twenties triangle, we go deeper into the meaty issues of relationships and career. Although you might be tempted to skip ahead to part 3, it's critical to read the first two parts beforehand because they provide background information and help you clear out a lot of mental clutter.

Throughout the book, I include many stories from women of various ages, races, and backgrounds who struggle with common issues that twenty-something women are facing. To respect the privacy of the women quoted, I have used pseudonyms. Reading about and relating to each of these women can provide insight into your own life. Also scattered throughout the book are words of wisdom and valuable advice from women who are well beyond their quarter-life years.

Finally, each chapter presents questions to ask yourself and a variety of exercises that will get your juices flowing. The purpose of the exercises is to help you gain clarity and to take steps toward making your twenties the time of your life. I highly recommend that you write down all your answers to these exercises in a notebook. Please don't just do them in your head. Think of how many times you've told yourself that you'd keep a journal but never got around to it. Consider your notebook to be your working journal. I promise, it will be more fun than studying, more rewarding than going to a psychic, and cheaper than seeing a therapist.

Some exercises ask questions about your past. If you have trouble remembering anything, ask your parents, family, or friends for input, if that is appropriate for you. It's not a big deal if you are unable to answer some questions. Keep in mind that these are proactive exercises that often ask you to draw your own conclusions. Some exercises are very specifically guided, while others are freeform and encourage you to amend them or to ask your own questions. I have learned that all the answers we search for usually are inside ourselves (and always have been there). Sometimes finding them just requires a little investigation.

At the end of the book, you will find a Resources section that lists books and websites addressing various topics discussed throughout the book that you might find helpful. Each resource was recommended by women I surveyed or is one that I have discovered on my own journey through the questions of the twenties triangle.

You have taken a very important step toward loving your life by reading this book and being open to the information within it. I hope it will inspire you to start making changes in your life and to follow your heart rather than turning blindly onto a road paved by someone else's expectations. Remember, only you can change your life, your mind, or your future — it is just a matter of commitment and choice. Soon, you too will call yourself a twenty-something crisis survivor.

PART I

The Twenties Triangle

Our twenties are like a Neverland between childhood and adulthood. Our ambition and excitement about our future meet the endless opportunities that lie ahead of us. But not knowing how to harness our energy and choose among a great number of possibilities leads us to ask questions about ourselves, what we want, and how to get what we want (or think we want). Twenty-something women spend a lot of time wondering, planning, and feeling overwhelmed while searching for answers.

Picture this: You get into the cockpit of an airplane, thinking of the thousand places you'd love to fly to. But then you panic because you have not visited any of the destinations before and you have absolutely no idea of how to operate any of the gadgets in the plane. You're all packed and ready to go, but to where? And how? Most twenty-something women want to answer these questions, and until we do, we're on the ground, waiting for takeoff.

In the past, a woman's role was clearer. Now that the recipes have been shelved and the glass ceilings shattered, a young woman's choices and possible roles are endless. Facing innumerable options generates confusion. We hear over and over again that our goal as modern women is to have it all. It is no longer enough to be a devoted wife and mother or an extremely successful career woman. We must have great careers, because otherwise we will not be successful or able to call ourselves feminists. We have to be married by thirty-five; if we aren't, we might as well get some cats and take up knitting. We must have children, or we will not be complete. We must have a fabulous figure, or we will not be considered sexy or desirable. We are on a treadmill powered by our own expectations and those of our families, society, the media, and even one another, which has us running out of breath.

Unfortunately, this treadmill is not the kind that burns calories and gives us tighter butts. Instead, it runs us smack dab into the middle of what I call the twenties triangle. In my research and my own experience, I have found that twenty-something women ask themselves three distinct questions: Who am I? What do I want? How do I get what I want? These three questions, and the concerns that are generated by them, form the three points of the twenties triangle:

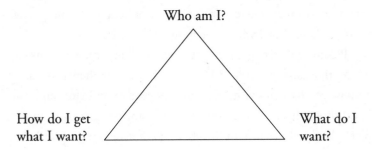

These questions are present in most, if not all, aspects of our lives: identity, independence, security, relationships, career and family.

Like the Bermuda Triangle, the twenties triangle can be mysterious, ominous, intriguing, and often scary. In fact, some of us find ourselves disappearing within it. The shape of a triangle visually represents many women's descriptions of life in their twenties: their life paths are jagged or go off in many different directions, and they feel confined. Many women confess to feeling that their lives are not flowing. Rather, everything feels haphazard, and they yearn for a sense of smoothness and ease. Since I am a visual person, another shape came to mind when I thought about that yearning: a circle. The balance, symmetry, smoothness, and completeness of a circle represent what we want in life.

If moving out of the confines of a triangle and into the peace and flow of a circle sounds appealing, begin by asking yourself the three questions of the twenties triangle, listed below in more detailed form. They are, perhaps, some of the most important questions we will ever ask ourselves. In your journal or notebook, thoughtfully respond to each question, writing as much as you can. Be honest (only you will ever see these answers), and avoid judging yourself or overanalyzing any of your responses. Take as much time as you need, and record your answers in list form.

1. Who am I? (Describe yourself. Include the reasons that you are the person you say you are.)

2. What do I want? (Take into account *all* aspects of your life.)

3. How do I get what I want or I think I want? (Include the ways in which you have already gotten or are in the process of getting what you want.)

Next, bookmark this exercise by dog-earing the page in your journal or notebook. These questions are each addressed repeatedly in the following three chapters, and you will be asked to refer back to your answers throughout the book's exercises. Again, please *do* try

"It was not until my late forties, after I had quit a career that I hated, that I realized I am the only person who can change my life. I am the deciding factor in my own happiness. I have the power to lead my life in any manner that I choose. I only wish I had gotten this in my twenties!"

— Shirley, fifty-two

to do the exercises (even if they seem silly or pointless), and remain open to the questions asked of you. Answering them may make a real difference in your life, and you'll get the full benefit of this book. Write and ponder as much as you can to jog your memory and jump-start your growth. The exercises are a good place for the overachiever in you to come out and play because they're designed to further your own development.

CHAPTER 1

WHO AM I?

From our first breath on this planet, we are influenced by our surroundings. Although each of us is born with an inherent personality and body type, for the most part we are molded by our environment. In our twenties, we have not yet had enough life experience to fully know who we are separate from our parents' and society's views of us. "Who am I?" we wonder. While this question about identity might seem somewhat ethereal, and the mystery of who you are cannot be solved by this book alone, we can start by breaking down the question into several smaller, more understandable parts. First, it is imperative to look at all the people and events in your life thus far that have had an impact on you.

TO BE OR NOT TO BE...LIKE MOM

When we are formulating our identity, we often look to role models for clues about how, what, and who to be. Perhaps our most significant female role models are the people who have been with us from the very beginning — our mothers. In fact, almost half the women I interviewed named their mothers as their primary role models and/or primary sources of influence. There is no doubt that our mothers — our relationship with them, their choices, their behavior, and our feelings about these things — have made significant impressions on us and will continue to affect our identity throughout our lives. If your mother was not in your life, think about the person you consider to be your main parental role model as you read through this section.

Heather is a twenty-five-year-old associate producer at a local news show. As the first woman in her family to go to college, she watched her mother live vicariously through her children while never doing anything for herself. Heather decided at a young age that she did not want to be like her mother, who never established an identity of her own. Her mother's life seemed boring, degrading, and, quite frankly, "beneath her." At her college graduation ceremony, Heather remembers, she gazed over at her mother, wishing she could truly connect and share the moment with her. Now, as Heather tackles the real world by herself, she is aware that "I often feel jealous of my girlfriends who have savvy working mothers who they can turn to for advice. I am even a little resentful that my mom did not really prepare me for the life I want. It sounds terrible, but sometimes I wish my mom had taught me how to balance a checkbook rather than how to bake banana bread."

Our Mothers' Role in Our Lives

Heather's experience highlights how the lives of our mothers (or whoever else our strongest female influences are) and our judgments of them affect who we choose to become. Our generation is the first to be raised in a time when women's roles were undergoing significant change. Our mothers were part of the baby boom generation, and most of their own mothers stayed home, instilling in their daughters the values of cooking, sewing, and attaining an "MRS" degree. Yet unlike Heather's mother, many of our moms began to challenge women's traditional role and fought to make a working woman as common as one with a killer apple pie recipe (Donna Reed, rest in peace). As the feminist movement gained momentum, more women chose to go to work and to have lives outside the home. Even if they didn't identify themselves as feminists, many of our mothers passed on to their daughters a desire to be part of the workforce. Gloria, twenty-five, says, "My mom is my role model. She had a great career as a pediatrician and has always been extremely supportive of my dream to pursue a career in medicine as well."

In my research, I found an even split between twenty-something women who had mothers who worked and those with mothers who stayed home. Ina, a thirty-year-old technology buyer in Dallas, says that having a mom who worked full-time had both a positive and a negative effect on her. "Her strong work ethic was an excellent example, but the negative side was that I thought she was Superwoman. She worked at least forty to fifty hours a week, kept a very clean house, and was always there when we got home from school because she worked nights. When I started working, I was struggling to pay the bills, get everything done, and spend time with family and friends, while working fifty to sixty hours a week. I kept telling myself, 'Mom did it and had even more to do! You're not trying hard enough.'" Ina's opinion changed after she finally talked to her mother about this. "She said that she struggled every day. It was hard for her; she would go into her room and cry after we went to bed at night, physically and emotionally exhausted!" Perhaps if Ina had been aware of her mother's struggle, she would not be so disappointed in herself.

Like Heather's mom, many of our mothers made careers out of being mothers and wives. They packed our lunches and attended PTA meetings. Yet even if we had great home lives and our mothers were happy, many twenty-something women still want more than their mothers had, and might have been encouraged to think this way by their stay-at-home mothers. Twenty-four-year-old Diana told me this when I asked her how having a stay-at-home mom has influenced her desire for a career. "My mom did stay at home, but she'd kill me if I called her a housewife. She did a lot of volunteer work and was always busy. She has influenced and encouraged me to work and strive hard for what I want. I want to raise my children, but I want to still have my career and use the skills I spent so many years building."

Some of us saw our mothers take on the roles of both parents as divorce became more common and our moms were forced to do it all. Maggie, twenty-seven, who was raised by a single mom, says, "My mom and I didn't really have such a great relationship. I respect her because she worked a lot, carrying two or three jobs to pay rent and support us. I got used to not seeing her and to being very independent. I respect her for being hardworking and having the guts to accomplish a lot." Explaining the downside, Maggie says, "My mom complains that I am too obsessed with the future and I work too much. Well, because I grew up with a single parent living from paycheck to paycheck, I want a better plan for my life. Sometimes it drives me crazy that I am like this, but I don't want my children to have to worry about money like I did."

Given all the different types of mothers we have, we are faced with a question: "To be or not to be like Mom?" Now, it's obvious that our mothers passed on to us some unavoidable traits, such as hair color, the size of our hips, or an undeniable love for the Beatles. And we fight tooth and nail *not* to inherit other things from our mothers, such as their fashion sense or the irritating way they offer "constructive" criticism. Finally, there are subtler things our mothers pass on to us, such as beliefs and behaviors, that are often more influential than their marital or professional status.

Annette, a twenty-four-year-old nurse from North Carolina, has always had a hot-and-cold relationship with her mother. Annette once thought this was because her mother was stressed out, but as she grew older she realized that her mom had deep issues she never had dealt with. "She never allowed her own self-expression but instead directed any emotion she had toward other people. She was a good caretaker and tried to be happy through other people. I've tried to learn how to express myself better. I'm sure it will be an ongoing challenge, but I'm confident in my awareness. My relationship with my mom and the emotional distance between us sped up the crisis during my twenties."

For those of you who have amazing relationships with your mothers — you consider her your best role model, you want to follow in her footsteps, and you are completely happy with who you are and where you are in life — I'd like to nominate them for mothers of the year. Most of us, however, have mothers who are *human*, and although they taught us a lot, we do not want to become exactly like them. One important thing to keep in mind as you continue to think about your mom is that our moms did the best they could given their life circumstances and experiences. Moving forward, it is in our own best interest to forgive our mothers for anything we hold on to and accept them for who they are. As savvy twenty-something women, we can look to our mothers for clues about why we are who we are, but we can no longer hold them responsible.

EXERCISE I

Your Mother's Influence

Now that you've read several stories of other women's relationships with their mothers, think about some of your mother's (or your most significant role model's) "ways of being" that you might consciously fight or unconsciously adopt. The following questions are designed to help you discover how the most influential woman in your life shaped your identity. Write the answers in your journal.

1. Among the women quoted above, whose story resonated with you most, and why?

2. What was your mother's role in your home? Do you think she liked it?

3. Did your mother work outside your home, and how did that affect your desire to work?

4. What did you admire about your mother?

5. What did you *not* like about your mother?

6. In what ways was or is your mother your role model?

7. Have you followed in the footsteps of your mother? In what ways do you think you are similar to her?

8. In what ways did you consciously decide to take another path? Why?

9. What advice did your mother give you that really has stuck with you?

10. Did your mother have any behaviors that you vowed *never* to repeat?

11. What things did your mother say to you that influenced the decisions you have made in your twenties?

12. Has your mother said, or does she continue to say, certain things to or about you that affect your self-esteem or self-image?

13. What was your mother's relationship like with your father or her husband (or with men in general)?

14. How was your mother's relationship with *her* mother?

15. How do you think your mother's relationships with others impacted how you behave in relationships with others?

After answering those questions, in what ways do you think your mother has influenced your definition of yourself? Overall, how do you feel about the influence she has had? Look at your answer to question number 5 and consider whether you need to forgive your mother for anything. This information is essential as we continue our journey toward a deeper understanding of ourselves.

"I wish I would have claimed my rights as a human being much earlier in life, instead of being so afraid and always listening to my mother define who I was."

— Maude, sixty-four

———

Who Is Mom, Anyway?

One of the most telling parts of my research was talking to women of our mothers' generation. Paying attention to how older women reflect on their twenties provides more insight into our experiences as we carve out our identity. We all think we know our mothers, but we knew or know them in their thirties, forties, fifties, and so on. We did not know who they were in their twenties — we were either too young or not yet born. Our frame of reference has always been from the perspective of a daughter.

Among my most fascinating interviews was the one with my own mother. I was surprised at how much I had not known about her. Although I'd always seen her as financially dependent on my dad, I learned that not only was she financially independent from her parents before the age of twenty-one, but she paid her own college tuition. I also thought she got married pretty young (twenty-four), and I never thought she had much of a life. Wrong again. She was out on the town, dating and having a great time. She told me that transitioning from having a career to being a mom was like becoming the CEO of a home. She approached it with a tremendous amount of pride and always knew she could go back to work if she wanted to someday (and eventually she did).

I had a significant realization after talking with my mother and her peers. We think we must decide in our twenties who we want to be for the rest of our lives, but we don't — our goals can and do change. This was a relief because I realized that the answer to the question "Who am I?" is not written in stone. Sure, some things about our identity remain constant throughout our lives, but we do have breathing room.

EXERCISE 2

Interviewing Other Women

You are going to interview your mother (if your mother is not living or is not in your life, pick the most significant female in your life) and two additional women around your mother's age. As you might have noticed already, I share bits of our preceding generation's wisdom throughout the book, but you'll find it valuable to do a little of your own research. Below is the list of questions that I asked women between the ages of forty-eight and sixty-three (roughly our mothers' generation) that you can use in your interviews. Feel free to stray from these suggested questions and make the interview more personal.

1. Overall, how would you describe your twenties?

2. What were your goals during your twenties?

3. What were your primary interests in your twenties?

4. What were the three most fun and exciting aspects or events of your twenties?

5. What were the three most challenging aspects or events of your twenties?

6. If you could go back to your twenties, knowing what you know now, what would you do differently? Do you have any regrets?

7. Do you have any other words of wisdom that you think could be of value to women in their twenties today?

Now that you have this information, it is up to you to decide what parts of it resonate with your life and experiences. Did the information these women, especially your own mother, shared surprise or inspire you? Remember, information from older women is often more valuable than the advice we get from our peers simply because it tends to be more objective and comes from experience rather than opinions.

Now look back at the list of questions above, and consider yourself in twenty or thirty years' time. How do you want to answer these questions then? Do you want to look back with fondness and pride or with regret? Are you making the most of your twenty-something experience? If not, what are you waiting for?

MOLDING OUR IDENTITY

Throughout our lives, we also look outside the home for clues about what kind of women we want to be. But when we open this window, a gust of mixed messages from our environment comes blowing in (as if the hodgepodge of roles our own mothers assumed wasn't enough!). We don't always choose who or what makes a lasting impression on us, so we might have conflicting ideas about who we are or should be.

Jessica, a twenty-seven-year-old pharmaceutical sales rep in Washington, D.C., was always told by her feminist mother that she could be whoever she wanted to be, but she was never given any specific ideas about how to determine who that was. So Jessica turned to television shows and movies that reinforced the notion that women can play many roles. She recalls the romance stories in which the dreamy-eyed woman is fulfilled by falling in love. She remembers seeing women portrayed in corporate roles who were sexy and smart and sometimes had families as well. Now that she is a full-fledged adult struggling with her identity, she is looking for real-life role models. She envies the women in her company who land the big accounts and earn big money. These women seem so together, intelligent, and sophisticated. On the other hand, she sees a lot of women beginning to settle into relationships and have children, and she envies them, too. They seem so secure, in love, and domestic. She observes satisfied women in her community and in the media with both families and careers. They seem to have and do it all. Each of these women seems happy to her, but whose situation is most ideal? Jessica's experience presents us with questions: Who is the prototype for the modern woman — Carol Brady, Kelly Ripa, Hillary Clinton, Oprah Winfrey? — and what is a woman's role right now?

What Is a Woman's Role?

When I asked twenty-something women how they would describe our generation, there was not a generic answer. Their feedback was an equal mix of responses such as these: "Independent, career-driven, and goal-oriented." "Confused and anxious." "Possessing a strong desire for and connection to a support system." "We want to have it all." Generally, we all see our twenties as *the* time to carve out an adult identity, yet with so many images and ideals floating around, this can be difficult. Fairly new to the grown-up world, we have not yet grasped the subtleties of appropriate behavior in a variety of situations. For instance, our role in the workplace can be particularly tricky. Do we act like men, assert ourselves, and hide our sexuality? Or do we climb the corporate ladder in stilettos and skirts while smiling? We are uncertain where the border lies between blending into a man's world and remaining feminine. If we dress too sexily or act too sweet, we might be considered airheads who rely on our looks to get ahead. If we dress too conservatively, we might be considered uptight. We are expected to be professional and unemotional, but if we are too assertive, we might be labeled bitches.

Catherine is a twenty-six-year-old junior architect at a large firm. As one of the younger people at her office, she feels that she is overly scrutinized and thinks that she should look and act a certain way. "All the senior women in my firm dress in designer suits, and they all have an attitude, and many of them try to act like the men. I want to been seen as a respected professional, so I overspend on clothes and put on a game face like they do. I am not really that comfortable with the money I am spending or the aloof person I feel like I am at work, but I do it because it seems to be the way it's done." Like Catherine, we take clues about how to be (or not to be) from individuals, particularly women, we observe in our workplaces, families, social situations, and the media. Often our only choice is to model ourselves on what we see in others: a "chameleon" way of being.

A chameleon nature can often be necessary in certain contexts. Like Catherine, many of us assume certain characteristics in order to fit in or be accepted. This becomes risky, however, when we start to let our outside circumstances dictate our identity. When that happens, we move farther away from who we really are. For example, Heidi, twenty-seven, recalls how a relationship molded her identity in her twenties: "I was with my ex for almost five years, and he was pretty overbearing and self-absorbed. But he was also charming, attractive, and brilliant (thus the attraction). I had always been a very outspoken person, but around him, I became more reserved. He commanded the spotlight, especially around his family. It wasn't until my best friend pointed out to me that I was becoming a 'mute woman behind the man' that I realized I missed that extroverted part of who I am."

EXERCISE 3

Chameleon Identity

If you find yourself struggling a bit with the question of who you are, perhaps some of your confusion might come from moments when you stepped away from or masked your core identity. You might have started doing this so frequently at such a young age that the mask became a part of you.

For instance, I was a very outgoing kid, but after being teased repeatedly, I hid behind an introverted mask. Acting withdrawn and quiet became part of my identity even though it was never who I really was. It wasn't until I asked myself the questions that generated this exercise that I realized shyness was not part of my identity.

Think of a time — or times — in your life when you tried to fit in and acted a certain way to get the result you wanted (such as acceptance, a promotion, a date, or to avoid an argument or appease someone). When and how have you turned into a chameleon? Consider these questions:

1. What was the event (or events), and how old were you when it happened?

2. Who was involved, and why did their opinion/reaction matter to you?

3. What did you think you should do, have, or be in that situation? Why?

4. What result did you want? Did you get it?

After completing this exercise, notice how you have adapted to situations or changed in the presence of others. Do you think those changes have for the most part been in line with who you are? Are there any masks that you might need to remove? A good way to answer these questions is to ask yourself if the role you took on felt right. Consider whether any modifications you made to your identity have suited you or stuck with you. For instance, if you were always passive in order to avoid conflict in your home, you might find you are still rather reserved and unassertive in your life. Ask yourself if you are truly docile or whether it's a characteristic driven by external circumstances that became a part of your identity.

—⚯—

Discovering that the answers to the question "Who am I?" can change depending on context is a stumbling block that many twenty-something women encounter. Many women admit that who they are changes in different situations or in front of different people. Tabitha, twenty-three, says, "I notice that lately I have been kind of irritable and withdrawn, yet if I am in an environment where I feel like I have to impress someone, I light up and become really friendly. I'll snap at a waiter but be nice to my boss." The next step in clarifying our identity is to bring our awareness into the present and identify which types of situations trigger chameleon behavior.

EXERCISE 4

Acting the Part

In this exercise, you investigate if and how your identity or the role you play changes in different situations. As you answer each of the following questions, try to picture yourself within the context of that situation and notice all the ways — no matter how subtle — in which you adapt, feel, or behave.

1. Who am I with my parents (separate your mom and dad if you want)?

2. Who am I with the rest of my family?

3. Who am I with my friends?

4. Who am I with men?

5. Who am I with someone I am dating/in a serious relationship with/married to?

6. Who am I with my coworkers? My boss?

7. Who am I with someone who intimidates me?

8. Who am I with someone I don't like?

9. Who am I at work?

10. Who am I with a group of people?

11. Who am I in social situations?

12. Who I am at a bar or party?

Add any other scenarios that fit your situation. Obviously, our identity and the roles we play are often malleable. Ask yourself which roles are most comfortable for you and most in line with who you truly are. Give some thought to times when you strayed from your true self and became an "identity chameleon." Hopefully, this exercise and the preceding one have shed some light on the roles you play and on the identity you have created for yourself.

———⊱⊰———

Who Is Your Role Model?

In researching this book, I asked women who they admired, and why. Women chose people ranging from family members to political and social leaders to celebrities such as Madonna ("Because she lives the life *she* wants") and the cast of *Sex and the City*. Most of us admire certain individuals based on what we think we want. Our chosen role models live the kind of lives and have accomplishments that we aspire to. However, it is difficult to really know what the individuals we put on pedestals are actually like. Many of us have had the unpleasant experience of being completely disappointed by people we look up to.

Talie, twenty-four, was over the moon when she was hired by a woman she had always admired and wanted to work for. "I thought it was the greatest break ever because she had the career I wanted. Things were great for the first few months, until her fangs started to show. I began to realize that she wasn't the mentor or type of person who I thought I had signed up for. She was mean and insensitive and had a terrible work ethic, and I don't think she was very happy with her life." This woman became a role model for what Talie did *not* want.

Many of us might feel that we have never had role models. This is not always a bad thing, because thinking a great deal about other people's lives can encourage jealousy and comparison. One woman in her late twenties said to me, "Most of the time I am blessed with the ability to see through what people have on the outside — beauty, fame, wealth, luck — and to see what they deal with on the inside — tough upbringings, unhappiness, insecurity. Usually, I'd rather have my life." Keeping our focus on ourselves is a very healthy attitude that can alleviate some of the pressure of the twenty-something crisis, and we will delve into this subject in more detail in part 2. Still, going through life without judging others for the traits and characteristics we find desirable or less appealing is rather impossible. Take a moment to think about the people who influenced your choice of who you would like to be.

EXERCISE 5

Who Do You Want to Be?

An appropriate follow-up to the question "Who am I?" is "Who do I want to be?" To dissect this question, take a moment to answer the following:

1. How would you describe your generation of women? Do you think you fit that description? Why or why not?

2. Who were your role models when you were growing up? If you did not have a role model, who had an important impact on you?

3. Who are your role models now?

4. Has any movie or TV female character had a significant impact on you?

5. Can you think of anyone who you consciously do *not* want to be like? If so, why?

6. Do you remember thinking about what it meant to be a woman when you were growing up? If so, what were your thoughts?

Often we pick role models without even knowing them. Look over the names you listed while answering this question: how many of them have you interacted with? Many women consider celebrities such as Oprah to be role models, but how many of us have ever actually talked to her? We might say we would love to have her life, her career, her influence; yet we know only the person we see on TV. We don't know who she *really* is.

Next, look back at your answers to questions 2 through 5 and think about the characteristics of each of the individuals you wrote down: their personalities, their traits, their accomplishments, and so forth. In order to provide a more individualized perspective on your role models (both good and bad), place each characteristic into one of three categories:

1. those you are able to emulate (i.e., characteristics you think you share)

2. those you admire but do not think you can emulate

3. those you do not like or want

Now that you've separated these characteristics into three distinct sections, it may become clear to you that looking to role models is just another way to identify the traits we have or strive to have. The bottom line: We cannot model ourselves after any one person or goal — our own identity will always distinguish us from other individuals. Who we are uniquely evolves over time, just as our characteristics, accomplishments, and realizations do.

When I asked Kimm, a twenty-nine-year-old philanthropist, whose life she might want, she answered: "Well, there is my neighbor, a 'casual' actress who makes occasional movies. She has an easel in her bedroom (I also like to paint, sew, and do arts and crafts). She rides horses (I used to take lessons), is very trim and healthy, and owns a house with her new boyfriend, who is the nicest man. She seems centered and happy with herself, has a great sense of humor, and is financially secure, beautiful, and creative. Even my good friend and boyfriend recognize that she's someone I would want to emulate."

Like Kimm, most of us have been guilty of modeling ourselves on people we view from a distance. Isn't that like buying a car based solely on how it looks? How do you know you would even like sitting in that car during rush-hour traffic? Most of us would want to open the door and check out the interior. Thus, instead of a role model we perceive from a distance, perhaps a mentor would be a more substantive source of support and guidance. A mentor is a trusted counselor or guide, rather than someone we want to be like without truly knowing them.

EXERCISE 6

Selecting and Getting to Know a Mentor

Write down the names of three people (including at least one woman) who you admire and could be adequate mentors to you. Choose someone who you know or could get to know. Over the next four weeks, establish a time to interview each of them. Do whatever it takes — make multiple phone calls, write a letter, send an email, stop by to set up a time to meet. Take your potential mentor out for coffee, meet in her office or home, or schedule a phone conversation. Aim high! If you've chosen an important executive at your office who you think would never give you the time of day, go for it anyway. You'll be surprised at how receptive people are when you ask them for guidance or advice. Think about how flattered you would be if someone told you that she respected you and wanted to ask you about your life. Let's be honest, we all love to talk about ourselves.

Below is a list of questions you can ask of your potential mentor (these are also great questions to ask of yourself). Feel free to modify and add your own.

1. At what point did you decide what you would do with your life?

2. Did a pivotal sign tell you that you were on the right track?

3. Did you have to make any sacrifices to pursue what you do?

4. Are there important things that you haven't yet done?

5. What do you wish you had known as a young woman that would have further advanced your life by this point?

6. What was your favorite part of your twenties, thirties, forties, and so on? What was your least favorite part?

7. Do you believe that you are following your destiny or that you have found your life's purpose?

8. Of the painful happenings in your life, which would you wish to keep?

9. Why do you think there is so much fear and jealousy in the world?

10. Do you listen more to your heart or to your head?

11. Do you trust others easily?

12. How important was money in your career choice?

13. What annoys you most?

14. What are some of the things you wish someone would have told you as a young woman?

15. How important do you think it is for people to have mentors? Who were yours?

16. Do you feel you have a fulfilled personal life? Do you consider your career to be part of your personal life?

17. If you could instantly have one talent, what would it be?

18. How much attention do you pay to the rest of the world?

19. What lessons do you think you still have to learn?

20. What is your favorite mode of communication? Why?

After you have finished your interviews, decide which of these people could be mentors to you. Then be proactive in building a relationship with that individual(s). Perhaps you'll have an email dialogue once a week or lunch once a month. Keep the person in your life, and go to them for advice and support. Mentors have wisdom and insight to share, but it is up to us to seek them out.

> "If you don't know a lot about life or what you want from it, set up a mentoring relationship with someone who does — it is often the best education you can get."
>
> — Maryanne, fifty-five

DEFINING OURSELVES

Now that we've looked at who we have modeled ourselves after, the next issue to consider is how we define ourselves. In your journal, flip back to your responses to the question "Who am I?" How many of the statements you wrote about yourself describe intrinsic qualities, such as "I am generous" or "I am intelligent"? How many describe physical characteristics or things that you do, such as "I am a redhead" or "I am a student"? Do you have a longer list of intrinsic, internal qualities or of external qualities? As young women in a materially driven, visual world, we are likely to identify ourselves by externals, the things outside ourselves. This habit indicates a lack of self-awareness and security that is at the very root of a twenty-something crisis (we'll delve into this more in part 2).

Lauren, twenty-eight, is an investment banker on her way to becoming who she always wanted to be: a successful businesswoman who makes a lot of money and will never need to depend on a man. During the holidays last year, she decided to take a short vacation by herself. Lauren had heard an expert on a talk show state that it is important for individuals in the rat race to spend time alone to "find themselves." Lauren thought she knew herself pretty well, but she was feeling rather stressed out after her latest promotion. Going to an island to find herself sounded enticing. She did not know how to go about this journey of self-discovery but assumed, as she did with most things in her life, that she would figure it out once she got there. At the very least, she could refer to the self-help book tucked away in her travel bag that she had heard about on *Dr. Phil.* She was destined to have some sort of epiphany. Well, she did. However, it was nothing like the one she had expected.

On the second day of her vacation, Lauren had what she calls a "mini-meltdown." Sitting alone on a beautiful beach, she realized she had absolutely no idea of what to do with herself. Without her usual life happening around her, she was clueless about how to spend her day. She could not think of anything she could do in that moment to make herself happy, despite the self-help book. "I thought of introducing myself to some people, which was usually easy for me, but in a setting where no one carries a business card, it felt foreign. I felt like I did not have anything to offer except a stock tip. I wanted to call someone, but who? I was overwhelmed with a sense of loneliness and, quite honestly, panic."

The Identity Crisis

As young women, we often become so focused on the things we do or have that we rarely stop to breathe and ask ourselves who we really *are.* This exhausting process keeps us in a perpetual identity crisis. How will we ever know who we truly are if we constantly define ourselves by what transpires outside ourselves?

I asked the women I surveyed how often they get asked, "What do you do?" Almost 100 percent of them responded, "A lot" or "Almost every day." Are we ever asked questions such as "What do you love about yourself?" "What brings you joy?" or "When you go to sleep at night, what do you wish for?" The world operates in a "doing" mentality, not a "being" mentality, so we become conditioned to identify ourselves by things that we do. We grew up during the very material Reagan years, when employment, disposable income, and opportunity were all on the rise. As children, we lived in an environment pervaded by mass media and technology to an extent greater than any generation that preceded us. Various representations of success were unavoidable. Images of money, sex, and power continue to surround us today. With so much emphasis placed on what we do and what we have, it is very easy to lose sight of (or possibly never even discover) our true selves. Distinguishing who we are from what we do and have is a powerful exercise in clarifying our identity.

Tara is a twenty-seven-year-old executive assistant at an insurance company in Tampa. She is a single woman who takes great pride in how she looks. During her sophomore year in college, Tara first noticed her body changing and has micromanaged her appearance since then. She spends a lot of time and money working out, counting calories, getting facials, waxing unwanted body hair, and shopping for the latest fashions. "When I feel fat or ugly, I just feel awful about myself. It ruins my whole day. Looking good makes me feel better about myself. Plus, I am a single woman, and I want to attract the right kind of man. With all the gorgeous women men are exposed to daily, the bar has been raised." Tara is not alone. This obsession with looks is very pervasive in her peer group. Every twenty-something woman she knows belongs to a gym, wants to find a guy, and talks about diets and beauty crazes. Tara also admits that the positive attention and compliments her looks bring are addictive. Being one of the most attractive women in any room has become part of her identity.

Tara's concern highlights a mentality that a lot of twenty-something women embrace. Many of us are taught that beauty is an extremely important quality, and we equate it with our physical looks. In this era of low-riding jeans, abs of steel, Botox, low-carb crazes, plastic surgery, and size-zero models, it is not surprising that there are more beauty magazines than news magazines in the stores. We are consumed with outward appearances — almost everywhere we look, images of gorgeous, thin, toned women stare back at us. Not only do we struggle with defining our identity according to what we do, but we are brainwashed by the notion that we should look perfect while we do it. It's no wonder our generation struggles with eating disorders and body-image problems! Despite the advances that women have made, let's face it: as long as there are heterosexual men with buying power, we will see women represented as sex objects.

We can spend a lot of time getting mad and talking about the bombshells all over billboards and television sets, but where will this get us? In an appearance-obsessed society, the latest diets, workout devices, and toning techniques probably will continue to headline the evening news. The real problem is the fact that we allow these images to affect us to such an extent. The subliminal message that we must appear a certain way to be attractive penetrates our being. We are at an age when most of us are trying to attract mates, advance in our careers, and be accepted and well-liked in our communities; therefore, we feel pressured to live up to societal standards and trends. The energy we direct toward these standards, and the importance we place on them, delays discovery of who we really are. Twenty-something women are especially susceptible to society's influences because we have not established enough self-worth to become immune to the images we see. We'll delve further into the topic of body image in chapter 5, but for now, consider how much your identity is tied to how you look. Do you think your perception of your body needs to change before you will be able to change your overall perception of yourself?

I had a fairly healthy self-image and relationship with my body until I moved to Los Angeles, where the "be skinny and spend money" disease is contagious. I admit that I invested too many of my resources (including my brain, which spent so much time thinking about it) in my physical appearance. Being a size two and carrying a Prada bag did not make me happier or help me understand who I really was. It did not give me answers to the questions I was asking about what I wanted out of my life. If anything, it distracted me from all my negative feelings about myself. But it did not make them go away. My own experience made me wonder how many other women obsess about their exterior as a way to cover up what they feel underneath it.

EXERCISE 7

Is Your Sense of Self Superficial?

You've heard "It's what is on the inside that counts" thousands of times. If we are so familiar with this phrase and agree with it on a basic level, why are so many of us still consumed by how we look? The following questions are meant to help you determine the depth of your sense of self.

1. On a scale of 1 to 10 (1 being "very bad," 10 being "no complaints"), how do you feel about your overall appearance?

2. On average, how much time do you spend each day on your appearance (grooming, exercising, shopping)?

3. How would you describe your relationship with your body?

4. What does the term *body image* mean to you?

5. Do you think you have a healthy body image?

6. Have you ever used your looks to get something?

7. Have you ever *not* gotten something because of your appearance?

8. Do you overspend on clothes, beauty products, and so on?

9. Have you ever thought that you do not look good enough to pursue something you want, such as a career, a relationship, and so on?

Look over your answers and contemplate how much the package you come in has become part of your identity. When you think about your sense of self, does the outside get more of your attention and count more than the inside? Perhaps it is time to bring your focus back to the internal — that is where all the really great stuff is anyway.

———

We began tackling the first question of the twenties triangle by uncovering some of the people and situations that could have influenced our identity. Also, by examining the ways in which we define ourselves, we've now armed ourselves with a more accurate picture of our self-worth. Keep your newly gained insights into who you are in mind as you read further. In the next chapter, we'll investigate what you want, and that question goes hand in hand with who you are.

"I wish I had not invested so much of myself in doing what was expected of me and obsessing about superficial things, but instead had figured out who I was."

— Penny, fifty

CHAPTER 2

WHAT DO I WANT?

Although we all ask, "What do I want?" throughout our lives, this question gains momentum in our early twenties, usually after we graduate from college. After spending years in the comfort of classrooms, we are thrust out into the working world, and suddenly we are supposed to know what we want to do with our lives.

Kouy is a twenty-three-year-old recent college graduate who is already stressed out about the future. "I began feeling pressure to find a great job and a great guy and to figure everything out before my senior year even began." Kouy always thought that by now she would have figured out what kind of job she wanted, but she is coming up empty-handed. She is not even sure of where she wants to live. She hears her parents' voices in her head like a broken record: "So what are you going to do next?" Lacking a specific answer to that question makes her feel like a failure. Kouy also worries quite a bit about her relationship with her boyfriend because it complicates her decisions. She does not want to move to a different city, away from him, yet she has heard so many negative things from her mother about allowing a man (especially one who is not Asian, as she is) to influence her choices. Although Kouy has not yet entered a profession, she worries about getting married and having kids while she establishes a career. At graduation, she was relieved that all-nighters and dorm food were behind her, yet she thought she would be more prepared for the next chapter of her life.

THE ROOT OF EXPECTATIONS

Like Kouy, we are told repeatedly that "your whole life is ahead of you" and then asked repeatedly what we will do in it. Although our prospects seem exciting, we have so many choices that we don't know which to pick. We feel that much is expected, yet we don't know where to start. Throughout our lives, many people have said things that set the stage for this uncertainty. Maybe it was a teacher who said, "You can be anything you want to be." Maybe it was your mother who said, "I know you will accomplish more than I did." Or a television show on which you saw successful women dressed in great suits with powerful careers. Or maybe you watched one too many romantic movies in which a woman is whisked away by an incredibly handsome man. We create pictures of what we do or do not want, and various people reinforce those pictures. The annoying thing is that there is no crystal ball that can reveal what we really want and what is best for us.

Discovering what we want is something we have to do by ourselves, despite the influence of others. Our parents might stand on the sidelines cheering us on, but they cannot tell us what we want. Even if they think they know best, this discovery is our own process. Furthermore, our moms' and dads' goals were generally simpler and clearer than our own: to make more money and to lead better lives than their parents did. If our parents don't pressure us to decide what we want, chances are someone else does — society, peers, and, most likely, ourselves. We are conditioned to believe that our twenties is the time to work toward achieving the American Dream. But what *is* that dream nowadays?

Many factors make the question "What do I want?" difficult for us twenty-something women to answer. Among the biggest roadblocks we encounter are expectations, which consist of all the pressure we feel to be and do certain things. The question I asked that triggered the most emotion and feedback was "What expectations do you feel as a twenty-something woman?" Not a single woman whom I interviewed or who completed my survey had trouble coming up with an answer. A common response was "So many — what expectations *haven't* I felt?" One twenty-eight-year-old woman put it very eloquently: "I'm supposed to have a devastatingly impressive life before I hit thirty (and it's always 'hit thirty,' as if it's this ghastly accident that leaves you disabled for life). I'm supposed to marry and to be the perfect match for that man in wits and success while also making sure that his socks match. I'm supposed to exceed what my mother achieved but not question or doubt her choices. I'm supposed to be my father's bright, accomplished young star. I'm supposed to be competitive and driven, yet soft and feminine. I'm supposed to be... everything."

Does fulfilling expectations put us at risk of never discovering what we want, of never setting goals based on what we actually desire for ourselves? Or are we so busy designing our lives around others' expectations that we never take the time to discover what we truly want? To remove the roadblock of expectations, we first need to understand their origin. During our formative years, input rushes over us like wildfire, and from it we create our belief systems, which are our basic opinions and thoughts about life. These belief systems cause us to frame our thoughts and actions in terms of "I should" rather than "I want to." The result? Living to fulfill expectations.

Follow me? If not, please don't think "I really *should* get this." Just keep reading because you *want* to. Everything will become clear.

Belief Systems

Theresa is a twenty-six-year-old woman who believes her life is not where it should be. Since graduating from college with a marketing degree, she has bounced from job to job and has never had a serious relationship. Theresa recently took a job as a waitress to make ends meet, and she is embarrassed to admit this because it does not fit her picture of what she wants in life. When she was growing up, her father was her biggest champion and always told her she was a "bright girl with a bright future." He prided himself on being able to send her to a top college and thus to ensure her a lucrative career. Since her parents' divorce, her mother has been itching to plan a wedding and tells Theresa she is a "great catch" who just needs to get out there and find the right guy.

As a child, Theresa loved to watch television. Shows such as *The Cosby Show* and *Family Ties* reinforced her belief that women can have both a career and a family. "I have always wanted a great career and a serious relationship. So I am looking for a job at an advertising agency, and I took my friend's advice and signed up for match.com." Theresa told me this as if she were describing a root canal. When I asked her if she was excited about pursuing a big career or dating, she leaned in as if to tell me a secret and said, "Not really. I kind of like the simplicity of my life, and I don't miss working long hours or dating."

"Then why are you doing it?" I asked her.

The floodgates opened: "I believe I should have a great job

that will lead to a fabulous career so that I can have an identity, and I want to find a man to have a family with, so I should be dating. There are other things I want to do, like go to Italy, but I have not pursued them because they may take me off the path I think I have to be on. Gosh, now that I say it out loud, it sounds ridiculous! But I'm afraid that I may end up alone and poor — or disappoint my parents, and myself."

Like many of us, Theresa holds beliefs that were significantly shaped by those around her, and she is not honoring what she really wants. The information that fuels our beliefs comes from a variety of sources: intimate places, such as our homes and schools, and public media, such as billboards and television shows. Lacking the life experience or mental maturity to discern what is true for us, we tend to adopt beliefs based on what we see, hear, or are told.

Licia, a twenty-six-year-old community outreach coordinator from Baltimore, thinks a big reason for her struggle to discover what she wants is that "society and media continually blast us with images of the 'ideal' — whether it concerns career, body image, fashion, or even the car you drive. It's hard to think on our own as we take in these force-fed messages (sometimes we are not even aware we are getting them) while trying to make decisions about our own values."

Remember the popular comeback from elementary school, "I'm rubber and you're glue; whatever you say bounces off me and sticks to you"? How empowered would we all be if we actually operated like that today? Unfortunately, we are more like sponges than rubber, and we take too many things personally. We must do some investigating to identify which of our beliefs are

"Don't let others decide what is best; decide what makes you happy (no matter how crazy it is) and follow it with all your heart (even if it means feeling lonely at times). Before you know it, the world will follow."

— Sharon, fifty-two

actually self-determined. If a belief has become reality because it is all we have known, how can we identify it as something not our own? Well, the first step is to thoroughly examine all our belief systems.

EXERCISE 8

Your Belief Bio

What we believe and what we are told to believe often become enmeshed in our heads. This exercise is designed to help you recognize which beliefs you now hold. Often, we are unaware of all our beliefs until we stop, think, and actually write them down.

This exercise asks you to write a list of statements. Begin each statement with "I believe." For example, you'd write, "I believe in God" or "I believe that my parents would be prouder of me if I had a great job." Try to generate at least ten beliefs that you now hold (trust me, they are there). Continue to write down as many as you can. When I did this exercise, I came up with twenty-two pretty strong beliefs that I had ingrained into my thinking. Yet recognizing them as belief systems, not actual, personal truths, took a while.

Next, look over your list and highlight the statements that you think might have been programmed into you. For instance, one of mine was "I believe I should have a big-time executive job and work a lot because I am smart." Truly, I do not believe that; I just took it on because various authority figures had told me that a big-time job was what I should do with my intelligence. Realizing that this belief was not my own value was one of the things that gave me the courage to stop trying to get a corporate job and write this book. Writing the book was what I truly wanted to do. But my belief system about my vocation blocked my view of that goal.

It is now time to reframe the beliefs that are not in line with who you truly are and what you truly want. These beliefs keep you in the life you are expected to live, rather than the one you *want* to live. Next to each highlighted statement, write a new statement that aligns with your true beliefs. Returning to my example, I replaced my old belief with "I believe I have the ability to do whatever I want because I am smart."

> "Identify your true values and choose to live by them. Find work that represents those values and that allows you to live them in the workplace. Throw away the word *should* and listen to your own voice. Don't allow anyone to ever tell you that you can't achieve something or that you 'should' do something else."
>
> — Lynn, fifty-seven

After you complete this exercise, make sure to save it. I encourage you to reread it and to add to your list of new beliefs. Doing so will help you ingrain these beliefs into yourself as you move through and out of your twenty-something crisis.

―――∞――――

The "Should" Epidemic

Once our beliefs are in place, we construct ideas of who we should be and the ways we should act. Since we believe that we should achieve certain things in order to become certain sorts of people, our lives often are fueled by expectations that stem from our belief systems. Each of the women I interviewed used the word *should* in at least one of her responses to my questions about her life experiences. Yet many twenty-something women find that doing the things we think we should do does not give us any sense of balance or direction. In fact, one of the main reasons that so many women are dealing with crisis-like symptoms is that so many "shoulds" race through our brains. We are truly suffering from a "should" epidemic that generates feelings of confusion and anxiety.

Georgia, twenty, is a junior in college. She and all her girl-friends from high school are doing what they are supposed to do: going to good colleges so they will have promising careers, getting into relationships, and concerning themselves with looking really good. "I cannot think of one friend who is happy. My friend who has her career mapped out for her is clinically depressed. My friend who has a great guy she wants to marry has a workaholic mother whom she never sees and a stepfather she can't stand. Another friend, who is just gorgeous, has an eating disorder. We are all doing the things we think we should be doing, but not one of us is happy."

Beginning in childhood, we take in endless information about the way we *should* be, pictures of how life *should* look, and ideas about what we *should* want. Our belief systems continue to welcome such expectations as we grow up, and thus the "should" epidemic continues to spread throughout our twenties. Helene, twenty-nine, still battles with shoulds even though she is at the end of her twenties and has a successful marriage, three kids, and a career. "I always think about the type of woman I assume my friends think I should be, the type of wife I assume my husband thinks I should be, and the type of parent I assume my parents think I should be. I display a much higher confidence level than I actually have. I am constantly questioning myself. People say, 'You just need to like yourself the way you are.' Okay, that sounds great, but I am too busy trying to be everything that everyone thinks I should be."

A great deal of confusion arises when we try to differentiate among parental ideals, relationship ideals, societal ideals, and personal ideals. A lot of us, no matter how smart and educated we might be, are not even aware of the difference between our own ideals and those of others. This is why uncovering our hidden belief systems is integral to our growth. The sooner we're able to uncover them, the sooner we will be able to create success on our own terms, not on someone else's. If we peel away, one by one, our illusionary ideals, which are disguised as shoulds, we can find the root of what we really want. You have already taken the first step by identifying your belief systems that are fueled by expectations and shoulds rather than by your intrinsic values. Next, we will learn to separate the things we think we should do from those that further our highest good. How do we recognize the values we should question and even change? It requires more digging, which is exactly what the following exercises are designed to help you do.

EXERCISE 9

Getting to the Core of What You Want

This exercise will help you peel back the layers of your belief systems and separate the "I shoulds" from the "I wants" in your life. Please move through this exercise slowly and thoughtfully. Write down each answer without looking ahead to the next question.

1. In your journal, look back at your answers to the question "What do I want?" (see the introduction to part 1). On a fresh page, list again each thing that you want on a separate line. Now rate the importance of each item: assign it a number from 1 to 10, with 1

being something that you are rather indifferent about and 10 being something that you will work your whole life to attain because it is very meaningful to you.

2. Now arrange and rewrite your list in numerical order. Omit anything that you ranked below a 2. Chances are, it is not something you really want, but you put it on your list because you thought you *should*.

3. After reviewing this list, write down your beliefs about what you want. Some examples: "I believe that I want to have a career" or "I believe that I never want to get married." You can also refer back to the end of exercise 8 and look at the beliefs you wrote down there.

4. Who or what do you think might have influenced the beliefs you have formed?

5. Which beliefs about what you want in life do you think might have been externally generated by your parents, peers, society, teachers, and so on? (These beliefs might fuel the expectations you feel during your twenties.)

6. Which beliefs do you think were internally generated from your own experiences or investigations? (These beliefs are true to who you are and what you want. Focus on them.)

7. Look over the list you made in response to question 2. Consider each item on the list and put a star next to anything you think was internally generated. If there is *any* chance you think it could have been externally generated, circle it and consider giving it up.

How does it feel to separate the "I shoulds" from the "I wants"? Many women have told me that they felt great relief after doing this exercise since their shoulds were such a weight on their shoulders. In the absence of your shoulds, you might feel at a loss to identify things you actually want. Beliefs that don't belong to you have drained so much of your energy that you might feel a little empty without them. Don't worry. This is an extremely common emotion when we start to deconstruct our belief systems. It's as if our training wheels were removed for the first time and we were apprehensive about riding without them. We don't know how it feels. But remember how awesome you felt once you finally learned to ride a bike? Well, discovering what you really want feels even more incredible.

Belief systems and shoulds are things that we learned in life. We were not born with them as if they were our eye color, and they can be changed. Anything we learned we can unlearn. If you are dubious, think back to your algebra class. You learned many formulas, but you might not remember them today if you found little use for them in your life. Similarly, once we discern learned beliefs, we can work on giving them less airtime, eventually deprogramming them from our brains and removing clutter from our consciousness.

The following advice from a thirty-year-old woman is appropriate to share here: "In the moment, things sometimes seem so overwhelming. But remember that in a few years, the emotion will be gone and it won't be such a big deal. You will be able to extract the wisdom out of the situation and learn from it instead of thinking, 'I should have...' You start to figure out what you want and where you want to go in life, rather than what you should want or where you should want to go."

EXERCISE 10

Exploring Your Heart and Head

This exercise can help jump-start your pursuit of what you deeply want. It might feel a little difficult or weird, but just read through it and *try* to do it. In it you will spend some time exploring two of your most significant parts — your heart and head — to get to know them better. Set aside ten minutes for each of this exercise's two parts, but do them on different days. Find a quiet place where you will not be distracted, and choose a time of day when you will not feel rushed or have a million things on your mind.

1. Sit comfortably and set a quiet mood (light a candle, burn incense, or put on soft music). Close your eyes and picture the inner workings of your heart in what-ever way you wish. Breathe deeply and imagine that you can speak directly to your heart. How often do you listen to your heart? What would it say to you? What does it truly desire? What does it yearn for? What makes it really happy and content? What makes it tight and anxious? How does it feel in your body? Continue to breathe, and keep your aware-ness right in the center of your chest. Do not worry about what happens; just take the journey and see what comes up for you. After you are finished, write down any wisdom from your heart.

2. On a separate occasion, set aside ten minutes to travel to the very back of your head (imagine that you're entering the subconscious part of your brain). Close your eyes, bring your focus there, breathe deeply, and listen. What would it say to you? Is anything back there that the more logical part of your head likes to ignore? Does it tell you to do anything that you constantly come up with reasons *not* to do? When you are done, write down the wisdom from your lead.

3. Finally, look over what your heart and head said. Commit to doing one thing or implementing at least one change from each list.

If this exercise feels too "woo-woo" or did not work for you, just jot down what comes to mind when considering the following: Which most rules the way you live, your heart or your head? In other words, which do you listen to most? Why? Write down specific examples of events in your life that relate to your answers.

Then write down one thing that you would do if the part you do not normally listen to were in charge. If you are usually a very cautious thinker and your brain leads, do something that seems to arise from your heart or emotions. For instance, the next time you need a gift for someone, be creative and make something for your friend rather than purchasing the most expensive gift. Or, the next time you want to do something — such as dancing — but fear you'll look stupid doing it, just go for it. Remember, the person who judges us most harshly is the woman in the mirror.

THE CONSEQUENCES OF EXPECTATION OVERLOAD

Becoming familiar with our beliefs and the "should" epidemic is just the first layer of the cake of expectation. We have to continue to cut through before we can truly enjoy the creamy filling of the things we really want. Next, we will look at the consequences of expectation overload, and examine how they complicate our answers to the question "What do I want?"

By now, most of us have deduced what is expected of us as women, daughters, sisters, girlfriends, wives, and mothers. Many of these expectations cloud our knowledge of what we really want. Even language can create problems: words that ooze expectations, such as *soul mate* and *passion,* infiltrate our daily existence and become part of our belief systems. As you read through the following list of expectations felt by women between the ages of twenty-three and thirty-three, pay attention to the ones that resonate with you:

- "To make a stand and breakthroughs in business world."

- "To find my passion."

- "To be thin and fashionable."

- "To support myself and take care of myself independently while looking for a companion to settle down with."

- "To create a foundation for career success so that my thirties can be dedicated to a husband and family, while also stepping onto a plateau of my own self-created financial stability and career identity."

- "To start doing something real, make a difference, and be on a path, because time is running out."

- "To develop a plan for my career and incorporate into it my 'family plan' and my plans to meet the man whom I will love for the rest of my life. To remain successful, raise our children, and be the happiest I've ever been. Not to mention to remain as beautiful as I was the day I met my Prince Charming."

I am sure you can relate to a lot of these expectations and could add even more of your own. By this point, you've gained a clearer sense of the sources of your expectations and the ways they shape your belief system and your sense of what you *should* do. Now it is time to move on to uncover how all these expectations impact our lives. Once that is revealed, we can begin to relieve the pressure of expectation overload.

The Expectation Hangover

When expectations rule our lives, we set ourselves up for disappointment and judge ourselves harshly. Rachel, a twenty-eight-year-old webmaster from Des Moines, remembers her most significant moment of crisis at twenty-five: "I basically freaked out as I took stock of my life, reviewed my experiences, both good and bad, and kicked myself for not having grown enough, experienced enough, gotten everything I wanted, or become a good enough person. I kicked myself for wasted time and laziness, procrastination, and stupidity." We beat ourselves up when we do not meet a standard that was set for us or that we set for ourselves. We are left with what I call an expectation hangover.

An expectation hangover occurs when we hold a certain expectation but things do not turn out as we thought they should or would have liked, and we then feel awful. It is far worse than a tequila hangover because it lasts much longer than a day, and no amount of aspirin can cure it. I am sure you have all had one. Think of a job interview that you were really excited and confident about. You wore your best suit, your resume and references were impeccable, and you felt like you nailed every question. You were on a high, just waiting for the call telling you that you got the job, but then you did not get it. You felt miserable and unmotivated, and you began to question your career path. You expected a certain result and then faced a huge letdown. Chances are, you found some way to blame this on yourself, and your self-esteem took a beating. You were suffering from an expectation hangover.

EXERCISE 11

Symptoms of Expectation Hangovers

Recall a recent time or times that you had a big expectation about something that did not turn out the way you had wanted or planned. Now write down a list of ways this situation affected your life. These are your expectation hangover symptoms. They could include items such as "I couldn't sleep," "I didn't date for months," or "I stopped being assertive at work." Try to identify all the characteristics and effects of your expectation hangover. As you look over this list, do you find any of these symptoms particularly desirable? Use this list to diagnose yourself when you feel off, and notice how often you suffer from expectation hangovers.

———— ∞ ————

So, if expectation hangovers are so dreadful, why are so many of us willing to endure them? Well, when we are at a bar, drinking the José Cuervo shot that is put in front of us is easier than saying no (even though we know we will regret it the next day). Similarly, it is often easier to fall into the expectation cycle than to let go and be okay with what happens in our lives. But does that mean avoiding expectation hangovers is impossible? Of course not. It is indeed possible, given a different perspective and the right set of tools.

We have an obligation to our own happiness, despite the outside obligations many of us feel to achieve certain things or to be a certain way. We sell ourselves short if we lead lives propelled by expectations and obligations. And yet we do it because we fear that if we stray from "the expected," we will face judgment, disappointment, isolation, or failure. Fear of the unknown keeps us from abandoning the rules and regulations we follow. If we do what's expected of us, we can predict outcomes. For example, if we go to good colleges and do well, we will get good jobs. The safety of the expected makes it alluring. But if we limit our experience of life to what we think we can control or understand or feel safe with, will we have the lives we want?

Denise, twenty-seven, is working at her dream job as a television producer and has reached the level of her career that she expected to at this point, yet she still questions her path and doubts whether it fulfills her. "Getting what you want is complicated. I ask myself, 'Does this measure up to what I thought it would be like? Is this the field I want to be in?' I see now there is much more that I want to do with my life besides television, but I never thought I would have to decide so early about where I should go from here. I want to do something that makes an impact, but I wonder if I even have it in me. Plus, I don't want to risk the security I have."

Like Denise, many of us have worked really hard to achieve things we always wanted, but, once we did, we still felt unfulfilled. The letdown we sometimes experience after an accomplishment is another symptom of the expectation hangover. When what we want is determined by a set of expectations, we are always trying to check the next accomplishment off the list. Any externally motivated goals and desires most likely will leave us feeling empty once we achieve them. So why do we do it? Outside standards are often clearer than those coming from inside, so we chase after externals. As we try to get what we want, we follow various signs that lead us in all kinds of directions, but we often feel that something is missing.

Discerning Expectations

To reduce the frequency of those nasty expectation hangovers, the first step is to identify what you think is expected of you and what you expect from yourself. Begin by identifying the expectations' original sources. The following techniques are designed to help you with this process and to separate your externally driven expectations from what you really want.

First, take a walk down memory lane. Thinking back to your past, imagine yourself as a sponge that constantly soaked up information. Think about things people said to you that could have felt like expectations or rules, ones that have influenced choices you made or still make. Write down each person's name, what he or she said, the message behind those words that made them seem to be an expectation, and the effect the expectation has had on you. For example:

Source: The most beautiful girl in your high school is crowned prom queen.

What was said or expressed: Your dad says to you, "She is so gorgeous; she has everything going for her."

Message/expectation: Beautiful girls will have great lives, so you have to strive to be beautiful so that you will have everything. If you are not beautiful, your life will be hard.

Effect(s): An obsession with physical appearance; insecurity; and jealousy of beautiful women because you perceive their lives to be easy.

Next, think about expectations that you placed on yourself and how they have affected you. Since these are self-imposed expectations, you might be unable to identify their sources. So just write down your expectation and how it affects your life. For example:

Expectation: I have to make a lot of money to be successful.

Effect(s): I work at a job I do not like and I have no social life, but I do have money in my bank account.

Now answer the following questions, basing your answers on what you've just written:

1. Among the various sources of expectations you listed, what or who was the most powerful, and why?

2. How have expectations benefited you?

3. How have expectations harmed you?

4. Think of all the things you did in the last week (for example, "Stayed late at work, went out with friends, volunteered, went to the gym"). Which of these activities did you want to do? Which were things that were expected of you or that you felt pressured to do? Which type of things do you do more often — desires or expectations? If you come up short on desired activities, plan out at least three activities that you truly want to do during the next week. Even

something as simple as sitting and reading a magazine is a great start.

Human beings are creatures of habit, and we follow routines that fulfill our obligations and manage our lives. But it is possible, with some practice, to break expectation-based habits. This week, pick one expectation to let go of. Obviously, do not pick something drastic, such as "I'm expected to go to work," and then end up getting fired. Rather, choose something workable, such as "I'm expected to go out every night to socialize or network." Over the next week, see what happens when you don't do what you think others expect of you or you expect of yourself. My guess is that you might feel relief.

> "Honor yourself and your truth as you know it at all times and regardless of how much you love anyone else or what anyone else wants for you."
>
> — Kathy, fifty-three

Having It All

As we transition from little girls to adult women, we sift through our expectations and determine which are in line with what we truly want and which we will discard. But, as we've already discussed, many quarter-lifers find it a problem to eliminate any of them. So, in addition to a hangover, another result of expectation overload is that we put tremendous pressure on ourselves to "have it all." Modern-day feminism supports the idea that a woman can and should have anything she wants. But if feminism really is about women having choices, we should give ourselves the option to choose what we want and let go of what others expect.

Our generation has been very fortunate, as we've had unlimited opportunities. Going to college and having a job are now more the rule than the exception for young women. We have seen women such as Katie Couric and Condaleezza Rice made it big in what was typically a man's world. Our career options have exploded. Women have become major contributors to the workforce. We are partners in large companies, hold government offices, and start our own businesses. We date, live with men before marriage, have lesbian relationships, bear and raise children on our own, and talk openly about our sexuality (thank you, Carrie, Samantha, Charlotte, and Miranda!). But is there a downside to all these options? Perhaps these limitless possibilities, combined with all the expectations we feel, are the reason that so many of us find determining what we want difficult.

Lisa, a twenty-eight-year-old grad student from Ohio, recalls, "It was hard for me to picture specifically what I expected of my life. Life after college just felt like a great big black hole. I always did well in school, and every teacher I had insisted that I go into his/her area (calculus, music, engineering). It messed me up because I couldn't decide where I really fit. It was like everybody was asking me to be in their club, but I couldn't pick just one."

The American Dream has evolved from the simpler days when white picket fences and color televisions were people's goals into a dream of having it all. One twenty-four-year-old says she feels tremendous pressure to make choices that will give her "the best education available or affordable, the perfect job that pays four times more than it would've paid my mother, the perfect husband, the perfect house in the new and upcoming area, and the perfect family, including the dog, while still maintaining my full-time perfect job and figure."

The entertainment media reinforce this have-it-all mentality throughout our lives. Think about the roles that women on the television shows we grew up with played: Claire Huxtable on *The*

Cosby Show was a lawyer, Elise Keaton on *Family Ties* was an architect, Maggie Malone on *Growing Pains* was a news reporter — *and* they looked beautiful while managing a handful of kids, a handsome husband, and a gorgeous home. The shows seemed totally believable, but did they skew our perception of reality? Is it really possible to have it all, or is it a myth?

When I asked women what they wanted out of life, I heard "I want to have it all" again and again. That is why I decided to take a closer look at what this catchphrase really means. I asked women to define "having it all." Here are some of their responses:

- "Having it all is having all the things that I want: a husband who I am totally in love with and who is totally in love with me, making partner, having at least two kids, making a lot more money, and, I don't know... just being happy."

- "Lots of children, a successful career that I enjoy and is satisfying to me, a stable and loving family life with as little stress and problems as possible, financial security, travel, the ability to have all of what I need and most of what I want, and continued spiritual growth and knowledge."

- "Getting everything I want, not just need."

- "I think it's the point in your life where you feel like you have accomplished a lot and can finally just enjoy where you are."

- "Having my life but with my friend's money and a perfect body."

- "Being free to choose what I want, when I want it."

- "Having it all means an influential career that allows you to touch individual lives but also enables you to reach the masses with an important message that improves the quality of everyone's life in some way. It means having a great personal life, with a family that you devote time, energy, and love to. It means being financially comfortable. It means having time left over to pursue your outside interests."

- "Being able to do anything on a whim!"

- "We all have a checklist in our heads of the things we want to do in life. 'Having it all' is what you write at the bottom of the list once you've checked everything off."

After I asked this question, I asked women how they felt about their goal to have it all, and for most it brought up angst. Hillary, twenty-three, says, "I am most confused when I think of how I am supposed to live the life that society deems appropriate, which is to do everything. Be fabulous at your career, have an amazing husband whom you just worship. Have children while still maintaining the husband, house, and job. How do we do all that? I am totally overwhelmed, and I am really scared I won't be able to pull it off." Clearly, having it all in our twenties is a pretty tall order, and few of us know exactly how to get it.

On further reflection, what interested me was the fact that not one woman responded that she already had it all. *All* was consistently defined as something to strive for or attain. This definition suggests that many young women have a future-driven mentality. This made me think that having it all is indeed a myth we have bought into. One of the women I spoke with, Kairol, thirty, echoed my thoughts: "*Nobody* has it all. That is a big thing that my twenties finally drilled into my head. I think that having it all is a very American concept, and it is worthless. It doesn't account for the texture of daily life, or the fact that luck and chance play a huge role in 'success,' or those incredibly important lessons that come from not getting what you want."

Perhaps "having it all" is indeed an unrealistic goal, one that arises when possibilities morph into expectations. Sure, having many wonderful things in our lives is possible, but if we strive to have them all at once, something will suffer. There is a direct correlation between the emergence of women's have-it-all goal and the rise of the feminine twenty-something crisis. We are stressed out and, quite frankly, self-absorbed. Having too much makes us consumption and achievement junkies. We will go through withdrawal whenever one element fades away, and we'll scramble to find something to replace it ASAP (ever tried to get over a guy by starting another relationship?). Of course, we still can go after everything we want (we are women, hear us roar!); however, it is important to review our goals. If we feel that in order to be happy or successful we must have it all as soon as possible and all at once, can we pursue what we authentically want, or will we just live to fulfill rather greedy expectations?

> "As president of a large company, I have young women ask me all the time how I balance having it all — career, family, marriage — and I always respond, 'I don't; I have dogs, and a husband who works from home.' It is impossible to do or have it all. Something will suffer. We have to make choices."
>
> — Amy, fifty-three

EXERCISE 13

What Does Having It All Mean?

The following exercise is designed to help you gain perspective on what this popular phrase means to you. In your journal or notebook, answer the following questions:

1. What does having it all mean to you? Specifically list all the things you want.

2. If you did have it all, how would your life look? For instance, what type of job would you have, what would you own, what would your family situation be, where would you live, and who would you be with?

3. Can you think of anyone who embodies the notion of having it all?

4. When you think about attaining "everything," does the idea seem overwhelming or actually possible?

5. How do you think you would feel if you didn't eventually get it all?

Look over your responses to questions 1 and 2. How many specific, tangible things did you write down? One of the biggest obstacles female quarter-lifers create as we try to figure out what we want is setting goals that aren't specific or realistic. We buy into the myth of "having it all" but don't often itemize what that involves. We list things such as "a great career" without really knowing what that means. We want "a wonderful romantic relationship," but we hate dating and expect our soul mates to just fall into our laps. We say we want self-confidence and balance, yet we judge and overextend ourselves. We moan and groan about our bodies, but we do not make exercise and healthy food part of our daily lives. The first step toward clarity and targeted action is to be precise and practical

> "Having it all means having a sense of peace and contentment right now, not some time in the future. It is not measured by how much money one has or what accomplishments one could list on a resume. It means having goals but not being attached too tightly to them. Simply find joy in every day."
>
> — Karen, fifty-three

in our goal-setting rather than clinging to the pie-in-the-sky notion of having it all.

—⊶—

EXERCISE 14

Demystifying Your Goals

This exercise offers a way to narrow your focus rather than just saying, "I want it all."

First, write a very specific list of your goals. For instance, instead of "A fulfilling career," write, "I want to work at a top-ten magazine in two years." If thoughts such as "I don't know" or "I don't know how" come up, keep it simple for now. (We will approach the third question of the twenties triangle — "How do I get what I want?" — in the next chapter.) For now, a statement that reflects a simple and immediate goal, such as "I want to work out at least twice a week," is enough. Also, do not worry about writing a lot. Maybe you actually want something very simple, and that's okay. There are endless options in the world, but that does not mean that you must complicate your life by taking on all of them.

Now that you have spent some time thinking about what you want, pause to reflect on how much you already have. We are all guilty of losing sight of this — especially in our twenties, when we are fixated on the future. Next, consider the following questions:

1. Look back at your list of things you want, which you created in exercise 13. Which have you already accomplished to some degree?

2. Have you done or accomplished something that was not on your original list of things you wanted?

3. What are the three most important things in your life right now?

4. What are you grateful for? Compose a "gratitude" list.

I also suggest keeping a separate journal, or "gratitude book," in which you frequently record things in your life that you are thankful for. This is an excellent way to remind ourselves of how rich our lives already are during times when we are stressed or caught up in the future. We often already have what we truly *need*, but it is human nature to *want* as well. Could it be possible that you actually have it all right now?

Throughout this chapter, you have focused on the question "What do I want?" Perhaps your answer is now clearer or differs from your earlier answer. As you review and adjust your goals, remember to adjust the expectations you place on yourself as well. Our goals and priorities change, but our expectations often remain the same. That's like changing the oil in our cars but never checking the air pressure of the tires. Remember, to avoid those killer expectation hangovers, try not to become attached to the outcome of your goals. Just moving in the direction of a goal is part of reaching it — so commend yourself for your effort.

EXERCISE 15

Drawing Your Life

Before moving to the last question of the twenties triangle, take some time out for a little arts and crafts project. You have been using your left brain (the rational, logical part) for many pages, and now it's time to exercise your right

> "In life you will discover that what you want may not be what you need, and that what you need is not always what you want. Life is a journey, and the less we try to control it, the happier we will be."
>
> — Glea, forty-nine

brain (the creative part). Get some paper and crayons, pencils, or paint. If you are thinking, "But I can't draw" or "I'm not artistic," you're getting in your own way. Just let your creative juices flow. This drawing is not going to be submitted to the Guggenheim.

First, draw a picture of how your life would look if you had everything you *want*. Are you hesitant about how to do this? Do you want more instructions? Sorry, there aren't any. Just stop reading, start drawing, and see what emerges. When you have completed your picture, then pick the book back up.

Next, evaluate how simple or complicated the picture is. Does it reflect how you feel inside? For instance, if your picture has many disorderly elements, do you also feel a bit chaotic?

Now take out another sheet of blank paper and begin to draw a picture of what you think you truly *need*. Again, don't overthink it; just start creating. Put down the book and draw.

When you are finished, compare this picture to the first one you drew. How did you feel while drawing the picture of what you need versus the one of what you want?

Similarly, pay attention to what you think and feel when you distinguish between what you want and what you need. At our root, we are all relatively simple creatures. What we need and want more than anything else is to express ourselves and to be understood. Perhaps the most realistic definition of *having it all* is having what you need, when you need it.

CHAPTER 3

HOW DO I GET
WHAT I WANT?

Now that we have a clearer perspective on ourselves and our goals, it's appropriate to address the final question of the twenties triangle: "How do I get what I want?" As twenty-something women, most of us strive to create a life plan based on how we answer the first two questions of the triangle: "Who am I?" and "What do I want?" Yet we often experience great doubt and difficulty in executing our plans.

Kristina is a twenty-five-year-old assistant at an advertising agency in Seattle who frequently suffers from anxiety and wakes up with knots in her stomach. "I feel like there is so much I need to do. My brain never turns off, and I feel like I will just never catch up." Kristina admits that she is hard on herself and faithfully abides by her "plan" for her life. When I asked her if she knew how she would accomplish everything she had planned, she replied almost as if she were reading from a script: "I need to continue working hard so that I can get promoted quickly and attain job security before having kids — I want at least two before the age of thirty-five — but I really don't know where this job will lead. I am searching for my Prince Charming, but I don't know where to find him. I miss no opportunity to network, because everyone says that is what you have to do. In my spare time, I try to exercise so that I can stay healthy; well, actually it's more about staying thin."

I ended the interview by asking Kristina how sure she was that what she was doing would lead to what she wanted, and whether she was enjoying the process. A rather disenchanted look came over her face. She paused and said, "I am not sure at all, which I guess explains the knots in my stomach. I think the only thing that would make this process enjoyable was if I knew that everything I am doing would lead to the happiness and success I want."

Modern culture gives us clear clues about what we should want from life: to be successful, to be happy, and to have love in our lives. However, life does not come with a road map showing us how to attain this. The world we are taking on is vastly different from that of our parents and elders (just remember how long it took them to use email). Our world generally has been more peaceful than that of our parents: until 9/11, our generation had not faced devastating events such as major wars and economic depression, or social upheavals such as the civil and women's rights movements. As we grew up, the world opened, and we were exposed to the finer things in life: other countries, other cultures, new forms of entertainment, and technology that made possibilities seem limitless. Yet as our options expanded, our contentment and sense of balance and direction contracted.

Many of us throw a lot of noodles at the wall, but they don't seem to stick. That was my predicament after I resigned from my job as an agent. I tried all sorts of new careers to make myself feel more successful: I went to nutritional school, I apprenticed with a Chinese herbalist, I interviewed at a consulting firm, I pursued freelance writing, and I even tried to get back into the entertainment business. Nothing I tried amounted to anything, and I felt like a directionless failure.

My own experience and the way it resonated with my research made me think about why those noodles we throw don't stick. This chapter offers suggestions on how to make things work in your life in a way that satisfies you, rather than feeling frustrated and misdirected.

To get started, refer back to your answers to the twenties-triangle questions (see the Introduction). Review your answer to the question "How do I get what I want?" Keep your responses in mind as you read through this chapter.

"NOT-ENOUGHNESS"

Valerie is a twenty-six-year-old grad school student who is quite clear about what she wants: a full life supported by a successful career. She is also very committed to how she will get it: she's at the top of her class, works part-time for a corporation, and spends her spare time studying. It seems that Valerie is right on track. Well, not according to her. "I am only in the top 10 percent of my class, and even though I already have an offer from a top firm, I really want to be in the top 5 percent. Sometimes I feel like my life is only about school, so I am trying to get involved in activities like working at the museum or tennis lessons — and I guess I should eventually date, too, so I don't end up alone."

I reminded Valerie that happiness and peace were on her list of things she wanted. She sighed and responded, "Oh, great — now I have to figure out how to get those, too!" Valerie's story is an extreme example of an interesting phenomenon among twenty-something women that I call "not-enoughness." It is a motivating force behind many of our actions and thought patterns. We go after what we want but often fall victim to thoughts that begin "I wish I were more...," "She's better than me at...," or "This should be different because..." This is not surprising, considering that we live in a "faster, better, and more" society. Enough never seems to be enough. It is hard to escape the materialism and immediate gratifications that surround us. Additionally, we measure ourselves against others and against our pesky expectations about where we think we should be.

In fact, many women I interviewed reluctantly admitted to lying about their accomplishments or contentment if they did not match their expectations. Maya is a twenty-seven-year-old artist who confesses that she often embellishes when she talks about her career. "I feel that I do this, especially since college graduation, because I feel a good deal behind wherever it is that I should be professionally. Thanks to my parents, I have always had access to the best in life, from clothes to education to experiences, so I feel as though not being an instant 'success' could only be a result of my own mismanaging of all the great things, information, and experience I have been given. Also, I come from a ridiculously accomplished family, and I feel like I, too, should be doing something damn good."

Discontent

Like Maya, many twenty-somethings suffer from the idea that something different or better is always just over the horizon. If we have fabulous careers but are single, we want great romances. If we have straight hair, we want curls. We want more money, more friends, more freedom, and more passion. I asked many women how their efforts to get what they want were going, and very few reported feeling content with where they were and what they had. If they were happy with one aspect of their lives (such as career), they were usually unhappy with another aspect (such as relationships).

April, an absolutely beautiful twenty-eight-year-old woman who is married to the love of her life, still feels that her life could be better. "Right now I am constantly reminding myself to 'keep my eyes on my own work,' often with great difficulty. I am terrified of not having the life I want and dreamed of, of not being successful enough on my own, especially if I am going to start 'breeding,' as I fondly refer to it. I am constantly fighting to keep things in perspective and denying my need to keep up with the Joneses."

As women, we tend to buy into a mentality like April's: the belief that there is always room for improvement. Thus we scrutinize every aspect of our lives. Getting what we want becomes a process of living under an analytical microscope, and that prevents us from enjoying what we already have. When is enough enough?

> "Life is never how you think it's going to be. If I had known how easy life can be if you just let it, I wouldn't have wasted so much time judging myself and keeping busy doing so many different things — I would have enjoyed the possibilities of my twenties."
>
> — Cynthia, fifty-seven

EXERCISE 16

Examining Your "Not-Enoughness"

When you're deciding how to get what you want, take into account how much "not-enoughness" affects your behavior and thinking. The following exercise is designed to help you distinguish whether and to what extent this attitude runs your life. This is a three-part exercise that moves from awareness to action.

Part 1

Write down your answers to the following questions:

1. When you inventory what you have in your life right now, do you tend to think of ways that your life could be *better* (such as making more money, dating more, or losing more weight)?

2. Is it difficult to let go of or accept something when it does not live up to your expectations or standards?

3. When you complete a task or goal, are you satisfied, or do you think of ways you could have done it better or differently?

4. When you get something you want, do you think of ways it could be better?

5. Do you think you should do more with your life?

6. Do you feel like a failure because you have not achieved what you wanted to by now?

If you answered yes to two or more of these questions, you might be getting what you want, but you're also living with the attitude that nothing is ever good enough. Consider what this costs you — probably peace of mind, satisfaction with simple things, self-confidence, and overall enjoyment of life.

Part 2

Now that you are generally aware of the extent to which not-enoughness infiltrates your life, let's get a little more specific. Make a "room for improvement" list to draw your attention to particular things in your life that you are not content with.

1. Write down all your important life categories (career, romantic relationships, social life, finances, health, physical appearance, and so on). Under each category, write down the ways that you would like to change, improve, or alter things in that arena of life.

2. Review your list, thinking about the time and energy you put into analysis and improvement. Do you think this could be keeping you from a natural process of discovery and fulfillment?

3. Are you too hard on yourself about certain things? Circle any item on your list that falls into this category. During the next month, commit to trying to let at *least* half of the things you circled go and to being content with where you are. Simply be gentler with yourself. Another good idea is to turn back to exercise 14 (see chapter 2), look at your gratitude list, and remind yourself of what you have. The next time a "not-enough" thought pops into your head, think of the things that make you smile.

4. Finally, make a separate list of the items you didn't circle. These are the areas of life to increase your focus upon; by doing so, you can make reasonable and positive changes in your overall happiness. You can add these items to your goals list, which you created in the first part of exercise 14.

Part 3

Complete this exercise by making an "action" list. This will help you to enjoy your life rather than looking at all the ways it is not good enough.

Write down a specific action you can take now to

help yourself get those things you want or to improve an aspect of your life. For instance, if you want to "work at a top magazine within two years," an action could be "Write two sample freelance articles and send my resume to ten major magazines this month."

Life is a lot less overwhelming when we are in "action" mode as opposed to "thought and feeling" mode. If we are anxious or obsessing about something, that usually means we need to *do* something in order to bring ourselves relief.

Overextending Ourselves

Once we put ourselves in action mode, we need to be cautious about overextending ourselves or getting out of balance. Natalie is a twenty-eight-year-old real estate agent who schedules every moment of her life. She works, she dates, she goes out with friends, she plans trips, she shops, she reads magazines, she volunteers, and sometimes she relaxes (when someone cancels). Natalie's sister, Amy, is twenty-six and works for a national car rental chain. When she looks at Natalie's life, she feels like a "big slacker." Amy feels that she should do more to achieve the things she wants in life, but she does not know what to do. "I am pretty happy overall, except I do feel like my life is just too simple and I may be missing out. Is that bad?"

Natalie and Amy represent flip sides of the same coin: feeling that we should always be doing, doing, doing until we arrive at what we want. Twenty-something women commonly overextend themselves. In fact, a third of my respondents stated that taking on too much and not saying no were among the characteristics they liked least about themselves. I can unequivocally say that quarter-life women are dedicated to doing a *lot*. In fact, most spend the majority of their time (ten to fourteen hours a day) and energy on the following things: working, commuting, sitting at a computer, making or thinking about money, talking on the phone, thinking about or working on their physical appearance/bodies, worrying about their relationships, and, most of all, checking off items on their to-do lists. Very few women spend any time or give any thought to reading for pleasure, learning about current events, spiritual practice, or doing things just for themselves.

We justify the stress that overdoing causes by rationalizing that we are setting up our futures. As we go after everything, it is tempting to put our fingers into many different pots, and we're even encouraged to do so. We spend a great deal of time trying to do as much as we possibly can to ensure that we will accomplish our goals and will not miss an opportunity or experience.

I was impressed by how much twenty-something women do today, from owning businesses to getting degrees to having families. This is not surprising: since the beginning of time, women have always done more. The men went out and hunted while the women gathered, cooked, raised children, and cared for the home. It is in our nature to do a lot at once; therefore, taking on many tasks feels natural. Unlike men, we are master multitaskers. Just try to have a conversation with a man while he is watching a football game (remember the dresser analogy)!

Doing a lot is not necessarily a bad thing. Our twenties are the time for exploration. But trouble begins when we do just to do and end up stressed out, confused, or overwhelmed. With too many

> "I think drama has become the sport of twenty-something women, making every decision such a big ordeal. Believe me when I tell you it will all work out and to stop agonizing. Instead, use those youthful bodies for real sports — try taking up tennis in your fifties and you'll get my drift."
>
> — Faye, fifty-six

things on our minds, we might have difficulty making major decisions, and even minor ones can feel like life-or-death situations.
Many of us believe that any choice we make during this building
phase of our lives will have life-altering ramifications. We have a
nasty habit of doing things because we think we have to, will miss
out if we don't, or think we should. If we are unsure of what we
want or how to get it, we try to do as much as possible and hope
that everything will just fall into place. It seems that doing, doing,
doing makes our twenty-something crisis keep going, going,
going.

Making Choices

Why does choosing what we want often involve so much drama
and deliberation? To answer this question, let's once again consult
Webster's, which defines *choice* as "the act of choosing; an option;
the best part; care in selecting; to be preferred; suggests the opportunity or privilege of choosing freely." Notice that nowhere in this
definition is anything said about self-doubt, obligations, fear, or
results. Yet so many of us make choices based on just these things.
Choice also is not defined as a process that completely eliminates
the possibility of something else. Perhaps one of the reasons we
struggle with decisions is that we forget we have *choices*. Making
choices is a powerful and empowering act. And isn't choice what
the feminist movement was really about? Feminism is not about
doing everything until we are exhausted, or about living up to
some fantasy of having it all. The trick is to not get into a complete
tizzy when we make a choice or beat ourselves up if we feel that we
made the wrong one.

Deanna, twenty-eight, told me, "What worries me most right
now is the direction my life should take. Try for a stable career and
buy a condo, go all out for my art, change it all and move to a new

city, or stick around and dedicate myself to a complicated relationship? I do feel like I am at multiple crossroads. I don't know what to choose and what to give up, so I end up just being paralyzed."

Keep in mind that deciding on one thing does not necessarily mean we have to entirely give up something else. For instance, if we decide to get married and have children, that doesn't eliminate the option of a career. We might go back to work later or start another career from home. It is not surprising that many of us in our twenties lack confidence in our decision making: we have not had a lot of experience in making choices on our own and seeing the results of these choices. Parents and advisors were once around to assist us. But as we pursue our goals as adult women, making more choices along the way, we will begin to see that we usually do know what is in our best interest. True, a big decision can be confusing at times, but in reality life has a way of taking care of us if we take care of ourselves.

> "Be confident in your choices and responsible for your actions. Don't have regrets, because with strength any situation can be changed."
>
> — Sue, forty-nine

EXERCISE 17

Taking a Life Inventory

Part 1

To get what we truly want, it is necessary to eliminate the things in our lives that do not align with our most important goals and values, and to commit ourselves 100 percent to the things we do want. Remember the discussion about having it all? Taking on too many tasks and ambitions makes it impossible to give any aspect of your life the attention it deserves. In this exercise, you'll inventory the choices you are making in your life.

First, write down all the important things you have recently done and are currently doing. Include everything from "Tried the South Beach diet" to "Read a self-help book" to "Went skiing for the first time" to "Aced the bar." Then assign each a letter from one of the following categories (if more than one category applies, write down both letters):

A. Something I do that I really enjoy (such as going for a hike).

B. Something I do that I do not enjoy, that I dread, or that completely overwhelms me (such as spending time with a negative friend).

C. Something I do because I am sure it will help me reach a desired goal (such as going to law school because I want to be a lawyer or working out to stay healthy).

D. Something I do even though I am unsure it will help me reach a desired goal (such as dating because I want to find a partner).

E. Something I do *solely* because I think I should do it (such as taking a job because it will look good on my resume).

Next, look over your list and answer the following questions:

1. How many of the things on your list were assigned the letters B, D, or E?

2. How many of them were assigned the letters A or C?

3. What do you think would happen if you eliminated the B-, D-, or E-rated items from your life? Try to eliminate *at least* one for the next week, and see what results.

4. What do you *not* do, even though you want to, because you are busy with all the things on your list? Pick one such activity or goal and, within the next week, do it, especially if that means you won't do something in the B, D, or E categories!

Part 2

Now answer these follow-up questions:

1. Is *overwhelmed* a word you often use to describe how you feel?
2. Do you feel that you never have enough time?
3. Do you tend to start a lot of projects but have trouble finishing them?
4. Is your stress reflected in your health and behavior? For instance, do you have trouble sleeping? Do you have complexion problems? Do you drive or eat too fast?

If you answered yes to these questions, you may be doing too much, and a lot of it might not accord with what you really want. Look over your list again and see what else you could (and might want to) eliminate. Remember, it's okay to say no to people or offers, and your reason can be "Just because." We are grown-ups now; we are allowed to use that answer.

PLANNING YOUR LIFE INSTEAD OF LIVING IT

Often the choices that we make in life are significantly influenced by the master plan we have in our head for how we would like our life to go. Why are so many of us addicted to planning? Unfortunately, life does not come with a crystal ball that shows us exactly how to get what we want. So, in order to feel somewhat in control of our fate, we end up making a lot of plans for our life. At age twenty-six, Alicia is finishing her MBA, interviewing with various companies, and well on her way toward a career in business consulting. She reports that her life is going pretty much according to a plan she initiated for herself in high school: attend college, then work two years to get experience so she would be an appealing applicant to top business schools, then get her master's, then get a great job, and along the way have some sort of social life. She does not have a lot of time to date but forces herself to do it anyway because she plans to marry before she is twenty-nine so she can have at least one child by thirty-one.

When I pointed out to Alicia that her life seems rather planned, she responded that she didn't know any other way to ensure that she will get what she wants. When I asked her if she allows herself to stray from the plan, Alicia said she is not totally rigid. However, she sees her twenties as the time to get all her ducks in a row. Finally, when I asked her if she is happy and fulfilled, she replied, "Not completely, but if everything goes according to plan, I will be."

Like Alicia, many of us live for "someday" rather than today. We think and reason in "when/then" and "if/then" terms: "*When* I get that job, *then* I will feel successful." "*If* I get married, *then* I will feel secure in my relationship." Driven by the weight of expectations and our urgency to get what we want, we focus on the future. The women I interviewed spent, on average, 60 percent of their time thinking about or planning for the future. Seventy percent reported they felt pressured to have plans for their lives, and of that 70 percent, the average amount of their plans they felt they had completed was 30 percent. The point is, a lot of us exhaust ourselves by trying to adhere to our "This is how I get what I want" plans, which many of us outlined before we could even vote!

Jennifer told me, "I just turned twenty-five, and my family and I celebrated as we always do. When they brought out the cake, singing 'Happy Birthday,' I started crying. I was so upset because I was not where I thought I'd be in my life. I am not married; I don't even have a boyfriend! No house; my career is up in the air; and there is no way I could have a baby by twenty-seven. This is the lowest time in my life. I feel like a loser because I have not met any of my life goals yet and my twenties are already half over."

Are You a Planaholic?

I thought my type A planning personality was unique until I started researching this book. Perhaps you have heard this piece of advice (my father regurgitated it when things did not go my way): "We must be willing to give up the life that we have planned so as to live the life that's waiting for us." Unfortunately, many of us quarter-lifers grip our life plans so tightly that we become planaholics. Setting an unrealistic timeline for our lives is a guaranteed way to provoke premature signs of aging, so why do we do it?

There are a few possible explanations. For the first time, we sense that we are getting older and feel it is time to create adult lives. Additionally, we believe that if we work hard now, we'll someday see the light at the end of the tunnel. And thus we become result-obsessed. But this obsession has a cost.

Take Kathleen, twenty-four, who spends so much time living in the future that she has begun to neglect her present. "I spend a lot of time thinking about the future because I need a plan of action so I'll know what's ahead. I like to think of myself in the future and to determine the way I am going to be. I've always done this, but it has gotten worse in my twenties." She explains further, "My relationship with my boyfriend, who is great, is on thin ice right now. I've been so consumed with work that I don't make a lot of time for him. In the little time we do have together, I always start the 'Where is this relationship going?' conversation. My boyfriend pointed out to me that all my stress comes from planning and thinking about my future and then being overly disappointed when things don't happen. He told me he's really sick of it."

> "Having a plan makes you feel more confident, but know that plans are great for setting goals and that's all. You will truly learn what you are made of when things don't go according to your master plan."
>
> — Priscilla, sixty-one

Taking time to "stop and smell the roses" might seem to be just another overused cliché, but it is something that we women in our twenties don't often do. Rather, we think things such as "I should plant some roses to make my yard look better" or "I hope someday he sends me roses" or "When I can afford a house, then I'll have a rose garden." Can't we just stop and smell the freaking roses? If you can't because it's not on your agenda, I would venture to guess that you have some anxiety in your life. When I asked Michelle, twenty-seven, how she was getting what she wants, she said, "That question makes me think of the future — I think of it all the time, and I am trying to stop! I think things like 'Okay, I am getting older; I should travel now; I may get married and have kids; I should really be into a career by now,' and so on. I totally think on a timeline, and I actually get stressed about free time, like I need to be doing something. I have to relax!"

Michelle is right: we have to relax, but most of us don't. I have heard it said that depression results from living in the past, while anxiety results from living in the future. This makes a lot of sense, since most of the knots in our stomachs are caused by things we are anticipating. It is natural to want to plan as much as possible in order to ease our fears about what lies ahead. However, in reality, no plan can control or predict the future, and overplanning can actually create more anxiety. As we journey into adulthood, we evolve away from lives in which everything was planned for us and taken care of by our parents, into college lives where we enjoy some freedom but our general structure is set, and finally into a reality that is devoid of a set curriculum. This absence of structure drives many of us right into planning mode. But what do we miss along the way? Does overplanning cause us to miss the very important steps of truly evaluating what we want and easing into our experiences?

> "Don't feel like you have to keep up with a time-line. You will just set your-self up for failure and disappointment. Have faith that everything happens for a reason and exactly when it is supposed to, and enjoy the moments of your life: you will never get them back."
>
> — Jo, fifty-five

To ease the woes of our twenty-something crisis, we can remind ourselves that just making the best decisions that we can every day is good enough. If we stop, take a deep breath, and check in with the present moment more often, a lot of the knots in our stomachs will loosen. A lot of us daydream about how things could be different or better in our lives because we hate our current circumstances. Although daydreaming can be valuable, true sanity comes from contentment with where we are. There is a big difference between the real pleasure of the here and now and the illusory pleasure of fantasy. Many dreams about how we *want* the future to be are simply ways to avoid reality. Living for the future and staying extra-busy with unnecessary activities keeps us from fully evolving and tapping into our present-day experience of life.

EXERCISE 18

Making Your To-Do List

Getting out of your head and into the present moment is actually not an easy task. This exercise will help you organize all the plans and dreams that float around in your mind. Once they are down on paper and you've committed time to thinking and acting upon them, it will be easier to let them go and focus on the here and now.

To start, write down your life's current to-do list — include everything from what you need to do today to what you want to do before you die. Include all the menial tasks that you remember when you are falling asleep (such as cleaning out that junk drawer) and all the things you dream about (such as going to Paris). Don't leave anything out!

Next, add a "goal-less" activity to your list that you will do sometime in the next week. Think of an activity that has no end result or won't result in any particular experience. For instance, leave your house and go on a walk. Don't take a watch, a wallet, or a phone. Just walk. See where you end up, see who you meet, see what you notice.

Now that you have your to-do list, schedule a specific time to think about it so its tasks won't echo throughout your day. Constantly thinking about everything you must do does not help you accomplish anything. It just makes you reach for the Pepto-Bismol or the glass of wine at the end of the day. Instead, schedule ten to fifteen minutes every morning to look at your to-do list, add to it, worry about it, obsess about it, and so on, and then do not allow yourself to do that for the rest of the day. Either take action on an item or decide when you will take action on it and then put it out of your mind.

Cross items off the list as you complete them. Whenever you feel overwhelmed, stay calm, take a breath, and know that whatever you can't do today, you can think about during your allotted time tomorrow. You might discover that planning a time to concentrate on your to-do list decreases the overall time and energy you spend (and waste) being consumed by it. You will feel less overwhelmed, more present and productive, and you might actually get to do more things you *want* to do.

———∞———

Designing a road map of our lives based on our beliefs and expectations can make us feel more secure. Yet, truthfully, we have to remember that the bottom can fall out at any time. Setting standards and making plans are great ways to set goals, but our circumstances do change. We cannot limit our experience of life to what we think we can control or understand or what makes us feel safe. As we cycle through the questions of the twenties triangle — "Who am I? What do I want? How do I get what I want?" — we must remain open and create fresh answers when they're needed. If we can accept that our answers will evolve for the rest of our lives, we will move one step closer to living in the flow of the circle rather than the jaggedness of the triangle.

PART 2

Building a Secure Foundation

Now that we have established what brings a twenty-something crisis to life and explored the questions that give it a pulse, you might ask, "Okay, now how do I get out of this crisis so that I can have the life that I want?" Well, if I had a simple formula for that, I would have bottled it and sold it and would now be sitting in a villa in Tuscany rather than at this computer in my sweatpants. What I *do* know is that your crisis is a natural result of trying to figure out so much at once.

Consider the following analogy. Our twenties are a time when we are building the house in which we'll live the rest of our lives. If you were actually building a house, how would you do it? Probably you would start by blueprinting a structure; then you'd gather all the materials, lay a solid foundation, and finally put up the frame and construct all the rooms that the house will contain. Many of us excel at the "blueprint" stage. We have plans for our lives, to the extent that we become planaholics. Most of us are also quite clear on where to gather the right materials. For instance, we go to college, date, establish ourselves in new cities, make friends, and so on. But then we skip a step. Often we are so anxious to throw ourselves into careers, relationships, or causes that we ignore the important step of laying a solid foundation and jump headlong into building the "rooms" of our lives.

What do I mean by a "foundation"? It is the overall sense of solid security on which we build our lives. The twenty-something crisis occurs as we struggle to make major decisions about our future while lacking emotional, physical, and financial security. We know better than to live in a house built on unstable ground, but do we consider the dangers of creating a life without a solid sense of self?

As we struggle with the questions of the twenties triangle ("Who am I? What do I want? How do I get what I want?"), we need to inspect our foundation. This part of the book shows you how to do that groundwork so that you can create the life you want. Here we assess the solidity of the foundations of the houses we live in now and the houses we are building. Each chapter in this part inspects a separate area of our foundation that either has not yet been laid or needs reinforcement. Given all the world's expectations — and our own — it is easy to feel dismissive about doing this inspection, excavation, and cementing. Yet we need to do it before we are consumed by the practical aspects of being on our own, such as paying rent, managing our finances, establishing social circles, committing to relationships, starting families, and finding jobs.

Even if you feel that you already have a solid sense of self, I encourage you to read carefully through these chapters. Consider it an archaeological excavation of your life thus far. You might not find anything new, but until you start digging, you'll never know what is there. As you read these pages, you will discover a deeper understanding of yourself.

CHAPTER 4

SECURING YOUR INDEPENDENCE

We face a lot of changes when we are on our own for the first time. As the protection and identity offered by our college circles, our hometowns, and our families recede, we experience a hodge-podge of emotions. Our habits, influences, and beliefs all color our experience of our new independence. We harbor many illusions about how this time in our lives should be, and, with our future-driven mentality, we tend to gloss over the phases and distinctions of this decade of passage. Thus we find ourselves in the middle of the twenties triangle. To alleviate some of the pressure we feel about being on our own, let's focus on the three basic phases of this time in our lives. I call them the ABCs of independence: adjustment, behavior, and creation.

PHASE 1: ADJUSTMENT

Moving from being a daughter, teenager, and student to being an adult woman is one of the most significant transitions in our lives.

It usually begins when we graduate from college and/or move out on our own for the first time. We are adjusting, learning to walk on new ground that often feels a bit shaky. Picture a baby fawn. When she first stands up, her legs are extremely wobbly and she is unsure of whether they will support her. Eventually, she learns to put strength, coordination, and confidence together and walk on her own. But it takes time and practice. The fact is, we are wobbly throughout a large portion of our twenties, and that's simply because we are in the adjustment phase of womanhood.

Jamilia is a twenty-three-year-old recent college graduate who is excited about her new adult life. She recently got her first apartment with one of her college friends, started her first job as a research assistant at a biotech lab (she was a biology major, so this job really fits), and leased a new car. She is off to a great start! Jamilia loves being free from homework and feels a great sense of accomplishment about graduating from college. She is relieved that she has a job and can generate her own income, because now her parents have less right to breathe down her neck. Yet, to Jamilia's surprise, although her independence is enjoyable, she feels that she actually has less freedom. "In college, even though my parents were still supporting me, there was a huge sense of independence because my responsibilities were not that great. Now I feel like I have independence without freedom. I have to be at work at a certain time or I won't get paid; I have to pay my bills or I'll get penalized; and if I turn to my parents for help, I'll feel childish. The burden of responsibility now is on a whole different level."

Jamilia is experiencing what I call the double-edged sword of independence. On the one hand, it is liberating to not have anyone tell us what to do. On the other, we yearn for someone to give us answers and guidance. No one can steal our thunder, yet we have no one to blame for our actions. Our lives are no longer scripted; nothing is written in stone; we can go anywhere and become anything. Yet now our closest support systems are gone, and we face our own destinies. If we move to new cities, we might feel a little out of place. We might miss our families and friends more than we thought we would.

As we discussed in the preceding chapters, this notion of independence is stressful since we face so many choices and questions. Furthermore, no class adequately prepares us for the "real world." The duties of a grown-up are not as clear-cut as those of a student. Getting a job, moving, finding a place to live, paying rent, paying back college loans, getting health care, managing credit cards, doing taxes, trying to save money, finding insurance, and making car payments become *present* realities. At the same time, quarter-lifers feel pressure to plan for the *future*. But how can we do that when the present is so overwhelming?

As Kat, a twenty-six-year-old from Alabama, puts it so poignantly: "We are expected to graduate from college and immediately be on our own. Of course, graduation is something we all look forward to when we are in college, but once we get out and are on our own, it is 'What the hell has happened to me!' Sometimes I still wish I could have Mom and Dad kiss my boo-boos and say that everything will be okay."

Transitioning to Independence

We all want to (or feel that others expect us to) be independent as soon as we reach our early twenties. Most of us approach this transition to independence in one of two ways: we adopt the mentalities discussed in chapter 3 — "not-enoughness," "doing, doing, doing," and "I gotta have a plan" — in order to prove we can make it on our own, or we remain dependent on an outside source, such as our parents or a romantic partner. Both approaches have one thing in common: they are solution-driven strategies.

In my early twenties, I took the former approach. School was always relatively easy for me, but I was very nervous about what I would do to achieve the fabulous career that everyone (including me) told me I should have. Hours after my college graduation ceremony, my car was packed and I headed to Los Angeles to conquer Hollywood. I was a resume-sending, cold-calling machine, and within two weeks I had a job and a place to live. Proving to my parents that I could make it on my own financially was very important given the substantial investment they had made in my education. At work, I never took time off because I figured there would be time for that later. I thought that getting established on my career track was more important. Cut to over four years later, in my plush office in Beverly Hills: I was completely burned out and questioning everything.

Transitioning to an independent life comes with a degree of discomfort. Most of us don't like this feeling, so we immediately look for a way to get more comfortable (i.e., a solution). If panic and urgency feel familiar to you, maybe you need to slow down and give yourself time to adjust. Think of it this way: If you hired a contractor to build your house, you would want her to get the job done well. If her approach was rushed, wouldn't that be a red flag? You would worry that she was doing things haphazardly. So why are many of us willing to rush into our lives?

Getting Comfortable with Being Uncomfortable

The twenties have a natural progression, and we need to just let it unfold, as uncomfortable as it might be. I realize this sounds rather simplistic, since life is not organized into stages and it's hard to let our twenties just happen. Questions about our independence are bound to come up, so how can we manage them? The answer is quite simple: we need to stop feeling that we must find all the answers at once. We can take comfort in the fact that our feelings are normal, and we can allow ourselves to experience them. Understanding that we are in a transition period is a critical part of securing our independence; this time teaches us how to take care of ourselves and offers us the freedom to just "be." How many of us give ourselves such a chance?

When we are in too much of a hurry to get comfortable, we often immerse ourselves in situations — such as relationships, jobs, or grad school — that we are not 100 percent sure about but that offer security or direction. Can this teach us true independence? Of course, we cannot be totally irresponsible, forget all our plans, move to an island, and meditate on who we are and what we want (although that does sound nice, especially if a cute island boy is there, but I digress). We simply need to give ourselves the gift of some time to be on our own. Take a vacation by yourself, visit a foreign country, take a community college class just for fun, read trashy novels, daydream, and perhaps take a couple of jobs that might seem directionless and "beneath you." We also need to give ourselves time away from our parents. That's easy for some, since parents can be pretty annoying. But love and guilt might keep others tied to their parents. Healthy separation from Mom and Dad is a natural and vital part of our development — we have to do it.

As we transition into womanhood, we also need to be gentle with ourselves. Maybe if we gave ourselves permission to relax and *discover* who we are rather than immediately *defining* ourselves, the phrase "twenty-something crisis" could be replaced by something more appealing, such as "twenty-something awakening."

EXERCISE 19

Reflecting on Your Independence

As you have ventured into the world on your own in your twenties, people probably have asked you many questions about what you want to do, where you want to live, and who and if you are dating. But have they asked you, or have you asked yourself, to reflect on how the transition to independence has felt to you? We can focus so much on outcomes that we forget that the process of adjustment and discovery is a key element of this transition. The following questions will help you acknowledge this process:

1. When did you feel "on your own" for the first time? Did a certain event make you feel this way?

2. How did you deal with this event?

3. What was your greatest fear during that time? What is your greatest fear now?

4. What did you learn about yourself during that time?

5. How do you think that *discovering* yourself differs from *defining* yourself?

6. Have you given yourself an adjustment period in your twenties?

7. Do you wish you had done something differently during these years?

8. Are any current experiences in your life making you feel especially on your own? If so, do they also make you feel a little unsteady?

9. Do you feel independent right now?

10. In what areas of your life do you feel truly independent? In what areas do you not?

Perhaps answering the above questions brought things to mind that you might not have previously considered or had forgotten about. Did you discover anything about yourself? Is there anything you need to accept rather than trying to change or fix? This type of self-discovery is designed to let us give ourselves permission to just be where we are, to let ourselves adjust as we become more independent. Did you ever give yourself this permission?

Taking "the lay of the land" is the first step in building a secure foundation. As you read about the next two phases of independence, keep in mind *your* experience of being on your own. Try not to focus on things you think you should've done differently, or on goals you think you should have accomplished by now.

PHASE 2: BEHAVIOR

Kelly is a twenty-three-year-old recent graduate who always envisioned her future in her hometown, Pittsburgh. Whenever her parents discussed her life, it was always set there. They would not even consider paying tuition for an out-of-state school. So Kelly went to college nearby and came home almost every weekend. Yet a desire to move away just burned inside her. She yearned for freedom and a fresh start but felt she couldn't make one. "The guilt from my family and my fear of leaving them made it seem impossible." Then a good friend living in Seattle encouraged Kelly to move there. She longed for new experience and loathed the predictable fate that awaited her in Pittsburgh. Despite her family's disapproval, she made the move.

Her first month in Seattle was exciting and liberating, but then reality hit. Her only friend there was busy with a job, a boyfriend, and her own circle of friends. Kelly feels lost, lonely, and a little homesick. "Sure, there were times I felt lonely at home, too, but at least there was the physical presence of family there." She lies to her family about how she is doing for fear they'll say, "I told you so," and urge her to come home. Kelly beats herself up because all she wanted was to be on her own and, now that she is, she isn't doing as well as she thinks she should.

Being on your own might provoke questions such as "What am I doing? What have I done?" You might feel apprehension about the destination you've arrived at. In my early twenties, I loved the song "Once in a Lifetime" by the Talking Heads. These lines really struck a chord with me: "And you may ask yourself — Well...How did I get here? / ...And you may ask yourself, Where does that highway go? / And you may ask yourself, Am I right?...Am I wrong? / And you may tell yourself, My God!... What have I done?" Each time I heard the song, I cranked it up louder. Its lyrics resonated with me because I was working at a job and living in a place I did not like. It became my twenties anthem, replacing "In Your Eyes," which had lasted right through my teens (I still expect John Cusack to show up in my front yard holding his boom box over his head). And as I researched this book, I learned that many twenty-something women feel the same bewilderment. As we struggle with the question "What do I want?" additional, related questions, such as "Do I even want or like what I have now?" also appear. And when they do, they are often more daunting than the first time we discover cellulite on our bodies.

Reactionary versus Intrinsic Behavior

The next phase in securing our foundation is to identify the motivations for our behavior as we establish independent lives. For the purposes of this chapter, I define *behavior* as how we make the decisions we make, as well as the actions we take. We need to answer one key question: "Do I behave in a way that is indeed independent?" If you (like me) are having a Talking Heads experience in your twenties and are questioning aspects of your life, chances are that the answer is no. As we become more independent, the questions of the twenties triangle become easier to answer. Conversely, the less secure our independence is the more we remain triangulated within those questions.

Take Kelly, for instance. She is desperately trying to prove to her parents and herself that she can make it away from home. Kelly equates independence with rebelling against what her parents told her she should do. The foundation on which she is building a life "on her own" is primarily her ego. For many of us, disregarding a "should," as Kelly did, is a commendable action that is important to our growth; however, we need to understand what motivates that action. In Kelly's case, moving to Seattle was more about her desire to challenge her parents' wishes than about her desire to start her life there. She had never even been to Seattle before, and she hates rain. Kelly's first step on the road toward securing her independence was *reactionary*, not *intrinsic*. Reactionary behavior happens in response to emotions (in Kelly's case, feeling restrained by her parents). Intrinsic behavior involves doing something because we feel it's in our best interest.

> "Be willing to change your mind, opinions, and views, but do it only from your own experience and what you want, not as a reaction to outside pressure."
>
> — Martha, fifty-three

Many of us are unaware of the distinction between reactionary and intrinsic (or internally driven) behavior. Of course, it's hard to distinguish them if we don't yet know who we are or what we want. Reactionary decisions are a direct result of the pressure we feel to *look* independent coupled with our limited independent life experience. We often make choices in our twenties based on our reactions to others' expectations or opinions. Yet it *is* possible to make intrinsic decisions free from outside influences. We need to look within ourselves to answer the major questions of our lives, and sometimes that might feel a little risky because we are unfamiliar with turning inward.

Joanna is a twenty-four-year-old who is just starting a career in hospitality. Immediately after graduation, she was expected to get a job. Everyone told her that if she didn't, she would fall behind and struggle in her career. But something inside her did not feel ready to get a job. "I felt so burnt out from pushing myself in high school and college that I did not really have the energy to even commit to figuring out what I wanted to do. So I took time off before I made any serious decisions. I followed a close friend to Colorado, and it was us against the world. It was the first time I had to pay rent with my own money and just figure things out. It was fantastic." Joanna feels that that experience was more rewarding than any job she could have gotten. It gave her an opportunity to follow her gut and learn how to "do life." She also learned that she had not fallen behind: the "real-world" life everyone was pressuring her to start was waiting when she got back.

Being a truly independent woman means making independent, yet responsible, choices, as Joanna did. Making independent and responsible choices requires honestly evaluating why we make the decisions we make. Many of us move to new cities to escape our parents or our past, not because we really want to live there. We take jobs because we are in a rush to start careers, not because they interest us. We get into serious relationships for companionship at a time when loneliness sets in, not necessarily because we have met

> "Don't get caught up in the instant-gratification style of thinking and acting. Think deeply about what you really want and why you want it. You can get a drive-through Happy Meal only at McDonald's, not in the real world."
>
> — Penny, fifty

our best match. During a twenty-something crisis, we often choose what seems to be the safe choice, but a safe choice can also be only a reaction to our past. Sometimes things seem safe because they are familiar, not because they are in our best interest.

EXERCISE 20

Examining Your Decisions

Making the important distinction between reactionary and intrinsic motivation will make your future decisions easier and better aligned with your true self. The following questions are designed to help you evaluate how many of your past decisions were reactionary or intrinsic.

1. Refer back to your answers to questions 1 and 2 in exercise 19 ("When did you feel 'on your own' for the first time? Did a certain event make you feel this way?" and "How did you deal with this event?"). Do you think the decisions you made regarding that event were driven by intrinsic or reactionary motivations?

2. Have you made any decisions or taken any actions to prove something to someone (your parents, peers, or even yourself)? If so, what were they?

3. Have you ever decided to do something because it seemed to be the safest option? If so, what was it? Were you/are you satisfied with that choice?

4. Now look at your answer to question 10 of exercise 19. There you listed areas of your life in which you feel independent. Do you feel independent in these

areas because you've done what *you* truly wanted for yourself?

5. If you could do anything you wanted right now, anything at all, what would it be? Think of an action you want to take, not something you want to possess.

Did you notice that many of your actions are motivated by outside sources or that you've often chosen what seemed to be safe options? If you did, congratulations — you are normal. Many of us try to ease the growing pains of independence through decisive behavior that's actually fueled by expectations (i.e., reactionary behavior). Yet we need to realize that making big decisions or engaging in grown-up activities cannot itself make us independent. Discovering and accepting who we are, what we want, and how to get it are the keys to true independence. We should remind ourselves that it takes some time to answer these questions and that we need to set realistic, individual expectations for ourselves. Practicing and eventually establishing more intrinsically motivated behavior will not only ease our twenty-something crisis; they also will give us a more secure foundation on which to build.

> "Choose with heart and mind — one without the other puts you out of balance."
>
> — Maude, sixty-four

PHASE 3: CREATION

Felicia, a twenty-seven-year-old accounts manager, has spent the past four years at a job she hates. She stays at it because it will look good on a graduate school application. She has been saving for grad school, which she wants to attend so she can make more money in her field. Her parents have offered to help her out, but since they paid for college, she really doesn't want any more of their money: "I feel like if I take their money, I'll owe them something. It's really important for me to do this by myself; I'll feel a greater sense of accomplishment when it is over." When I asked Felicia why making a lot of money is so important to her, she told me that, one, she enjoys the finer things in life, and, two, although she wants to get married, she doesn't want to become financially dependent on a man.

Felicia recently decided to move to her own apartment because she thought it was time to live alone and she was tired of her roommate. She hired movers and did not ask anyone for help — Felicia hates asking for help or looking needy. "One of the things I like about myself is how independent I am — I have all the resources I need to take care of myself." To Felicia, independence means not relying on anyone to make her happy. When I asked her how people, especially her peers and guys she has dated, react to her independence, she said, "Well, they do notice that I tend not to get too close. I've even had people tell me I should get better at letting others contribute more or help, but that feels weak." Felicia got very quiet and then looked sad. I asked her what she was thinking, and she said, "Sometimes I wonder if my independence is a little isolating."

Defining Independence

Is independence overrated? Must the pride and sense of accomplishment we gain from being completely on our own always be mingled with the stress and loneliness that Felicia feels? Once we've allowed ourselves a period of adjustment and have learned to make truly intrinsic choices, we still must live with those choices and create lives entirely on our own. So many women in their twenties find themselves struggling as they try to prove they can make it. As

I talked to twenty-something women, I repeatedly heard things such as "I am exhausted because I am trying to do too much by myself," "I hate the thought of ever having to depend on anyone," "I feel like I am burning the candle at both ends," "I always feel behind," and so on. When we feel overwhelmed, we often do not ask for help because that might be perceived as weak or somehow offset our independence. If "independent" is one of our answers to the questions "Who am I?" and "Who do I want to be?" we can become very adamant about securing this independence.

> "There is nothing you have to prove to anyone else, and don't be shy to ask for help along the way — we all need it, at any age."
>
> — Sandra, sixty-five

Many fiercely independent twenty-something women hold the strong opinion that the best way to extinguish any sense of independence is to become financially dependent on a man. As Rita, twenty-six, says, "I would never be financially dependent on a spouse, because I garner great pride from taking care of myself. I have seen too many women lose sight of their own goals and desires and cave in to what their spouses want. Not every situation is that extreme, but I like to be prepared for the worst-case scenario. I will share in expenses and savings with my husband, but I will be sure to always plan for my own adventures and dreams." Few twenty-something women reported feeling okay about complete financial dependence on a partner. Most who were open to it said they would do it only if they were raising children. However, if you are fine with eventually being supported by a partner, that is 100 percent okay, too, as long as that support is not enabling (we'll discuss enabling a little later).

Brandy is a twenty-eight-year-old living in Cincinnati who feels that she has coasted through her twenties so far. After she graduated from college, Brandy did not know what she wanted to do and just bounced around from job to job. She volunteers, goes out with her friends, shops, and keeps herself very busy. "I feel that I never fully developed survival skills because I had a 'cush' life. Maybe I was born without that drive for success, money, or recognition. While briefly living on my own, I was bad with saving money and with finances in general. Being self-sufficient is such a hard thing to do, and when I tried I was defeated by all the stuff you have to do and gave up. Thank goodness I had my parents around to help me." Brandy now lives with her boyfriend, who supports her financially. She wants to be more independent, but she has gotten very comfortable with the current situation. Brandy is beginning to "feel very behind the curve in terms of being a grown-up. I guess I am pretty happy, but I feel like I need more of my own thing."

EXERCISE 21

Your Definition of Independence

Now that you have read about how some of your peers define independence in their lives, it's your turn. Assess how you define independence by answering the following questions:

1. What does independence mean to you?

2. Do you consider yourself completely independent?

3. If not, what would it take you to get there?

4. If you do consider yourself independent, why? What have you done and what are you currently doing that make you independent?

Since how we define things often influences our actions and decisions, keep your definition of independence in mind as you continue to create your independent life. Perhaps your definition needs a little refining.

Interdependence

The input many women gave me led me to question how we perceive independence. Once again, I consulted my trusted friend Mr. Webster, who defines *independence* as "not subject to control by others, self-governing; not affiliated with a larger controlling unit; not requiring or relying on something else; not looking to others for one's opinions or for guidance in conduct."

Most of us would define independence in a similar way. However, many of us also have a major misconception about independence that significantly fuels quarter-life feelings of stress and burnout. We believe that in order to be independent, *we must do everything on our own.* Yet this is a completely ridiculous notion. Think of it in the simplest of terms: survival. We need three basic things to live — food, clothing, and shelter. Very few of us actually grow our own food, make our own clothes, and build our own homes. If we do not fulfill our basic needs by ourselves, why do we put so much pressure on ourselves to do everything else on our own? Just what are we trying to prove?

We are all naturally interdependent beings, and knowing when and who to ask for help is an essential aspect of true independence. Remember, *Webster's* does not define *independence* as doing everything alone, but rather as not being controlled by, reliant on, or guided by the opinions of others. Giving and receiving support is part of being human. So another necessary part of our foundation is a healthy support system composed of people, things, and activities that are part of our interdependent lives.

Angie, twenty-five, told me, "The biggest challenge I face in my twenties is searching for a place to call my own among people. I seek to surround myself with people who allow me to grow, to become stronger, smarter, happier, and more fulfilled." It is natural to want a trusted group to belong and turn to at a time when so much of our lives seems up in the air. In our newly independent lives, we will encounter bumps in the road — such as accidents, breakups, illness, or losing a job — that threaten our overall security. Creating a solid support system is crucial because it is our safety net when we feel off balance. Some of us confuse being supported with being enabled, which means being overly dependent on someone or something to the extent that it becomes a crutch. But being supported does not make us less independent. Remember Felicia, who is so afraid to jeopardize her independence that she refuses any kind of support? People in her life tell her that she is hard to get close to. Her fear of being supported and her need for control might push people away. She is securing a rather lonely life, not a truly independent one.

We all need support, and we all like to feel supportive. To put this in perspective, think about a time when you did something for another person. It probably made you feel great. And it probably did not make you perceive the person on the receiving end as weak or less independent than you. Support becomes enabling only when we become overly dependent. Remember Brandy, the woman with the cush life? She went from being enabled by her parents to being dependent on her boyfriend. This cost her the opportunity to learn how to do things on her own and generate her own support system. She is not strengthening her own foundation; instead, she is living on the foundations of others.

"Find people like you, who get you, and who help you to be yourself, and surround yourself with them — trust me, they are out there."

— Joannie, fifty-one

Identifying and eliminating the tendency to be either too controlling or too enabled are fundamental to the creation of our independent lives. If we play it too safe, we will always wonder, "Could I have done it on my own, and what would my life have been like if I had?" At the same time, no medals are handed out to those twenty-somethings who handle all the changes and challenges of these years totally alone. The only thing at the end of that road is high blood pressure.

EXERCISE 22

Independence versus Interdependence

Time for another perception check to see how you are assembling your foundation. The following questions will help to further clarify what independence means to you, and will also help you discover the approach toward independence that you've taken.

1. For the most part, do you prefer to do everything on your own? If so, does this way of securing your independence cost you anything?

2. For the most part, do you prefer to be supported or held up by someone or something? If so, does this way of securing your independence cost you anything?

3. In your journal, make two columns labeled "independence" and "interdependence." Filling them in is more basic than you might think. In the independence column,

just list all the things that you do on your own. For instance, if you always pay for or make most of your own meals, put "food" in that category. In the interdependence column, list all the things and people you depend on in your life. For instance, if you take the bus to work, put "public transit" in that category.

4. Now go back through your independence list and highlight anything that you would like or could use some help with.

5. Go back through the interdependence list and by each item write either "enable" or "support." Distinguish the things that support you, such as the bus that takes you to work, from those that enable you, such as permitting your sister to fight all the battles with your mother for you.

6. Look at what you highlighted in question 4. Pick at least three things on that list that you will commit to getting assistance with. This is a way to facilitate healthy interdependence in your life.

7. Look at the two categories you made in question 5. Pick at least two things that currently enable you and, over the next month, commit to taking steps to break those patterns.

Building an External Support System

The first time that we are cut off from our parents, geographically, emotionally, and/or financially, is the classic defining moment of independence. But merely breaking away from our parents does not secure our independence. We also must establish healthy, secure support systems of other people. In our twenties, surrounding ourselves with as much healthy input as we can helps us to feel more grounded. This decade is a formative time when others' assistance and support might save us from a lot of credit card debt or therapy down the road. Since a support system is like the cement in our foundation, we need to look at how it was created and determine whether it enables us or is weak. We cannot control the families we are born into, the students we went to school with, our college dorm culture, our colleagues, our exposure to the media, or our overall environment. However, as we set up our independent lives, we *can* choose our support systems. And they don't have to include relatives. We often forget that just sharing DNA with someone does not necessarily entitle them to be part of the inner circle of our support systems.

"Dedicate time and energy to developing and maintaining quality relationships. In the end, people are all you have, and they are the most fulfilling part of your life."

— Diana, forty-nine

Creating new social lives and circles of friends who can become part of our support systems does require effort. Whether we have moved away or just grown apart from old friends, we look for new people to connect with during our twenties. Many women find it's now more difficult to relate to childhood and/or college friends. Kate, twenty-six, just transferred to a new city because of a job promotion. She now finds she has nothing in common with her friends in her Texas hometown. "They are all getting married and having babies, and it's weird not having things to talk about with women who I grew up with. I want to call my best girlfriend and yap, but she is more interested in breastfeeding." As we graduate and enter the world of grown-ups, a social life does not just show up, the way it did in college. We search for new friends but often don't know where to find them. If we are new to a city or company, breaking into established cliques of women can also be hard. But just because it's hard or intimidating does not mean we cannot do it. If we do not make an effort to surround ourselves with like-minded people in our twenties, when will we do it? When we are playing Bingo in our nursing homes?

> "Life's too short to think critically of people, to think they're not 'good' enough for you. Lots of people have a lot to offer once you let them."
>
> — Donna, fifty-nine

Our needs, desires, and goals have changed since our teenage years, which is why we need to amend the support systems that we relied on as teenage girls. If we withdraw, either emotionally or geographically, from our previous support systems without setting up new ones, we will be lonely. Let's return to the analogy of your life as a house. You can look at your support system as another important element to include in your foundation to ensure a reinforced, stable home.

EXERCISE 23

Your Twenties Toolbox

The next exercises center on the things, skills, and people you will need to have in your "twenties toolbox" as you lay your foundation. As any good builder knows, you need more than one tool in a toolbox, and you will use some more than others.

Begin by making a list of the "tools" or components of your current support system. Just think of your everyday life, and identify the individuals and external things that support you. Separate your list into two categories: people and things. "Things" can be material things, such as your car, which is a tool that helps you get from home to work, or they can be non-material things like going to church.

After you have completed your list of tools, answer the following:

1. Which tools do you use most?

2. Which tools can you always rely on, no matter what?

3. Do you think you might need to upgrade any tools?

4. Have you become too reliant on any tools?

5. Do you know which tools you are missing?

6. Could you use any new tools that you haven't yet thought about? Take a look at your answers to the questions "Who am I?" and "What do I want?" (see the introduction to part 1). Now think about the question "What do I like?" List activities, groups, and new things to get involved with — anything that you like, from a church group to a belly-dancing class to visiting a sports bar; it doesn't matter. If you include places where you'd like to spend your free time — not those where everyone else spends theirs — chances are that you will meet like-minded people there, and they'll be great additions to your toolbox.

7. Commit to trying at least one thing that could add a new tool to your toolbox.

Building an Internal Support System

A year ago, Shirin's father was diagnosed with cancer, and she had no idea if he would live. He had always been her biggest source of support, and she, at the young age of twenty-six, was scared of losing him. She was struggling with other issues as well. She didn't get the promotion she had wanted, and she felt that she couldn't relate to a lot of her peers. Shirin had always been pretty independent, but her experience during this time forced her to go within for support. "It spotlighted the idea that no matter how many great and supportive people I have (or don't have) around me, sometimes I am just on my own. Sounds depressing, but it does not depress me, because it made me stronger on the inside — I have my faith and my belief in myself."

As Shirin discovered, an equally important aspect of our support system is how we support ourselves internally. Throughout our twenties, we grow more reliant on ourselves. Balancing our external responsibilities with taking good care of ourselves reinforces our independence and our sanity. The things we do to nurture ourselves are tools that we need to take out of the bottom of our toolboxes as we build our foundation. We tend to overlook a part of our growth: consistently being aware of how and if we support ourselves from the inside. If we do not invest energy in internal support, we could find ourselves depleted, irritable, and stressed. And once we feel this way, we'll look for someone or something outside ourselves to lean on, which will throw our independence off balance.

An internal support system is one of the perks of being a grown-up (in addition to staying up late and eating dessert for dinner whenever we want). This system consists of things we do in our private time to refuel or center ourselves. Knowing we can do things for ourselves that are free from obligations, expectations, or outcomes is another element of independence. We are discovering fulfilling activities that we can do 100 percent independently. Some women might take up a spiritual practice, such as

"After investigating my foundation, I realized the solutions that I was coming up with still weren't working, that I had to go deeper. A voice underneath was screaming, 'This is really about you not taking care of yourself.' I stopped exhausting myself on the outside and began to look within."

— Patty, fifty-two

going to church or temple or meditating. For others, the activity might be physical, such as going to the gym or playing sports. It could also be reading, going to movies, watching television, painting, listening to music, taking a bath, spending time in nature, or all of the above. Our options are endless, yet the opportunities to practice them seem limited when we're grappling with the questions of the twenties triangle.

As we discovered in part 1 of this book, most twenty-something women do not spend a lot of time nurturing themselves. We find it difficult to turn our attention inward when we have so much to think about every day. If thinking about the outside world burned calories, the fitness and diet industries would go out of business! Yet a securely independent woman develops skills to ground herself despite all the stuff happening inside her head. Such skills take practice and commitment. Many of us *say* we are going to take better care of ourselves, but then something always seems to come up. We want to take an art class, but then an invitation to spend money on something else appears. We say we are going to work less and relax more, but we find ourselves staying late at the office. We want to read a book, but we cannot seem to pull ourselves away from our computers and cell phones. We have every intention of going to the gym, but the days are short and it's easier to go on a fad diet or just keep hating our bodies. We want to check out a new organization, but we are scared to attend the first meeting alone. We are overextended, but we feel guilty saying no to people. Does any of this sound familiar?

If we do not stop making excuses for why we avoid focusing inward, what will happen when our outside world becomes more chaotic? Will we be able to go within when we have families of our own, more responsibilities at work, or parents who need care? One possible reason for the midlife crisis is that people do not spend time learning to take care of themselves during their quarter-life years. Our twenties give us a priceless window of time between being taken care of and taking care of others. It is the perfect opportunity to develop the habit of nourishing ourselves.

Additionally, as we become better at caring for ourselves on the inside, we will enhance our ability to gracefully deal with the everyday pressures and questions of the outside world. A strong internal support system is like a healthy immune system. If your immune system is weak, you will be susceptible to colds, and if you walk into a roomful of sniffling kindergartners, it will be very difficult to ward off a virus. However, if you do things that strengthen your immune system, such as eating a lot of green vegetables, taking vitamins, avoiding toxins, and exercising, your body will be better equipped to fight off viruses and you will get sick less often. Similarly, as we learn to feel secure by taking care of ourselves internally, we will feel more grounded and better equipped to cope with the many stresses that are an invariable part of life.

> "It occurs to me that in our twenties, we are so insecure that it is impossible to appreciate what we don't know we have. It is fascinating that we are the only species that cannot directly teach life experience to our offspring. Birds for generations can teach their baby birds not to eat a certain berry, but women have yet to teach other women how to adore themselves."
>
> — Nancy, forty-seven

EXERCISE 24

Nurturing Yourself

It's time to strengthen your immune system — and I don't mean with a multivitamin! Think back to the last few days. How much time did you spend doing something completely for yourself? I hope it was a lot, but I venture to guess it was not enough. (Can you even say that you are reading this book and doing all its exercises completely without expectations? Are you hoping to make a part of your life better, or would you be happy with just a little more internal solace?) As you go through this exercise, remind yourself of how important taking care of yourself is (and how much you deserve it!):

1. Once again, look into the toolbox that you are using to build your foundation. What do you use to nurture yourself? For example, do you do yoga, pray, read, receive spa treatments or take walks?

2. Might any tools — alcohol, unprotected sex, junk food, an overly critical parent — in your toolbox be unhealthy or not in your best interest?

3. Which tool works best? Which parts of your internal support system are very solid?

4. Do you think you have enough tools to take care of yourself?

5. On a scale of 1 to 10, rate your internal support system based on how grounded you feel daily (1 is "completely anxiety-ridden and frazzled" and 10 is "calm, peaceful, and clear about my actions and decisions").

6. Do you feel you lack the correct tool for any particular situation? Look back at exercise 23 where you created your twenties toolbox. Could someone in your support system help you find that tool?

7. What types of situations are hardest for you to deal with?

8. Why do you think these situations are hard for you? Can you think of anything you could add to your

internal support system that would help you build internal strength and make these situations less daunting?

Now stop reading. Yes, put this book down and go do at least *one* thing to nurture yourself now. No excuses — go do something that brings you joy! Oh, and next time, try not to wait for permission to do something for yourself. Just do it.

We all want to be secure in our independence. Being an independent woman means knowing ourselves and our strengths and weaknesses. It means knowing when we ask for assistance out of laziness, bad habit, or insecurity and when our requests for help are in our best interest. It means identifying the areas in which we need to build skills or confidence. It means taking care of ourselves on all levels. Yet few of us equate total self-reliance with total self-fulfillment. We all want friends, lovers, and families around us, and being supported by them is 100 percent okay and normal. I invite you to look at independence as a way of being, rather than as an overwhelming or isolating notion. It is the freedom to be interdependent while independently choosing what we want and who we want to be.

CHAPTER 5

SELF-SECURITY

Women experiencing a twenty-something crisis find that feeling totally secure is often more challenging than trying on a bikini in December under fluorescent lighting. I don't think any of us float through life without an ounce of insecurity or self-doubt (unless you live on an island and Mother Teresa and Gandhi were your parents). After all, we all fear something, and usually our fears come from a lack of self-security. A well-known fact is that more people fear speaking in public than fear death. Isn't it remarkable that so many of us are more scared of how we will be perceived than of our own mortality? It goes to show how many people struggle with self-doubt.

In my research, I asked women between the ages of twenty-three and thirty-two all across the country to rate their self-confidence. On a scale of 1 to 10 (with 10 being the best), the average rating was 4. Yes, 4. This number is discouraging, but not that surprising. As we struggle with the questions "Who am I?" "What do I want?" and "How do I get what I want?" our insecurities confuse our answers. If we do not establish a secure sense of self in our twenties, how can we ever authentically answer these questions which will affect the rest of our lives? This chapter addresses the various components of our self-security and how to enhance them.

EXERCISE 25

Rating Your Self-Security

The following exercise asks you to rate your own self-security in several areas. As you do this, be completely honest with yourself — no one will see your answers but you. Rate yourself in each category on a scale of 1 to 10, with 10 meaning you have no doubt or judgment about that area of your life and feel completely secure with it.

- Overall happiness
- Romantic relationships
- Success/career
- Health
- Physical appearance/body
- Intelligence
- Social life
- Self-confidence/image
- Finances

Average of the above categories:_____

Next, consider how and why you rated yourself as you did. How did this exercise feel to you? Even the simple process of rating certain aspects of our lives can stimulate a lot of self-judgments.

Beth, twenty-six, shared the following with me: "I only wrote down a 6 for happiness because I am nagged by thoughts such as 'I don't have a big picture. Why don't I know what my passion or purpose in life is?' But I feel a little guilty, because with all the blessings I have, I should be a 9 or 10. I'm just not the happiest with myself, which brings down the score." A lot of us have experienced a sense of angst without being able to pinpoint the exact reasons for it. Kathy, twenty-three, second-guessed her ratings as well. "My moods surrounding each category change too quickly for me to cement a number for them. I climb up and down the ladder between 3 and 10 on most of these issues. One problem is that I know I can and should achieve a 10 on most of these. When I'm not at 10, I feel as though I'm not living up to the image I've created for myself." Did you also feel that some of your numbers should be higher, or were you disappointed with some of your answers?

———— ✸ ————

Disappointment and dissatisfaction about ourselves go hand in hand with the sense of angst mentioned above. We might be able to do things to temporarily relieve them, but these feelings keep popping up, possibly appearing in one aspect of our lives after another. These feelings are even more frustrating if we do not know exactly where they come from. I am sure it is no shock to hear that insecurities underlie most of your doubts. In fact, you probably knew this already but, like me, have not known how to change it. If I could tell you where to buy self-security as easily as I could tell you where to get the best deal on a pair of trendy jeans, I would win the Nobel Prize. But I can share with you what I have learned and observed, and possibly offer you some insight into your insecurities. Just becoming more familiar with who you are and how you evolved into the person you are is the first step. Liking who we are now, not who we will become, reinforces our foundation. In this chapter, we'll look at when and how our sense of self was formed, examine feelings that weaken our self-security, and explore what we can do to build and reinforce a healthy sense of self.

> "Honestly love the life you have created for yourself. Accept the decisions and choices you have made and the outcomes they have brought. If you are happy with yourself, the rest of life will fall into place."
>
> — Susan, fifty-four

THE ROLE OF INSECURITIES

I'd like to share my own story of how insecurities can negatively influence one's sense of self. I was always an extroverted, bright, and happy little girl. Then, in middle school, things shifted. Like so many adolescents, I was teased and completely ostracized by my peers, mainly girls. I was a late bloomer, became rather quiet, had glasses and braces, and was liked by teachers and other parents because I was smart and polite. This made me a bull's-eye for my peers. They formed an "I hate Christine" club. I was pinched by boys; girls passed around notes about me; and I sat alone at lunch. My mom got me a medical excuse from PE because I just couldn't stomach changing in the locker room with all those girls. This feeling of being different and disliked continued from the fifth to the tenth grades. I had only one friend. I always admired the "popular" group from afar, wanting desperately to be accepted by them. I longed to be like them, to look and act as cool as they did.

Around the age of thirteen, I started getting migraines, grew depressed, and isolated myself. I even saw a psychiatrist, but I was so ashamed that I had the doctor's office white out the word *psychiatry* on my excuse notes so no one at school would know. I began to hate myself because I believed that no one else liked me. Television became my escape from self-loathing. I would come home from school every day and watch show after show — I could probably recite the *TV Guide* from the years 1988 to 1993. Even though my social life improved a little in my last two years of high school, I was still incredibly unsure of myself. When I went to college, I picked a school far from home where I knew no one. I wanted a clean slate, a chance to reinvent myself and maybe even to be popular. Unfortunately, my insecurities followed me all the way from Dallas to Chicago, making it impossible for a new, cool "me" to emerge.

I always had trouble relating to and especially trusting women my age because I still thought I was not interesting enough to be liked by them. I feared they would turn on me. I did not know how to make friends because I had only one best friend growing up. I faked it as best I could, and even joined a sorority, but I never really felt part of it. Actually, I did not like college as a whole very much and could not wait to graduate. At the time, I thought this was because I was more mature (that's what my parents told me) or because my ambition made me anxious to get on with my adult life (that's what I told myself). The truth is (and I did not realize this until I began to face my twenty-something crisis), my insecurities led me to believe that I was unlikable, which prevented me from liking any situation I found myself in.

The wounds of my adolescent experience had never healed, and I kept myself extra busy with two majors, a minor, and four different jobs. I even took off a quarter to work, and still graduated in under four years. My overachievement became a mask covering how badly I felt inside. I bought into the notion that I could be liked for what I did rather than who I was. After all, I believed for years that I did not have much to offer. I clung to the fantasy of one day being popular and admired, which would prove everyone wrong! Consequently, I went off to pursue a career in the entertainment industry because I figured if I could make it there, I would finally be liked. Telling off those girls who had tormented me in middle school as part of my Oscar or Emmy acceptance speech became part of the fantasy. But the higher I moved in my career, the more I hated it. Finally, I realized I had spent years working in the industry because it symbolized an adult version of the popular group I had longed to be part of, not because I was passionate about it.

My self-doubt affected more than my career. As the years went by, my ball of insecurities gained momentum, barreling over other aspects of my life. In college, I dated a guy who treated me like a second-class citizen. I think I was attracted to him because he agreed with my negative opinion of myself. He was also so self-absorbed that it was easy for me to model my life after his, which was great for me since I didn't like my own life very much. My social life suffered as well. I was intimidated by my peers and did not believe I could be a good or worthy friend, and I did not want to get hurt again. Independence became isolation. Then the body issues started. Keeping up a front of having it all together and looking good on the outside became distractions from the pain I felt on the inside, which I did not really understand. Needless to say, nothing was really satisfying. Finally, enough was enough. I got a great therapist, I began talking to people in my life about my insecurities, and I became willing to clean out those old wounds that I had covered with Band-Aids for years. During this process, I became inspired to write this book.

Pain from the Past

Many women I spoke with made similar connections between their past and present insecurities. Kristi is a twenty-nine-year-old receptionist who is completely bored by her job. She really wants to get her real estate license, but she does not think she is smart enough to pass the test. I asked her if she struggles to understand things in her everyday life. "Well, not really," she replied. "My job is so easy, my finances are in order, and I've never had trouble managing my life. I guess I am just not super-book-smart. I am pretty average. I always did okay, but not great, at school — except for biology. I loved biology, and I got an A in that class."

Kristi comes across as a very together and intelligent woman. I told her that I did not understand why she did not go after what she wanted. Her claim that she wasn't smart did not make sense. If she liked real estate as she had liked biology, why wouldn't she do well on the test? She thought about it for a minute and then said, "Well, when I was applying to colleges, my dad and a few of my teachers always told me I was average and not smart enough to get into the schools I wanted, and I guess I believed them."

Amanda, also twenty-nine, is content in her job but hates being single. She wants to fall in love but says that she has zero dating confidence and does not believe she is a good catch. "I was obese when I was younger, and I think that made me see myself as fat and ugly. My father would poke fun at me, and so would the kids at school — it always hurt. I got the message that I wasn't good enough. No matter what grade I got, I was asked why I hadn't done better. I internalized all that and never thought I was good enough, smart enough, or pretty enough. I date guys who are not right for me because I don't believe I deserve any better."

Kristi's and Amanda's stories are perfect illustrations of the cause-and-effect relationship between the self-concepts we formed in the past and our feelings about ourselves in the present. Kristi's belief that she is not "smart enough" keeps her from the career she wants. Amanda's belief that she is not "good enough" keeps her from the love she wants. Each seed planted during our formative years eventually sprouts into a belief and has a huge impact on our perception of ourselves. Two of the questions I asked the women I surveyed were "What are your best characteristics?" and "What don't you like about yourself?" Almost without exception, they had a hard time coming up with answers to the former but could rattle off a laundry list of things they did not like about themselves.

EXERCISE 26

How Much Do You Really Like Yourself?

Now it's your turn to answer the same questions. First, list what you identify as your best characteristics: the things you have always liked about yourself, you are good at, or compliments you actually agree with. Don't be modest. List everything from personality qualities such as "I am outgoing" to physical traits like "I love my hair." Next, list all the things you do not like about yourself: the ways you feel "less than" other people; things you don't like in your life; your personality flaws; your bad habits; and so on. Leave nothing out. It can be as silly as "I hate the way I sneeze" or as serious as "I feel unworthy of falling in love."

Notice how you felt when writing each list. Did you discover that the list of things you don't like about yourself is longer than the list of things you *do* like? Even if the "don't like" list is shorter, you probably have at least a few items on it. As you continue reading, consider how long you've been aware of disliking these things about yourself and how those opinions impact and affect your life.

After putting all your insecurities down on paper, you might feel a little low and ask why it is necessary to look at them. It's necessary because we cannot forget our pasts when we're learning about self-confidence and security. I have found that being consciously aware of things I do not like about myself or my life and things that I would rather ignore heightens my ability to make positive changes. To get out of our twenty-something crises, we need to be aware of *all* the things that keep us in them, not just obvious factors such as the stress we feel in our careers or relationships. During our twenties, when so much in our lives is changing, there are endless opportunities for our insecurities to be triggered.

Insecurity, like belief systems, is learned. We are not born with it in the way we are born with red hair or green eyes. Our sense of self develops over time and is molded by our experiences. For instance, as a little girl, I did not believe I was a nerd until my peers told me I was. Then I took on that identity and always saw myself as a nerd, never believing anyone "cool" could like me. Again, human beings are sponges. From the moment we are conceived, we take in information, and most of it affects us on some level. Everything we witness, experience, and decide molds our self-concept. Ignoring our past can be an underlying reason that the questions of the twenties triangle are so difficult to answer.

We have all been hurt, teased, treated badly, or judged. Unfortunately, those events that stung us most or were reinforced most frequently are the hardest to shake. Have you ever noticed that you tend to remember more critical things that were said to you than compliments? One hundred nice things could be said to us in a month and may be forgotten, but over the course of a lifetime, the mean, judgmental, or critical things usually stick with us. And if they were said by important people in our lives, they are even more damaging. Libby, a twenty-eight-year-old designer, shared with me, "When I was a little girl, my mom said to me, 'Libby, stop being obnoxious,' when I wanted her attention. Without realizing it, as I got older I became very withdrawn and would shut down in social situations — I am shy and quiet — while the real me, the vivacious, funny entertainer, became lost. I didn't realize until recently how that one phrase had such power over my life. My mother, the woman who was supposed to protect and nourish my self-esteem, taught me that I wasn't okay just being me."

The nasty little insecurities we carry with us crack our foundation. They are behind the things that scare us and keep us from what we want. The time to deal with our insecurities is *now*. Think of it like this: starting to exercise when you are fifty is a lot harder than beginning to work out in your twenties; when you reach fifty, you won't be overweight, weak, and unhealthy. Similarly, if you confront your insecurities now and understand why they are there, you will have a head start on figuring out what makes you tick. Then you will not need to buy a red Porsche when you turn fifty!

EXERCISE 27

Examining Old Wounds

This exercise is designed to help you investigate how old wounds continue to bleed into your current life. Warning: This will not be the most fun exercise, but it is one of the most crucial. Judging by my own experience, I cannot stress enough the importance of such self-investigation. You can really start to love your life when you understand and like your*self*.

1. Referring back to exercise 26, look at each item on your list of things you don't like about yourself. Think about who initiated, agreed with, or reinforced that

particular insecurity or trait. In your journal, write down each insecurity/trait and the name of the person(s) who corresponds to it. For example, in my case, I had written, "Nerd and not cool" on my "don't like" list. Next to it I wrote, "Classmates from fifth grade who teased me and called me a goody two-shoes." If you cannot think of a particular person or group, just focus on those items that do trigger specific memories.

2. Look at your list of names. How many of these individuals are still in your life and continue to reinforce or remind you of the particular trait or insecurity?

3. How many of these individuals are completely out of your life?

4. In exercise 4 in chapter 1, you were asked to list who you are in various situations and around certain groups of people. Turn back to that page in your journal and look over your responses. Do you think that any of your insecurities might affect who you are in various situations? Can you think of any situations in which your insecurities keep you from being your true self?

> "Learn from life's events and challenges — they will always be there. Allow your loved ones to love you, and, most of all, love yourself for the extraordinary person you are. If you don't think you are extraordinary, work at it until you know you are. Then give that joy and uniqueness to the world."
>
> — Deanna, forty-nine

After reflecting and writing down anything that comes up, let this information marinate. Consider any ideas you have about how to heal old wounds.

The Lure of Quick Fixes

Core things that we do not like about ourselves get in our way more than the external factors to which we often attribute our unhappiness — such as the wrong job, a bad relationship, or ten extra pounds. Many of us fixate on investing time, money, and energy in temporary confidence uppers, which I call quick fixes. We've all gotten sucked into glamour magazines at drugstores and left with bags full of cheap makeup and creams that promise to make us beautiful. Another degree, a gym membership, a new wardrobe, or a cute boyfriend become the answers to our insecurities. This dynamic inspires "once/then" thinking: "*Once* I am a size six, *then* I will feel better about myself and attract the perfect man."

Audrey is a retail store manager who believes she will be more content with herself as soon as she makes her body and health higher priorities. "I'm thirty, and I don't look the same as I did when I was twenty-two. I'd like to work on that and at least feel great in my own skin. Once I do that, then I will feel better when I go out, and probably would get asked out more. That is why working out and watching what I eat have become a major part of my new routine." Audrey's commitment to a healthy change is commendable; however, quick fixes such as a better diet and exercise might have temporary results. Yes, feeling good about external things such as our weight can increase our confidence, but wouldn't it be great if our confidence didn't depend on our waistlines? Imagine being secure without the new job, lots of dates, the gym membership, or calorie counting.

EXERCISE 28

Your Favorite Quick Fixes

We have all been lured by quick fixes and have hoped that they would make a part of our lives better or clarify an answer to the twenties-triangle questions. We even try the same quick fixes over again, thinking, "Well, this time it'll be different." This exercise will fine-tune your quick-fix radar.

1. Again, refer to the "things I don't like about myself" list you made in exercise 26. Next to each item, write down any fixes you have tried or continue to try. For instance, next to "Not popular/well-liked," I wrote, "Moved out to Hollywood to prove myself to the world."

2. Look over your new list. How many of these fixes actually made the insecurity or disliked characteristic fade?

3. How many of these fixes did *not* make the insecurity or disliked characteristic fade?

4. What are you currently doing to change things you don't like about yourself?

As we continue to discuss building your foundation, think of quick fixes as temporary repairs to deeper problems. A trip to the mall and a great new outfit might make you smile for an evening, but racking up credit card debt will just make you suffer more stress. Think of it this way: If you had a leaky pipe in your bathroom, you could tape it up for a while, but the leak would still be there and eventually you would need to replace the pipe.

———— ❧ ————

Healing from the Past

The stories and exercises you've read in this chapter might have stirred up a lot of emotion or frustration or even brought you some enlightenment. So, now that our insecurities and our past are on the table, what do we do? How do we fix our "pipes"?

The first step is to recognize and understand all the influences on our sense of self, which was the purpose of exercise 27. The next step is to use that information to construct a securer sense of self and thus strengthen our foundation. Many twenty-something women have people or situations in their lives who reinforce their insecurities. Sometimes this is unavoidable, but often it is not. For instance, we cannot avoid an intimidating boss at work unless we are willing to switch jobs; however, we *can* avoid or set boundaries with critical colleagues, friends or family members. Many women I spoke to admitted that often they feel obliged to spend time with people or in situations that reinforce insecurities.

Jessica, twenty-eight, told me, "Whenever I talk to my mom, she makes some comment about my being single. Even if I feel really great about my job or my social life, just one comment from her about how I need to work on becoming more 'datable' totally brings me down." It would be difficult for Jessica to avoid her mother, but she could set a boundary with her. For instance, she could say: "Mom, please do not comment on my love life anymore. I know you may be trying to help, and I appreciate it, but I'd rather not discuss it — there are lots of other really wonderful things we could talk about."

Refer back to the list you made in question 2 of exercise 27. Do you need to set boundaries with anyone on it? Or is limiting your exposure to anyone a good idea? Twenty-seven-year-old Jenna realized that spending less time with one friend was in her best interest. "One of my friends constantly talks about how men are cheaters and liars. This is a sore spot for me since my dad cheated on my mom. The more time I spent with her, the more my doubt that I will meet a trustworthy man got reinforced. I finally realized her negative attitude was toxic to my security, and now I spend a lot less time with her." As we reinforce our foundation, it's best not to expose it to elements or tolerate conversations that threaten our positive sense of self and overall growth.

Consider whether anyone on your list, although they might no longer be physically in your life, continues to negatively affect your life. Just because people are out of our lives does not mean their influence has faded. Are you willing to finally let them go? And if so, how can you do it, other than get a lobotomy? I learned one technique, which replaces painful memories or experiences with positive actions, from Gloria, twenty-seven. "I have been over-weight my whole life, and I have always been teased about being fat. Obviously, this made me extremely insecure. In my early twenties I lost weight, but insecurity about my body did not go away. I still heard the voices of those kids echoing in my head. I decided to start teaching exercise classes on the weekends. I thought that motivating others would help me get out of my own head. I am surprised at how it has worked — my voice for my students finally became louder than the voices of the past."

Can you think of a way to use Gloria's technique to reframe a negative perception of yourself by creating a new, positive experience that will make an old, unhappy one fade into the distance? Write down any ideas in your journal. If nothing comes to mind immediately, write a reminder to yourself to return to this question and brainstorm several ideas.

"Don't let insecurities stop you or get in your way. I heard Barbra Streisand was so nervous every time she went on stage that she would get sick to her stomach. But did she ever let it stop her? No way."

— Lila, sixty-one

Another technique for reframing negative experiences, one that has been extremely beneficial to me and many women I spoke with, is therapy. It has helped us to understand our insecurities and why they became roadblocks. Having an objective, well-trained person in our lives (our girlfriends, mothers, and sisters do not count) is very helpful to many of us. If you do feel stuck and suffer from many crisis symptoms, you might want to consider therapy to help you clean up your inner atmosphere. I mentioned in chapter 3 that anxiety is created by living in the future, and depression by living in the past. A lot of our sadness comes from old hurts and events we wish had happened differently, and a good therapist can help you sort through these issues.

If you are considering therapy, make sure you find the right therapist. If money is an issue, find someone with a sliding scale. Try to choose someone based on a referral rather than picking at random. Find someone with whom you feel safe and who does not judge you, someone who inspires you to be your own advocate and helps you to find your own answers. As my own therapist reminded me, a good fisherman teaches his student how to fish but does not catch the fish for him.

I am not here to preach therapy — I realize it is not an option or a requirement for everyone. But because healing work of some type is an imperative part of securing our foundation, I asked women what actions (other than therapy) have helped them to deal with their insecurities. Their answers included spiritual work, prayer, travel, spending time alone, support groups, writing/journaling, yoga, meditation, being willing to take risks, and doing things outside of their comfort zone. It doesn't really matter what we do — what matters is that we do it! Until we are willing to not only look at our insecurities but also to really *change* the way they affect our lives, our foundation will always have a little crack in it.

COMPARISON LAND

I interviewed Kathleen, a twenty-eight-year-old event planner in New York, over lunch. Within only ten minutes of meeting her, I found her dynamic, funny, intelligent, and charming. She has an amazing job that other people (including me) would dream of going to each day. As Kathleen spoke about her work with much passion, I found myself comparing my life to hers, especially since she was so accomplished in her career while I was struggling to create mine. She was not bragging, but I still felt "less than": I did not have her success, ambition, or glamorous life.

When I was honest with Kathleen, telling her that my life as a personal trainer and aspiring writer felt ordinary and that I envied her career and lifestyle, she laughed. "Are you kidding? I cannot believe you envy me when I am sitting here comparing myself to you — your healthy lifestyle, your commitment to deeper things. . . . Being around you makes me think I need to start working out, eating better, and doing something that matters." Before our iced teas had even arrived, Kathleen and I had sized up each other and begun comparing ourselves.

I would bet that every woman has felt insecure in some aspect of her life because she has compared herself to someone else, be it a girlfriend, a model in a television commercial, or the woman behind the perfume counter. It is almost impossible not to notice other people or societal representations of happiness, love, beauty, and success. It is even more difficult not to evaluate ourselves or our lives based on these people and representations.

> "Never take advice or model your life based solely on someone's age or life experience. There are a lot of confused people out there. But if you do, listen to women who are at least sixty years old."
>
> — Cassandra, fifty-eight

If we pause to look at those we compare ourselves to, we might realize how unfair we are being to ourselves. We measure our bodies against those of airbrushed cover models. We evaluate our beauty against standards set by actresses who have stylists, personal trainers, and private chefs. We compare our careers to those of women whose lives and sacrifices we know very little about. We strive for the type of relationships we see in television shows and movies or read about in romance novels. We even compare ourselves to individuals whose lives we know, deep down, we would not even want. The ways that we women compare ourselves to people on completely different paths are almost comical.

Take Maggie, for instance, a twenty-eight-year-old marketing manager who is accomplished in her career and has a loving lesbian relationship but says that she wishes she were more like "the blonde bimbo next door. She's pretty, so she gets an older man as her 'sponsor.' She has other love interests on the side; she doesn't worry about money; she doesn't need to work; and she's so busy going to parties and getting pretty that she doesn't have time to feel lonely. I would love to not need a plan all the time and to be a bit more carefree, too — with either relationships or life."

EXERCISE 29

The Comparison Game

This exercise will help you to determine how often you play the comparison game. Think about the last few days: how many times did you compare yourself to someone? It might be a girlfriend, a coworker, a person on a television show, someone you noticed on a billboard, or anyone else. List all these people. Next to each name, write down how and why you compared yourself or some aspect of your life to that person. Consider how you feel less than, different from, or envious of that person.

After doing this exercise, try to notice how many people you compare yourself to each day — even in the smallest of ways. Is it fair to say you are the MVP of the comparison game? If so, do you think that this benefits you?

———— ∞ ————

Focusing on Others Weakens Our Security

The expectations we feel and the insecurities we battle can blur our identities so much that we set up, and compare ourselves to, completely unrealistic standards. We take advantage of opportunities to compare particularly when they touch our worst vulnerabilities. The area(s) in our lives where we feel most "less than" is usually the area most likely to earn us frequent-flyer miles to comparison land. For instance, if you are insecure about your physical appearance, you probably notice every attractive, thin, and well-dressed woman with flawless skin, a "ten" body, and fantastic hair. You probably base how good you think you look on cues from other women or the number of compliments you receive. You probably think you won't feel good enough until you have a body suitable for *Fitness* magazine. You might run up your credit card bill to imitate *In Style* magazine, thinking this will make you feel better.

Along the same lines, if you are insecure about your capabilities, intellect, or career, you will be triggered by individuals whom you perceive as smarter or more successful than yourself. You might diminish your own accomplishments whenever you encounter someone you perceive as more accomplished. If you meet a successful woman with a great corporate career and an MBA, suddenly your college degree and job become diddly-squat. Similarly, if you are unhappy in the romance department, you might notice affectionate couples everywhere. You might compare yourself to your girlfriends who are in love and feel less desirable than them. You despise Valentine's Day. As your friends get married, you assume that something is wrong with you just because you are single. Notice a pattern? Comparing ourselves to others throws our internal security off balance, which makes our foundation unstable and, even worse, prevents us from ever really loving ourselves.

EXERCISE 30

Is Comparison Making You Insecure?

Refer back to exercise 29 and take another look at your comparison list. Do many of the ways you compare yourself to others correlate with your insecurities? In other words, do the people or type of people you put on a pedestal embody some characteristic that you feel you lack? Write down any correlations that you notice.

⎯⎯⎯⎯ ∞ ⎯⎯⎯⎯

When we travel to comparison land too often, we risk tying our self-worth to external standards and to our expectations that we should be more, better, or different. Our security becomes defined by how well we measure up rather than by our self-acceptance. In our twenties, especially our early twenties, we do not yet have faith in the fact that every life is different and that everyone is on a unique path. Each one of us is dealt a different hand of cards, and it is up to us to play them. We forget the meaning of the old saying "The grass is always greener on the other side of the fence." The comparison habit diverts us from our inner knowing, which is the true source of answers to the questions "Who am I, what do I want, and how do I get it?"

The truth is, there will *always* be someone prettier, thinner, smarter, funnier, richer, more in love, more successful, and so on than us. We forget to truly look at all our own innate abilities, personal experiences, and traits that make us unique individuals (recall your "gratitude" list from exercise 14 in chapter 2). This keeps us from becoming secure in our individuality and the progression of our lives. In an unpredictable world with an overwhelming number of options, it's natural to want to model our lives after someone whose life seems to "work" or based on a plan that we invent for ourselves and believe we can control. Fear of the unknown and of failure makes such modeling even more tempting. Until we give up the act of constant comparison, our answers to the questions of the twenties triangle will always be based on things outside ourselves — and we might never feel complete.

Investigative versus Comparative Living

So how do we stop taking unfulfilling trips to comparison land? We must become more conscious of when and how we do it. Quite simply, we need to break a bad habit. Naturally, many of our decisions stem from our observation of and experience with other people. Self-development requires looking at the world. Yet there is an important distinction to be made between observing and comparing, between *investigative* and *comparative* ways of living.

As women in our twenties, we seek answers to many questions in many places — we just need to make sure we return to ourselves to find the final answers. So, as you think about the people you compare yourself to, also investigate whether your visions of their lives truly fit *your* life. Consider that having someone else's characteristics would make you a different person living a different life, with a different perspective and most likely a different set of problems as well. Is that really what you want? When you answered the question "Who am I?" did you put down someone else's name? If not, then why answer "What do I want?" based on others' lives? Seek and contemplate, but take advice only from people who you know are happy with themselves and their lives. For example,

Jaxie, twenty-seven, realized, "Once I stopped comparing my relationship to and taking advice from a friend who was miserable in hers and always picking fights with her boyfriend, my own relationship improved."

EXERCISE 31

Becoming an Investigator

This exercise will help you become an investigator, instead of a connoisseur of comparison. Put on your investigative-reporter hat and find out if people you compare yourself to *really* have something that you want.

Again refer back to exercise 29. From the people on that list, select at least three with whom to have a conversation. Ask specific questions about the qualities you envy or admire most about them. For instance, if you compare yourself to an acquaintance whose job seems really fabulous and you think your career pales in comparison to hers, inquire about how she got there, what hours she works, what sacrifices she's had to make, and what she does not like about her job.

Repeat this exercise for each of the three people you selected, and feel free to interview more than three. List what you learn from each individual you investigate. Now separate these new lists into categories of things that you do want and those you do not. If you learn that you actually do not want what they have, then whew, what a relief! Give yourself permission to stop comparing yourself to them. If you discover that you do indeed want some of the things that they have, use them as a source of inspiration and information rather than as a basis for comparison.

When you're done, ask yourself if this exercise brought any clarity to the questions "What do I want?" and "How do I get what I want?" Record any new insights in your journal.

———— ∞∞ ————

Comparison Jet Lag

When we take many trips to comparison land and don't focus on ourselves and what we want from our lives, we are likely to experience what I call comparison jet lag. It consists of the undesirable aftereffects and behaviors that result when we analyze whether we measure up. Take Heather, twenty-seven, for instance. When I interviewed her, she immediately struck me as a woman whose life was a fulfillment of her dreams. She is eloquent and intelligent without being arrogant. She has a job she likes, is surrounded by great friends, and feels generally confident. She discussed her family and career with pride and enthusiasm.

Once we began to talk about her relationship, however, her whole body grew tense. Recently she has become very insecure about this area of her life. "I compare my relationship too much to others'. Deep down, I know that everyone is on their own path, but when I see everyone getting married and engaged except me, it makes me feel like I should be seeing some kind of red flag. I don't want to look back and wonder why I didn't see it and act on it." Essentially, Heather feels she is falling behind. She worries that there might be something wrong with her or the relationship because it is not at the same point as her friends'. She feels insecure about herself because her boyfriend has not proposed. Heather admits that this insecurity is sabotaging her relationship: her incessant questioning of her boyfriend about the future is causing him to pull away.

EXERCISE 32

Is Comparison Harming You?

Consider all the essential aspects of your life: career, relationship, body image, finances, social life, spirituality, and so on. Recall Heather's story, and ask yourself if you make unnecessary or excessive comparisons in these areas of life, and whether they actually have detrimental effects. Write down anything that comes to mind and consider how you can transform comparison into investigation.

Competition

Another nasty effect of comparison is that it often leads to competition between women. You all know from middle school that girls can be cruel and two-faced. Why are so many grown women guilty of such behavior as well? Perhaps because we were taught as girls to be polite, proper, and well behaved. We were not allowed to forcefully express ourselves physically or verbally. Yet competition continues into our young adulthood, when we know better. Most of us also have experienced a negative attitude or noticed a lack of support from another woman for no obvious reason. Why? It's caused by the dangerous habit of comparison and competition, which is fueled by our insecurities. We become jealous of one another, and instead of owning that jealousy and realizing it is only our insecurity talking, we often lash out, compete, gossip, or decide not to like one another. Of course, I am simplifying here, but I am sure that every woman has felt competitive with or jealous of another woman.

Because of these dynamics, bonding with and trusting other women can take time. It is especially hard to break into an established group of friends when we are new to a city or company. Clarissa is twenty-six years old and recently moved from Michigan to Washington, D.C., to work at a magazine. She is having a hard time being accepted by the other young women who work there. "I feel like there is this big clique that I don't know how to break into. All the women are so competitive with each other, and it's like every man or, I guess, woman for herself. My first few weeks there, only the men went out of their way to introduce themselves to me. I don't know if the women there see me as a threat or if they really just do not like me, but I don't get it. I always feel self-conscious and like I am being talked about."

Almost every woman I interviewed stated that she felt for the most part that women do not help one another. Additionally, the majority of the women I interviewed told me that they never had female mentors to offer guidance. This is sad and disappointing for many reasons. First, women are strong, sensitive, loyal, and loving, and if we could celebrate one another rather than competing, imagine how much more pride we would take in being women. We would be more empowered and powerful as a gender and as a force in society. The glass ceiling would vanish if women above it shattered it and reached their hands to those underneath. We forget that there's enough for everybody and that useless competition simply divides us and makes the difficulties we face in our twenties even more isolating.

Furthermore, by competing with one another, we miss out on the incredible power of female friendships. No one understands a woman better than another woman. Our mates, fathers, buddies, and brothers will never get us like our girlfriends do. We need to remove competition from our female friendships to truly connect to other women. The more we can do this, the stronger our support system — which reinforces our security — will be. Charlize, twenty-nine, articulated the importance of female friendships so eloquently: "My closest girlfriends celebrate one another's successes, their hearts break when others are mourning, and they want nothing more than to see one another blossom into completely free, confident, joyous beings."

The energy we waste in competition can be redirected toward making our own lives more complete. I was very competitive with one of my girlfriends, Casey, when we both were trying to get freelance work in the same field. I would hear of an opportunity, send in a submission, and not tell her about it. (Could I have acted any more like an eighth grader?) When she would book an assignment, she would call to tell me about it and I would fake happiness. Inside I thought, "Why did she get it? It's so annoying that she is calling me to brag. Why can't I get a gig? It's not fair that she is not helping me more." One day, realizing that this type of thinking was getting me nowhere fast, I decided to turn my jealous, competitive energy into supportive energy. I told Casey about jobs; I asked her for help instead of pretending I knew everything; I proofread her submissions; and I celebrated each job she got. It was challenging, but I started to accept where I was. Eventually, it came full circle. Because of my support, Casey started to help me find freelance work.

Of course, we cannot give with the expectation of getting something back, but giving beats the other option: isolating ourselves in a world of jealousy, comparison, and competition. Creativity and productivity do not thrive in that kind of environment. So, if we save our competitive energy for the tennis court or our next game of Scrabble, we can redirect our focus toward building our foundation. As we learn greater self-acceptance, the temptation to compete with others fades, bringing the answers to our twenties-triangle questions into better focus.

EXERCISE 33

Transforming Competitive Energy

In this exercise, you'll think about women with whom you compete. Don't feel ashamed or worry that competing makes you a bad person. We all have had thoughts such as "I hope she gets fired" or "I hope he dumps her" or "I hope her thighs balloon to the size of tree trunks." They do not make us evil; they just make us human beings with insecurities of our own.

1. Think about the women in your life with whom you compete in some way. Even if the competition is very subtle or exists only in your head, consider anyone who you secretly want to do better than or you hate to see succeed. In your journal, write down their names and the ways in which you compete with them.

2. Look over your list and consider why you feel competitive with each woman. Why don't you want her to achieve? Why do you feel a need to do better than her? What would happen if she did "beat" you or get something you wanted?

3. Pick one way in which you can transform your competitive energy into supportive energy in at least one of the relationships you listed. Write down your idea. It could be as simple as a phone call to check in and actually listen to what is going on in that woman's life. Take at least two supportive actions every week for at least three weeks. After three weeks, notice how your relationship has changed. Perhaps your friendship seems more valuable and less stressful or your

friend spends more time listening to you. At least you may feel less consumed by the relationship.

4. Afterward, return to this section of your journal and record what you experienced while doing this exercise.

In a recent yoga class, one of my favorite teachers made a comment that resonated with me. The class was in a pose, and he advised us to stop looking at one another. He said that yoga was classically taught on an individual basis so that students would not compare themselves to others. Instead, they learn to listen to their own bodies to dictate how their practice should look. If students can't compare their flexibility or the level of their practice to others', they are fulfilled by where they are. I began to consider that my practice could be more authentic and that I might listen more to my body if there were no others in the room to compare myself to. Could the same be true in the rest of my life?

Imagine if there were absolutely no one and nothing to compare ourselves to. Would our foundation have fewer cracks? Comparison is a strong force driving the confusion and crisis symptoms we experience in our twenties. Like ivy, comparison is tough to kill and just grows and grows, invading our lives and intertwining the answers to the questions we ask about ourselves with the external world. So, the next time you feel yourself extending your stay in comparison land, divert your thoughts to another, more internal destination. Imagine being alone in a yoga studio, exulting in the perfection of a pose without thinking about or seeing anyone else.

BODY IMAGE

As mentioned above, one way in which we cruelly compare ourselves to others is physical. We do this because our awareness of our appearance, which starts in our teens, becomes especially acute in our twenties. There is no question that we women invest a great deal of time in enhancing (or criticizing) our appearance. Just think about the money we spend on grooming, new clothes, and gym memberships, and the effort we put into dieting, working out, and judging one another's appearance, all in an effort to feel better about ourselves during a time of self-doubt.

After taking a trip during which she lost weight and was constantly complimented for it, Sandy, twenty, has become obsessed with her weight and what she eats. "I constantly think about my body and what I eat; I punish myself for eating something I shouldn't; if I go out to dinner, I think about what I am going to order. I don't like eating in front of other people because then I can't do my neurotic 'Sandy' stuff. It's like I've lost freedom and control with food." When I asked her if she talks to her friends about her struggles, she said no. "My friends always say things like 'Oh, I shouldn't eat that,' or 'I am only going to order dessert if you have some.' Not a single meal with one of my girlfriends goes by when we don't talk about food or our weight, but we never talk about how we are really feeling emotionally."

I shared with Sandy that my body image and my relationship with food started to feel less out of control when I started to talk about it. When I did, I found that many other women had the same demon inside their heads. I began to feel less crazy and less ashamed. So many of us stay in our heads and allow the issue to grow. As we become more honest and give voice to those out-of-control feelings, we feel more balanced and less alone.

As I talked to women about their body image, most of the feedback I received was negative:

- "My self-confidence really goes up and down depending on my weight."

- "I feel the extra fat around my middle."

- "I need to get up and go to the gym, and when I think about what I had for dinner, I am usually disappointed in myself."

- "My appearance is a major burden and I am never satisfied."

- "I've always struggled with my weight."

- "I fight to even stay a size ten, which is very frustrating."

Scores of books are devoted to body image and eating disorders. For the purposes of this book, we will focus on how body image can threaten the sense of security we seek to establish in our twenties. A common tendency among young women struggling to find their identities is to allow their body image to rule their self-image. When this happens, the questions a twenty-something woman asks herself become even harder to answer. A negative body image that becomes a negative overall self-image has a ripple effect on other areas of life. Some twenty-something women report feeling so insecure and unhappy with their bodies that these feelings keep them from going after the things they really want. This dynamic affects everything from jobs ("I always wanted to be a performer, but I am not thin or pretty enough, so I never went for it") to social events ("Every summer my friends go to the beach, but I never go because I know I would need to be in a bikini; now I kind of feel like I am on the periphery of my social circle because I've missed out") to relationships ("I don't date much, and when I do I usually end up sabotaging the relationship before it gets physically intimate because I hate the way my body looks naked").

One story that deeply touched me — and made the ramifications of not establishing a healthy body image in our twenties crystal-clear — came from Kristin, a beautiful thirty-year-old makeup artist living in Los Angeles. "When I was younger, I was a model and actress, which meant one needed to be 'perfect.' There was no such thing as 'too thin.' Casting directors told me that I looked 'amazing,' which was scary considering I was a gaunt and spiritually dead five-foot-seven, 104-pound woman." That message had a significant effect on Kristin's life: "All I see are my flaws; I never feel as though what I have been blessed with is good enough. It can get to the point where it is almost hard for me to leave the house, as the feelings of self-loathing and insecurity are so thick." She continues, "I am torn between my desire for decadence — to celebrate life in everything that I do, whether it is food, drink, or luxuries — and my desire for control over my imperfections. I wish that I could feel comfortable and free from body shame, the object of other women's envy and admiration. (We all strive to be skinny for women, not men.)"

Kristin's recovery has been slow. "I had to leave behind success with my career as an actress, as I cannot live with my body under constant scrutiny and in the spotlight. My body image has in large part become my self-image. From the moment I get out of bed, it is a struggle to not let these feelings into the forefront of my thinking, to not let them control my attitude, and to try to remind myself that my value as a human being and a woman does not lie in my measurements, my ongoing cellulite safari, or the number on the scale."

If you identify with any aspect of Kristin's experience, your self-image might be intertwined with how you feel about your body. Looking back at times when I felt bad about my appearance, I can see that it affected my relationships, my attitude at work, how I related to other women, and even my quality of life. This insecurity perpetuated my own crisis because my standard for the way I should look became just another thing on the list of issues that caused me anguish.

When I asked women, "On a scale of 1 to 10 (1 being 'Not at all' and 10 being 'I can't get it out of my head'), how much time do you spend thinking about your body's physical appearance?" their average answer was 7.5. That is a lot of time. Why do we expend so much energy on our physical appearance?

First, as we all know only too well, we feel pressured by the images constantly thrown in our faces and the ways that they define beauty. Alluring promotions for age-defying, fat-reducing, and physical-enhancement techniques are ubiquitous. Even plastic surgery is on the rise among women in their twenties.

Second, during our twenties, when so much is up in the air and our confusion about who we are and what we want feels so out of control, we might fixate on things we *can* control. And, for the most part, we are the direct bosses of our bodies. Some of us become obsessed with diets, exercise plans, and making *carb* a four-letter word. We feel that if we put our time and energy toward achieving a certain dress size, maybe we can delay dealing with questions that scare us, such as "What am I really scared of?" Beauty magazines, fitness gurus, and diet fads offer us quick-fix answers to the question of how to *look* good on the outside. However, answers to the harder question of how to *feel* good on the inside can't be found in the aisles of our local drugstore. We need to take a good, hard look at how much our appearance determines our security. If we do not address our insecurities about our bodies and how those insecurities affect us, they will continue to weigh us down, cracking our foundation.

Separating Our Bodies from Our Sense of Self

So, if a healthier body image will reinforce our foundation, how do we get one? It starts with our self-perception. Throughout my research, I asked women, "How do you feel about your body?"

Very few women said they loved their bodies or did not think about them much. Women consistently expressed discontent with how they looked. Some of us become obsessed with micromanaging our bodies, while others say, "Screw it" and find solace in a tub of Ben and Jerry's. These reactions are flip sides of the same self-sabotaging coin. Somewhere in the middle is a healthier option. Coming to peace with your body is such an important part of securing your foundation and sense of self; after all, you spend twenty-four hours a day in that body.

EXERCISE 34

How Do You See Yourself?

Start by examining whether your self-perception and insecurities weaken your foundation. Turn back to your answers to the question "Who am I?" (see part 1). How many things on your list are related to your appearance? Write each of those external things down again on a fresh journal page.

Now look at the lists of things you don't like about yourself and insecurities you lsited in exercise 26. How many are related to your body or physical appearance?

Finally, grab a piece of paper and a pen and sit in front of a mirror. Set a timer for five minutes. Now just look at yourself (warning: this is not easy and might feel awkward). Write down your observations of your physical self. Don't worry about whether you like it. Just write about everything you see. Notice whether simply looking at yourself causes any discomfort.

Our bodies are vehicles for true self-expression. The body is not who we are. Instead, it is one of our greatest tools, so we need to learn how to love it, use it, take care of it, and not confuse it with our sense of self. The first step in becoming secure with our bodies is to distinguish things we can change from things we cannot. Some of you might be familiar with the Serenity Prayer: "God grant me the serenity to accept the things I cannot change, the courage to change the things I can, and the wisdom to know the difference." Accept that some things about your physical appearance are permanent, and stop comparing yourself to standards that are not physically possible for you. You do not compare your math ability to Sir Isaac Newton's, so why compare the size of your hips to a movie star's?

Meanwhile, take action on those things that you *can* change, if they really bother you. I have heard from countless women statements such as "I know there is so much more I can do to keep myself looking good, but I just don't feel like it — so I deal with feeling insecure about myself and try to compensate in other areas." Well, that is not a very empowering approach! Again, looking better on the outside is not the cure for insecurity; however, if you don't try to change the things that make you unhappy — those things that you both *can* and *want* to change — ask yourself what else in life you aren't doing, even though you can and want to do it.

Talie is a twenty-four-year-old from Texas who finally learned to accept her body. "I don't succumb to the pressures that society supposedly puts on women to stay thin. What I have is what I have. I work out to stay healthy, to keep my body in shape, and because it makes me feel better mentally. I eat what I want because I don't concern myself with every piece of food I put in my mouth and what effect it will have on my body."

EXERCISE 35

Knowing What You Can and Cannot Change

Look back at all the things you wrote down in the last part of the previous exercise, when you observed yourself in a mirror. Relist them in two categories: "Things I can change" (column A) and "Things I can't change" (column B).

Now look over these columns. Recognize that you simply have no control over some things in column B — you are the way you are. Accepting those things just takes practice. Each time you think about these characteristics, recite the Serenity Prayer or immediately shift your thoughts to another topic, such as something about yourself you love.

Now look at column A and create an action plan. If losing five pounds is on your list, toss the Hershey's Kisses and set up a time within the next two days to exercise for at least thirty minutes. You are not going to change your body by just thinking about it. You have to move and be committed. Get creative as you plan how you'll change the things you can and want to change, and then *do it*. Once you begin to see results, you will notice a shift in your overall confidence level.

Taking Care of Our Bodies

The next step toward a secure relationship with our bodies is to treat them like the gifts they are. If we are careless with ourselves on the most basic level, how strong can our foundation really be? Actively taking care of our overall health is more important than looking like

> "Take care of your body, and I don't mean with fad diets and beauty products. I know it seems indestructible, but how you treat it now will very much affect your life later."
>
> — Pattie, fifty-eight

supermodels and more productive than being self-critical. Being in good health strengthens our sense of security because we are proving to ourselves that we can nurture and nourish ourselves. The results of good health are tangible, so don't wait until you are unhealthy! Women who take good care of themselves have more energy and confidence because they put their time and thought into being healthy rather than looking perfect.

EXERCISE 36

How Well Do You Take Care of Yourself?

Take this short inventory to determine if you take good care of yourself on the physical level:

1. Do you smoke? If so, how much?

2. Do you drink? If so, how much?

3. Do you exercise?

4. If you exercise, does what you do make you feel good? (For example, do you take a kickboxing class that makes your body ache so that you can fit into a certain pair of jeans, or do you take walks through the woods or runs in the park that invigorate you?)

5. Do you eat fruits and vegetables?

6. Do you consider junk food a basic food group?

7. When you are stressed out, does it affect the way you eat? Do you become an extremist — either pigging out on pizza and candy or not eating at all?

8. Do you turn to alcohol when you are stressed out or nervous or need a pick-me-up?

9. Do you have unprotected sex?

10. Have you been tested for STDs?

11. Do you go to the dentist and the gynecologist at least once a year?

12. Do you have health insurance?

13. Do you take a multivitamin and calcium?

Now review your health inventory. If there are unhealthy habits in your life, make a commitment to take better care of yourself. For example, if you smoke, come up with a reasonable program to stop. If you have not been to the doctor in years, go. If you do not treat your body the way you would like life to treat you, you will just extend your twenty-something crisis well into your thirties, forties, and fifties. Becoming empowered in your own body will free you up to discover who you are, what you want, and how to get it.

When we are secure with the package we come in, we glow. Confidence comes from within, and others are drawn to us. Look at someone such as Oprah Winfrey, who has struggled with weight and insecurity her whole life yet has come to accept the body she has. She is not beautiful by model standards, yet she radiates beauty. Her foundation is solid, and millions of people watch her show and read her magazine. Oprah reached this place of acceptance later in life, but through awareness, empowerment, and a willingness to amend our perceptions and behavior, we can secure our body image while we're still in our twenties. Working to forge a healthy perspective on our bodies in our twenties is an investment in our overall security that carries us through the rest of our lives. Please refer to Resources, at the back of the book, for additional sources of support and information on body-image issues.

CHAPTER 6

FINANCIAL SECURITY

Security with our bodies obviously is not the only challenge we face as twenty-something women. Financial security also becomes essential for us to address as we become primarily responsible for ourselves for the first time in our lives. Just as starting to care for our bodies later in life would be more difficult than doing it now, we might incur stress later if we do not build our financial foundation now, when we face fewer economic responsibilities. Many women in twenty-something crisis feel unbalanced when it comes to money. Finances become yet another area in our life where we ask, "Is enough ever enough?"

When she was twenty-four, Bethany moved to Los Angeles after graduating from the University of Kansas. She wants to make a lot of money, feel and look glamorous, and prove she can make it in the big city. But L.A. has turned out to be a lot more than palm trees and movie stars. The realities of high rent, taxes, car expenses, and insurance costs and the competitive job market have been a rude awakening for Bethany. Since she comes from a family that

earns a comfortable living, the responsibility of budgeting is new
to her. As she bounces from job to job, Bethany is not making as
much money as she expected. She also feels the need to create a life
for herself in a new city by going out a lot, which leads to more
expenses. "I never realized how fast I could go through a hundred
bucks on food alone," Bethany told me. "I've had to seriously curb
my latte habit in order to afford lunch, and dinner is often a can
of soup."

Just two years out of college, Bethany has a lot of anxiety over
her unpaid credit card bills and significant student loans. She
admits to restraint problems with her credit cards, and finds it difficult not to buy something she really wants. She figures she'll
worry about the cost later. She compares herself to her twenty-six-
year-old brother, who has a steady income and a secure job that he
likes and is dating, going out, and taking weekend ski trips. He is
even investing money, which Bethany has not even considered. "I
can't even save for the weekend, much less put money away. Plus,
I don't know anything about investing."

Bethany could ask her parents for financial help, but she is too
proud. After all, she is an adult and should be able to take care of
herself. The truth is, Bethany has never felt more like a little girl
than she does now. She always thought her twenties would be the
time of her life, but instead the need to support herself financially
has turned these years into the most *stressful* time of her life.

Money can represent different things to each of us, from freedom and flexibility to stress and anxiety, yet we all need it to live.
Just as we must deal with our emotional and physical issues as we
build a strong foundation for the future, we need to acknowledge
the necessary financial component. Like Bethany, many of us
struggle to accumulate and budget our money. Self-awareness, a
solid support group, and self-confidence are critical, but unfortunately these intangibles do not pay the bills.

Personal finance is something that we young women today have to think about and manage on our own. Thanks to all the courageous and strong women who came before us, we are no longer limited to being "bread-makers" — we can be breadwinners. We no longer have to hurry up and find men to support us, so making and managing money are priorities in our twenties.

Among a hundred women who I asked, "On a scale of 1 to 10, how important is having a lot of money to you?" the average response was an 8. Obviously, money is on our minds and is something we want. During our twenties, we long for financial freedom, which means we need steady incomes and jobs. However, if we don't yet know the answer to the question "What do I want?" how can we know what we want to do in order to earn money? Often our desire to be financially independent adds to the pressure and expectations we feel to start on a career track. We can't take sabbaticals in the wilderness to figure out what we want to do with our lives, so we become consumed with finding jobs and making money. Of course, some of us do pull a Scarlett O'Hara and say, "I'll think about that tomorrow." That decision can lead to a different set of problems, including massive credit card debt and/or staying reliant on someone else.

To build a solid financial foundation in our twenties, we need to create balance. This is a time to learn how to be financially savvy but also a time to have some fun before really big responsibilities, such as paying a mortgage and caring for children, come our way. In other words, it's a time to think about the future but not to become *too* consumed by it, since we have plenty of time to live a "grown-up" life.

To put our finances into perspective, this chapter discusses how money affects us and why becoming *financially secure* is an essential component of our foundation. For the purposes of this book, the term financially secure does not mean that we must be debt-free. Instead, it means that our financial affairs are in balance. Balance comes when we understand how money works and how we can create financial flexibility and security. To feel more financially secure, we need to reframe the ways we look at money. In this chapter, we examine your finances in three time frames: your financial past, present, and future. Hey, if it worked for Scrooge, it can work for us.

YOUR FINANCIAL PAST

Deb, twenty-six, works in a doctor's office and does not think about money very often. She does not live by a budget and has a wallet full of credit cards. Deb makes enough to pay her rent, and financial assistance from her parents supports the lifestyle to which she has become accustomed. She is not in love with her job, but she does not have huge career aspirations, the people she works with are nice, and it is an "easy gig."

Hadley, also twenty-six, currently works over twelve hours a day at a tech company, not because she loves her field, but because jobs in the technology field pay well. Hadley is entirely on her own financially and is very frugal. She has taken a total of eight days off since she started at the company three years ago and is determined to get a promotion and a raise within a year.

Deb grew up in a well-off family in which money was always available. Her parents cover the bulk of her car payments and also pay for her health insurance and one of her credit cards. She feels that their monetary support is fine because she has assumed enough adult responsibility by having a steady job and living alone. "After all, it's just money, and my parents have enough of it. It's not like I am still totally dependent on them. There are more important things to worry about than money, and, quite honestly, I don't want to work a lot more just to be able to say I am financially independent." I asked Deb what would happen if her parents cut her off financially, and she admitted that she would be "really scared and really mad. I would be afraid that I would not be able to live the way I want to live anymore."

Hadley's mother raised her alone after her dad left the family when she was eight. Hadley watched her mom struggle as she made the transition from supported housewife to single working mother. Hadley's teenage years were spent clipping coupons, going to sales, and moving to more affordable apartments. There was never enough money. Hadley remembers being unable to do certain things as a child, such as team sports or Girl Scouts, because her mother could not afford the additional expenses. "I remember feeling so angry about how everything required money and how we never had enough. Each month it was a struggle to make rent and pay the bills. I knew this was not the life I wanted to live as an adult." Hadley's mother recently pulled her aside and told her she was concerned about how much Hadley was working. Her mom fears Hadley is not enjoying her life; she doesn't date, go out, or do anything for herself. Hadley was upset by her mother's words of caution, since she saw firsthand that lacking money and a career can leave a woman powerless. "I don't mind sacrificing my life now. It's what I need to do so that I will *have* a life and choices in the future. I don't want my children to grow up with the anxiety I had around money — I'll do whatever it takes to get there."

As Deb's and Hadley's experiences demonstrate, there is no escaping our past, even when it comes to money. The role it played in our lives as we grew up influences how we spend, save, and earn today. Additionally, we made judgments about money when we were children that can affect the importance we place on it today.

In my family, my dad worked extremely hard and was an excellent provider. We were not wealthy, but we never struggled. Money was never a source of stress. In my midtwenties, I struggled with money for the first time. I was in debt and didn't make a substantial income. I was not overly frivolous; "life" just happened, and I did not budget accordingly. Looking back, I think I was under the false impression that money would always just be there, as it had been when I was growing up. I found myself getting really mad at the cutbacks I needed to make. Money management became about balancing my checkbook and transferring my credit card balances. For the first time, I had to adjust my lifestyle, and I eventually put my tail between my legs and asked my dad for help. I was humiliated because I was unable to support myself. My parents had always told me that money meant freedom and power, and I felt that I had lost mine. I had always banked on my maturity and desire to be independent. The reality that money was *not* there significantly contributed to my twenty-something crisis. Yet I learned that hundreds of other twenty-something women in crisis feel overwhelmed by their transition to financial independence.

EXERCISE 37

What Role Has Money Played in Your Life?

We each have our own relationship with money that is dramatically influenced by our financial background. The next set of questions is designed to help you investigate the role that money and finances have played throughout your life, which might deepen your understanding of how they affect you today.

1. How would you describe your financial situation when you were growing up?

2. How does your financial situation now compare to that of your childhood?

3. How do you feel about the differences and/or similarities between your present and past situations?

4. What patterns of earning, spending, and saving money did you learn from one or both of your parents?

5. Was money a source of stress in your family?

6. When you think about money, how do you feel?

7. Look at your answers to questions 1 to 6. What overall role did money play during your childhood and early adult years? How do you think that experience has influenced your major life decisions?

8. On a scale of 1 to 10, how important is having a lot of money to you?

9. Look at your answer to question 8. Do you think your answer was influenced by money's role in your life so far?

10. Look back at your answers to the twenties-triangle questions in the introduction to part 1. What role did money play in your answers? Was having money a motivation behind any of the things you said you wanted?

Your answers to these questions will help you create a sense of financial security because they clarify your financial past.

———— ⌾ ————

Your Accumulated Beliefs about Money

As you read the following story think about how your past experiences with and understanding of money might influence your current financial state. As a kid in the suburb of Northbrook, Illinois, Malia, now twenty-six, got whatever she wanted from her parents. Her mother was the main breadwinner in her family and hated going to work every day. Malia's mom told her she envied other mothers who stayed home and were cared for by their husbands. She repeatedly told Malia to marry a rich man so she would not have to work. Consequently, as Malia thought about her future, she believed she should marry a wealthy man or at least someone who would eventually be a big earner. Malia works, but she admits that, in the back of her mind, she thinks someone will just bail her out if she gets into trouble (like her mom always has). Her belief that there can and should always be someone to come to her financial rescue has influenced her sense of financial responsibility. Currently she spends much more than she saves, and she dreams of being a rich housewife.

Our beliefs about money affect the expectations we create about how we will get it. We all have our own ideas about how money should enter our lives. Like Malia, many of us expect certain things, such as the right job or person, to come along and provide financial security. However, expecting this to happen or believing that it should keeps us in crisis mode. Many twenty-something women make decisions about finances based on their accumulated beliefs. As we discussed in chapter 2, our beliefs can interfere with our ability to make reasonable and rational decisions. We can find it hard to separate the question "What do I believe is the right choice?" from "What is the right choice?" Since many of us do not always know the "right" answer, we find it easier to cling to our belief systems.

EXERCISE 38

Your Money Memories

The next step in uncovering our financial past is to examine our belief systems and the expectations they have created. In your journal, answer the following questions:

1. Can you remember anything you were told as a child about money and the role it would play in your life? If so, write down what was said and who said it.

2. How did money influence your parent(s) or family?

3. What were you told about how (or whether) you would be financially supported in your twenties? For instance, were you told that you should and would work to make your own money? Were you told that you would always have financial support? Were you told to marry or find someone wealthy enough to support you?

4. Based on your answers to questions 1 to 3, what beliefs do you hold about money? Do you have any expectations about how it will come to you?

5. How have these beliefs and expectations influenced important decisions you have made?

After completing this exercise, are you able to identify belief systems or expectations you hold about money that might weaken your financial security or keep you off balance in any way? Write down anything that comes to mind; recall these insights the next time you are out shopping, paying your bills, talking about your finances, or engaged in any other behavior that involves you and your money. Take note of how much your beliefs about money influence the way you handle it.

Is Your Financial Past Haunting You?

Tatiana is twenty-five and eight thousand dollars in debt. After college, she took time off to travel around Europe, an experience she would not trade for the world. What she would trade, however, is the amount of debt she racked up. In college, she acquired credit cards by filling out a few of the applications that bombard college seniors. "When I got my first credit card," Tatiana recalls, "I was so excited. I felt so grown up. I was amazed at how great credit cards were. I could spend and not have to pay it all back right away." Tatiana was not aware of the high finance charges that came with her credit cards. She thought she needed to pay only the minimum each month but was lazy about meeting payment deadlines. Now her credit rating is low, and chipping away at her debt is hard since she is just starting her career. Tatiana is embarrassed about how completely unbalanced her finances are, and she never feels completely free.

Like Tatiana's, our past might catch up with us in the form of credit card bills and student loans, which add to the stress already present in our lives. Those of us who are concerned about debt and/or want to become more financially aware need a plan that supports financial responsibility and security. We can start by realizing that debt is not the end of the world. In fact, a history of making on-time minimum payments on debt is actually good for our credit ratings. We just need to manage our debt and credit while not going overboard in our spending. Fortunately, we are only in our twenties, so we have not had a lifetime to make financial mistakes or rack up mountains of debt. As we get our finances in order, we will gradually become more financially secure and confident in our ability to make and manage money. It is also important to remove the expectation many of us feel that we need to make a lot of money right away. There is time to increase our salaries — right now our focus should be on balance, not excess.

EXERCISE 39

Taking a Financial-Past Inventory

Clearing away our financial fog allows us more clarity as we answer the questions of the twenties triangle. In order to do this, bring your financial past into focus by examining where your money has gone and the debts that you owe now. Again, not all debt is bad. Having an overview of it helps us to manage it more responsibly.

First, gather any credit card bills, loan statements, or other documents that will help you complete this exercise. You might also want to grab a calculator and put on some relaxing music — for some of us, looking at our financial picture can be a rude awakening. But you do need to know the exact amount of your debt because, unlike a pimple, ignoring it will not help it go away.

1. Do you have any student loans? If so, how much do you owe?

2. What is your interest rate (percentage) on your student loans?

3. How much do you pay in interest per year on these loans?

4. How many credit cards do you have? (Don't forget credit cards other than those issued by your bank, such as department store cards.)

5. Do you have credit card debt (*debt* means any balance that you do not pay in full on a monthly basis)? If so, what do you owe?

6. How much do you pay monthly in finance charges on your credit cards?

7. Do you make your minimum payments on time on your credit cards?

8. What are the interest rates of each your credit cards?

9. Do you have any other loans (e.g., car, computer, appliance, mortgage)? If so, how much do you owe?

10. What interest rate do you pay on these loans?

11. Do you owe any money to people? If so, how much?

Next, add your answers from questions 1, 5, 9, and 11. That will give you an idea of the size of your debt. If your total is zero or low, your financial past is in good shape. Those with a higher number should take a deep breath. Often, our debt might seem manageable until we look at the total amount we owe; then it can seem overwhelming. Don't worry: you have time to pay it off, and resources are available to help you deal with the anxiety you might feel (we'll discuss those resources later).

Now look at your answers to questions 2, 6, 8, and 10 to get a handle on how much you pay in interest and finance charges. Often, these rates can be extremely high, forcing us into even more debt than we started with (this is how credit card companies make money).

Your assignment: Call each financial institution you have debt with and investigate whether a lower interest rate (also known as an annual percentage rate, or APR) is available. Credit card companies and banks will often work with you to find a lower rate because they do not want to lose your business. In general, a good APR is between 7 and 12 percent. If you have a good credit history, 5 percent is possible. If you pay over 12 percent, you should explore your options, such as transferring your balance to a card with a lower APR.

&oo&

Well, wasn't that a pleasant trip down memory lane? Looking through old photo albums might be a lot more fun, but becoming aware of our financial past makes dealing with the present less confusing. Before we move into the present, however, ask yourself again how your financial past has influenced your answers to the questions of the twenties triangle.

YOUR FINANCIAL PRESENT

Now that we have delved into the role money played in our past, let's look at the here and now. Our financial state can have a tremendous influence on our everyday state of mind. Patty, twenty-four, admits that she is just now forming a concept of how important money is, because her parents recently told her they will cut her off financially in one year. Patty is not even close to being financially independent: she still relies on her parents to pay the majority of her bills and loans. "I work hard, and I am not a big spender. I save up when I want something, but other than that I haven't thought about money much. I guess I have always thought of money as this nebulous thing; unless it was passing to or from my hands, it has not been that big of a deal."

Men no longer completely control all the money in this country. Women play the stock market, run large companies, work at financial institutions, and buy real estate. We live on our own, make investments, have credit cards, and file our own tax returns. Yet despite our economic power, many of us, like Patty, start our twenties rather indifferent toward or ignorant about our finances.

Although we are expected to be financially independent, many of us aren't taught the skill sets that enable this independence. Most school systems and universities do not offer courses on how to prepare for the fiscal responsibilities of an adult life. If we do not learn these skills from our parents, how do we acquire them? And what skills and knowledge might we already possess that we aren't aware of? In other words, what is our financial IQ?

EXERCISE 40

Your Financial IQ

The first step in taking responsibility for your finances is to ascertain your financial intelligence. If you feel that you don't know enough about money, that does not mean you are stupid. Lack of exposure and education, not brain cells, is the main reason that our financial IQs are often low. The following questions are intended to give you perspective on areas where you might need some enlightenment.

General Finances

1. Do you currently save money?

2. Do you have enough money to pay your bills each month?

3. Have you set any financial goals? If so, what are they?

4. Do you spend more than you can afford?

5. Do you feel that you are aware of and take advantage of all the financial tools available to you, such as saving, investing, tax deductions, free checking, and lower interest rates on credit cards?

Banking

1. Do you monitor your checking and savings accounts?

2. Do you know where to find a local ATM that won't charge you any fees?

3. Does your bank currently charge you fees for check writing or teller assistance?

Credit Cards

1. Do you know how much interest you pay on your credit cards?

2. Do you use your credit cards for cash advances?

3. Have you ever transferred balances? Are you aware of the fees that accompany such transfers?

4. Are you often late on credit card payments?

5. Do you normally pay just the minimum amount due on your credit cards?

6. Do you know your credit rating?

Investing

1. Does your job offer a 401(k) plan? If so, do you take advantage of it?

2. Do you know the difference between a mutual fund, a bond, and a stock investment?

3. Do you own anything of significant value (such as a car or property)?

Review your answers and determine which area(s) of your present financial picture is blurriest. Can you think of anything else about finances and money that you do not understand? What is the most stressful financial issue you face?

If you got uncomfortable, confused, or possibly even bored during this exercise, you are not alone. Educating ourselves about money is not always at the top of our "What do I want?" list, yet having and/or making money is. For many of us, the topic of finances brings up fear and anxiety. The good news: We are only in our twenties, so there is time to get all our questions answered. The only catch is that we actually have to do it. Now is the time to increase our financial IQ. In the Resources section at the back of the book, I list books and websites that can help you learn about money. Additionally, the financial tips section at the end of this chapter is a good place to start.

Financial Interdependence

Janet, twenty-five, is a college-educated waitress whose finances are even less organized than her closet. "My father always handled the finances in my family, and I was never really interested in learning about them. He has made investments in my name that I know nothing about. I have never been good with money, and I don't understand a lot, but I have always been good at spending, which is getting me in trouble." When Janet gets statements from her bank and credit card companies, she never reads the fine print. "I just make the minimum payments and stuff all the paperwork in a drawer. I could ask my dad to explain it to me, but I don't want to look stupid. Plus, I have so much on my mind and so many things I feel I need to do, I just don't have the time to figure it all out."

Like Janet, some of us could really use a financial tutorial but do not ask for help or take a proactive role in managing our money because we want to be perceived as independent. Remember the common misconception about independence addressed in chapter 4, that being on our own means never asking for support? But true independence requires *inter*dependence. Sometimes we need help in building our financial foundation.

Janet has another common and dangerous tendency that I have noticed in myself and other young women: when we are overwhelmed by something or do not understand it, we often run from it. We do this particularly when we perceive other things in our lives as more important or more fun and thus dedicate more time to them. We run out of steam as we exert a lot of energy on these other things. And if certain aspects of our lives are stressful, thinking about APRs and 401(k)s is the last thing we want to do. As long we are "getting by," we think we are doing okay. But some of us face expanding debt and shrinking financial freedom. The more we ignore our present financial situation, the weaker our foundation becomes. If you ignore your finances, it is time to run *toward* your present financial situation.

You have already taken the first step. In exercises 39 and 40, you identified the weak areas in your financial past and present. Now it is time for reinforcement. Those exercises gave you some tips to deal with debt and raise your financial IQ. If feeling overwhelmed prevents you from dealing with your finances or pride stops you from asking for help, return to the question "How do I get what I want?" (see part 1). Ignoring areas of weakness and protecting your pride are probably not the answers. Since this book is about getting what you really want, dive in. Figure out which areas of your financial foundation need reinforcement, and gather the tools to shore them up.

Your Current Relationship with Money

After looking at where we stand financially, we need to examine another element of our financial present. Each of us has a relationship with money — influenced by our past — that affects more than just our bank accounts. That relationship, just like relationships with people, can fall anywhere on the spectrum between healthy and dysfunctional. Although investigating the dynamics of the relationship offers us crucial insight into how to answer the questions of the twenties triangle, many of us never find time to do it. After all, sitting around and talking to our girlfriends about a recent date, a project we are working on, or reality television shows is much more interesting than examining our finances.

Some women's answers to the question "Who am I?" are largely rooted in the material realm. Farrah, twenty-seven, reports: "I tend to define myself by my financial independence. If I'm making money and investing, I feel great about myself. If I need family support because I can't pay my bills, I get really down on myself." When we let our relationship with money determine our self-worth, we are once again in danger of defining ourselves by an external standard, as discussed in chapter 1. Let's face it: Money cannot truly solve our self-confidence problems. If we think it can, then we are simply using money as another "quick fix" for our sense of self. What money *can* do is purchase basic requirements such as food, shelter, and clothing. It can also help us acquire skills for our future, as when we invest in our education. However, money should never dictate our self-worth. If we allow money to control how we feel about ourselves, the answer to the question "Who am I?" will be a number rather than a person.

Another trap that many twenty-something women fall into is allowing pride to motivate decisions about their finances. Martha, twenty-nine, has parents who have always been willing to help her with money. These days, she feels that she is "too old" to receive any monetary support from them, so when they ask how she is doing financially, she says, "I'm fine!" The truth is that money is the one area of Martha's life where she still feels a bit stunted. However, she does not admit it to her parents or anyone else, because she thinks it makes her appear weak.

Being too proud to ask for help when we truly need it is dramatically different from being proud of our financial independence, which is a much healthier stance. Emily, twenty-eight, says, "I really like the idea of paying for everything on my own and not having to call Mom and Dad and ask for money. I take pride in spending 'my money' on whatever I want. After I graduated, I was making very little money, so I had to call up and ask for help now and then, but I worked to become financially independent as soon as I could. It feels good to be earning my own way."

The main difference among Farrah, Martha, and Emily is that while Farrah and Martha see money as something that defines them, Emily sees it as something she can use to empower herself. Money influences how Farrah and Martha feel about themselves, whereas Emily takes pride in assuming control of her finances, and they are not part of her identity. As we face the questions of the twenties triangle, it's important to distinguish between being empowered by our relationship with our finances and being overpowered by it.

EXERCISE 41

How Do You Relate to Money?

Farrah's, Martha's, and Emily's stories are just a few examples of the ways we relate to money. Money is energy, just like everything else in our lives, and the way we relate to it impacts how it flows in and out of our bank accounts. The following exercise will help you analyze your own relationship with it. For this exercise, think about money as if it were a person. Let's call money George. In your journal, answer the following questions about your relationship with George:

1. Overall, how would you describe your relationship with George?

2. Why do you think your relationship with George is as you described it?

3. Do you think you ever take George for granted?

4. Which of the following statements best describes your thoughts about and interactions with George? (More than one might apply, and if none are accurate, please write down your own.)

- I am a bit obsessive about him.

- I am rather oblivious to George.

- George plays a significant role in my life.

- I keep George on a short leash.

- I am a bit intimidated by George and keep him at arm's length.

- I am a bit confused by George; I don't really understand everything about him.

- I am a bit annoyed or angry that I have to think about him.

- I am happy and enjoy a very balanced relationship with George.

- I want a lot more of George.

After determining which of these statements best describes you, is there anything in the relationship that you think might be unhealthy? Do you see any red flags? In other words, if one of your girlfriends were describing a relationship that sounded like the one you have with George, would you be concerned? In your journal, write down any concerns about your relationship with money. Consider how these concerns around money might interrupt its flow in your life.

———◦◦◦◦———

Your Financial Behavior

Our relationship with money directly affects our financial behavior. If we have a secure and grounded relationship, chances are our checkbooks are balanced, our debts (if we have any) are manageable, and *save* is not a four-letter word. If our relationship is not grounded, our financial behavior might be erratic.

In chapter 4, we discussed the difference between intrinsic and reactionary decisions. It is abundantly clear that many of our decisions about money are reactionary. We see something we like, and we buy it. It is no secret that most women love to shop, but many of us spend more on things we want than we do on things we truly need. This impulse will probably never go away, but how we deal with it today affects how solid our financial foundation will be tomorrow.

Alicia, twenty-seven, brings up her credit card debt in daily conversation. "Well, it's sort of a joke with my friends and family, me and my spending. Like yesterday: I bought a ticket to Paris so I can go shopping! A lot of my friends are buying homes. I'm traveling. I go to all the latest clubs and restaurants. I'm single, and I'm certainly not going to meet someone sitting at home watching TV. I may have some debt, but I'm fine with it."

When we ask ourselves, "What do I want?" debt is usually not on our list. Yet each time we say to ourselves, "I want that new dress" or "I want to go to Europe" louder than we say, "I want to lower my debt" or "I want to get my MBA," we delay our financial security. Our lifestyles need to be in balance with our current financial state. To return to the topic, addressed in part 1, of the pressures we feel in our twenties, many of us live beyond our means because we feel pressured to do so. Saying no to things we want or feel others expect us to do or have is difficult because of the "wanting it all" mentality. We want to have fun. We want to go out. We want to look good. We are constantly tempted. We feel pressure to keep up with our peers and society. We might even overspend to impress others. Our perception of how much is needed for a sensible lifestyle is distorted when our financial lives are dictated by what we want rather than by how much we earn.

Remember the "doing, doing, doing" mentality discussed in chapter 3? In the financial realm, this translates into a "spending, spending, spending" pattern that many of us follow. Instead of slow, steady accumulation, we go for fast acquisition. The immediate gratification we get from this behavior allows us to forget about our credit card debt, which will last longer than the new outfit we bought will stay in style. We need to consistently remind ourselves that our lifestyles are a function of the choices we make. If we choose to blow our savings on clothes, we will look great at dinner but might drown in a sea of debt. On the other hand, choosing to borrow a dress rather than buy one for a cousin's wedding might afford us extra cash for the weekend getaway we need. As we make choices about money, we also need to be on the lookout for unrealistic expectations. For instance, if we become too attached to dreams of fortune, we risk always feeling dissatisfied, and we might miss the important distinction between what we need and what we just want.

We might say that we want to be financially secure, but do we understand the choices and behavior that will get us there? Some of us think that working hard and making a solid income are enough. Sometimes they are, but often they aren't. Take Jennifer, twenty-nine, for example. "I did not have a lot of money growing up. Now that I have more money and don't have to watch every expense, I think it is harder to manage. I need to do a budget again because I am finding that the more I earn, the more I spend!" Jennifer's story shows the importance of nurturing a healthy relationship with money that remains consistent regardless of your income level. This relationship is similar to a healthy marriage. Sometimes times are good; sometimes they are not. But if the relationship is built on a healthy foundation, getting through the rough times is possible.

EXERCISE 42

Is Your Spending in Sync with Your Income?

Life is full of necessary and unnecessary expenses. Usually the unnecessary ones are more fun. However, to be financially secure, we need to ensure that our lifestyles are in sync with our income levels. This exercise is designed to help you do just that.

1. Think about your recent spending habits. Look over your credit card or bank statements from the past few months, if you need to. Next, list at least ten unnecessary items or activities you spent money on and how much they cost you.

2. Record the total spent on unnecessary expenses.

3. Go back over your list and put a star next to each expense that really was an indulgence beyond your means, something you probably could have lived without. Then calculate the total of all the starred expenses.

Now that you've done this exercise, how far beyond your means would you say you live? Does your level of financial security dictate your choices, or does your lifestyle throw your financial security off balance? If financial independence is our destination, we won't get there via reactionary and overindulgent spending. It is wonderful to treat ourselves, but if we do it in excess, treats become an expectation rather than a special occasion, which diminishes their value.

— ∞ —

Budgeting... Everyone's Doing It

As a personal trainer and nutritional consultant, I know for a fact that despite all the fad diets and workout crazes out there, the secret to maintaining a healthy weight is monitoring calories in versus calories out. The same is true of a healthy and secure financial foundation. The only way to attain it is to monitor money in versus money out. We do this by preparing and living according to a budget. This is the best way to know how our spending and saving habits affect our present financial state. Many of us keep a budget in our heads or keep track of major things we have to pay for each month. Others avoid budgets altogether and live paycheck to paycheck, month to month. Starting a new habit of budgeting is a surefire way to gain more financial balance.

EXERCISE 43

Creating a Budget

Creating and living by a well-thought-out budget is about as fun as waiting in line at the supermarket (except there are no trashy magazines to read while we do it). We don't necessarily want to live on a budget and save, yet we want to be financially secure. But sometimes things that we don't necessarily *want* to do right now must be on our list of *how* we will get what we want down the road.

Using the chart that follows, create your budget (even if you don't want to or think you need to, recall Jennifer's story — her spending habits sneaked up on her). This will help you gain perspective on how much money goes out versus how much comes in. Often we do not remember the things that we spend money on, but having this knowledge empowers us financially. This exercise could bring to mind areas that you have not considered to be part of your current budget, such as a "speed-bump" fund that you set aside to cover life's little surprises — such as a parking ticket or an emergency root canal.

Please gather whatever information you might need to complete the chart, and feel free to amend the categories so that they are more applicable to you. In the "Estimated" column, rely on your spending history and previous bills to calculate your estimated expenses. This figure will stay the same each month. Then, each month, write down what you really spend in the "Actual" column. This figure might fluctuate from month to month, which is why revisiting this budget monthly will be crucial.

Wntr Budget

MONTHLY BUDGET

	Estimated	Actual
1. General expenses:		
Home:		
Rent/mortgage payment	500	
Property taxes		
Homeowners' association dues		
Home/renters' insurance		
Home maintenance/repairs		
Cable/TIVO/satellite	50	
Electricity		
Water	50	
Gas		
Home telephone		
Cell phone		
Housekeeper	5	
Internet access		
Education:		
Student loan payments	375	
Class fees/tuition		
Car/transportation:		
Car payment	415	
Gas	60	
Maintenance/repairs/oil changes		
Insurance	67	
DMV registration/smog check		
Public transportation/cab fare		
Parking/parking permits		
Credit card minimum payments	150	
Other		
Subtotal	$ 1672	$
2. Food expenses:		
Groceries/household items	100	
Meals out	100	
Coffee/snacks	40	
Other		
Subtotal	$ 240	$
3. Entertainment and social expenses:		
Movies/video rentals	15	
Hobbies/clubs/sports	99	
Theater/sporting events		
Vacation/travel		
CDs/tapes		
Drinks/cover charges	25	

	Estimated	Actual
Cigarettes/alcohol Other		
Subtotal	$ 139	$
4. Health expenses:		
Insurance Medication/prescriptions Doctor/dentist/vision Counseling/psychotherapy Co-payments Health club membership/dues Other		
Subtotal	$ 0	$
5. Clothing expenses:		
Clothes/shoes/accessories Dry cleaning/laundry Other	0	
Subtotal	$ 0	$
6. Grooming and personal expenses:		
Hair care Cosmetics/toiletries Manicures/massages/facials Magazine subscriptions Other	75 25	
Subtotal	$ 100	$
7. Miscellaneous expenses:		
Holiday/gift expenses Birthdays/weddings Charitable contributions Pet costs Other	25	
Subtotal	$ 25	$
8. Safety net expenses:		
Speed-bump fund (for unplanned but necessary costs) Contributions to savings/investments		
Subtotal	$ 0	$
Total monthly expenses:	$ 2176	$ 2200

Next, if you are up for it, try a little experiment with your budget. After figuring out how much money you predict you will spend in one month, withdraw that amount in cash and see if you can actually live off that amount for a month. Use only that cash to pay for everything. For bills you have to write checks for, write the check and then re-deposit that cash amount back into your checking account. This is a very powerful way to see where and how fast your money goes and to prevent yourself from spending what you do not have.

———⊶⊷———

Achieving Financial Balance

Doing a budget was probably not the most exciting or relaxing way to pass your time, but you might have noticed that it has already given you a sense of accomplishment and control. Creating a budget is valuable because it is a way to understand how *your* money works. That knowledge alone is empowering. It forces us to align our choices with what we want and can afford. As Jamie, twenty-nine, explains, "Creating a budget in my early twenties when my finances started to get out of control was the smartest thing I ever did. Since then, I've been forced to be resourceful. I remember losing confidence when money first became tight for me. This was actually a blessing because it made me explore what I believe in. When I have money, I'll probably be smarter with it because I have practice in managing it."

Living by a budget is not flashy or fun — and a lot of us in our twenties do crave flash and fun. Yet sometimes we need to make sacrifices and adjustments to stay within our means. Take

Meghan, for instance: "I moved in with my parents to save money. It's a very family-oriented area, not too exciting for twenty-four-year-olds. But increasing my financial stability is more important to me than decreasing the status of my social life, so I had to sacrifice something. I know living here is not permanent, and it saves me a lot of stress."

One of the simplest sacrifices we can make is to give up that "wanting it all" mentality. Letting go of our attachment to or even obsession with the green stuff can be very freeing. Janae, a thirty-year-old writer, articulates the importance of a healthy perspective on money: "Money is really nice now that I have it, but I know I could always live and be happy without it. Frankly, if there is one thing really wrong with our generation — and specifically women in their twenties — it's that many of us actually feel entitled to having nice things even when we can't afford them. Something might be a nice luxury, but if you don't have the money, don't buy it." And remember, even if something is on sale, that does *not* mean you will save money if you buy it; you are still spending. Justifying spending with sales is a bad, yet common, habit.

Getting by and making ends meet can be challenging in our first phase of adulthood. As you think about where you currently stand financially, do you feel that you control your finances or that they control you? If you feel a little out of balance, refer back to exercises 42 and 43 and brainstorm about sacrifices, adjustments, or new behaviors that might be appropriate. Make simple changes, such as putting aside twenty bucks a month or cutting back to only one latte per week (you can make a great cup of coffee in a French press and buy a milk foamer for eight dollars). These are steps you can take today toward a more secure financial foundation. Everything we do in our twenties to improve our present financial picture makes for a brighter future.

YOUR FINANCIAL FUTURE

In our twenties, we become more conscious of the rest of our lives. We map out our lives. We set mental timelines. As we've discussed, many of us are planaholics, and that can get in the way of living in the moment. But is there a way to put our obsession with planning to healthy use? *Yes!* Planning for our financial future is a healthy habit we can create in our twenties.

The urgency we feel about the questions "Who am I?" and "What do I want?" drives us to constantly seek answers. Wouldn't it be nice to have a crystal ball that tells us if the decisions we make will lead us in the right direction? Yet two things that we *do* know is that we will get older and that we will need money. But how much thought do we give to these facts? In our twenties, we are preoccupied by other, seemingly more pressing issues that keep the distant future off the top of our lists. Myopic thinking becomes common. We say we want it all, but do we pursue our goals in a way that guarantees results?

Planning for the Future

Financial planning is an integral part of building a foundation that will last a lifetime. So how do we do it? Well, let's first look at how *not* to plan for our financial future. Some of us might compare ourselves to others on the basis of material possessions. If what others have directs our fantasies about what we want financially, we won't set realistic standards for our own lives. Take Dana, twenty-seven, who is heavily influenced by the lifestyle and financial portfolio of her aunt. "She married a multimillionaire and has two live-in maids and basically shops for a living. I envy her because she literally has no housework or financial issues to worry about. This seems like the ideal life, but ultimately my dream of marrying a guy with *that* kind of wealth is just a silly fantasy. To marry some-one with a more normal kind of wealth, like a doctor, is definitely more within my reach." Dana's plan to secure her financial future by marrying the right person is not empowering and is even less romantic. She is setting a standard for herself based on a comparison and faces her future wearing blinders.

EXERCISE 44

How Will You Get What You Want?

Knowing what we want is easier than knowing how to get it, especially when it comes to money. If only we all could just win the lottery or score millions on a reality television show. To answer the question "How do I get what I want?" we have to consider financial planning. In your journal, answer the following questions:

1. When you think about your financial future, what do you envision? *Not having to worry.*
2. What do you do right now that you consider to be financial planning? *Budget*
3. Do you plan to be financially independent for the rest of your life? *Yes – Hopefully*
4. What does financial security mean to you? *taking care of myself*
5. How many things in your overall life plan offer the guarantee of a certain financial result? *Many.*

Answers to these types of questions can feel rather fuzzy to many of us. So let's talk about the real nuts and bolts of financial planning. What do I mean by nuts and bolts? Things such as 401(k)s, IRAs, money market accounts, mutual funds, savings, stock portfolios, and investments. Many of us avoid thinking about this kind of financial planning simply because we are intimidated or uninformed. The rewards of a great job or a grad school degree (or even a rich spouse) might seem obvious: they help us to achieve a higher financial tax bracket. However, we might not be so clear about the rewards of financial planning. Most of us have little experience or knowledge in this area, which prevents us from any real planning. But our twenties are a great time to start saving and investing for the future.

Mariana is a twenty-seven-year-old actress/model who recently inherited some money that she wanted to invest. She went to a bank to ask questions about what to do with her money but left feeling more ignorant. "I felt like the biggest idiot. The bank representative started asking me all kinds of questions about what I wanted to do, what kind of interest rates I wanted, how risky an investment I was willing to make, and so on. It was like he was speaking a different language." Mariana decided to just put the money in a savings account because she got overwhelmed. "Eventually I'll figure out what to do with it; right now I just don't have the time or energy to investigate all my options." Many twenty-something

> "Most people don't think about saving in their twenties — you think you'll get to it later — but in your twenties you have less financial responsibility, so you can sock it away, and it will grow."
>
> — Eleese, fifty-eight

women can relate to Mariana; we avoid financial planning because we are intimidated by or feel ignorant about it. Moreover, we do not even think we have the money to invest.

When we are in our twenties and just starting out, we find it difficult to think about money in terms beyond earning and spending. A lot of us think financial planning is something we can do later in life. Hillary, twenty-four, explains her financial plan like this: "I want to reach a point in my twenties where I feel financially successful. I'm confident I'll work hard and make it happen; and then I will know internally I am capable of reaching my goals. At that point, I'll be smart about my earnings and invest them wisely." If we are similar to Hillary, our financial planning might be rooted in "when/then" thinking, which gives us little control of our fiscal future.

Many of us avoid financial planning because we feel too stressed out by our current financial state and see little relief ahead. Those of us who struggle with money find it hard to see investing and saving for the future even as possibilities. Jessica, a twenty-eight-year-old grad student, states, "Being in school makes finances a very tense issue. I'm living on loans and totally broke, with the promise 'You'll be making more than enough to pay them off easily in about ten years' ringing in my head. Ten years? I'm going to be collecting Social Security before I actually have an income."

If you relate to Mariana, Hillary, and Jessica — if your feelings about financial planning keep you from doing it — you might need to reframe your financial future. Being proactive about our financial future is the type of tangible planning we can do in our twenties. Although we might not have extra money, there are plenty of small steps we can take to begin this task. Even beginning to expand our financial knowledge is a proactive step.

EXERCISE 45

Becoming a Proactive Financial Planner

This exercise suggests things you can do to overcome feelings of hesitation, ignorance, or anxiety about financial planning. All you need to do is review the list below, pick at least *one* suggestion, and act on it.

1. Throw a "money party." Get your girlfriends together and talk about money. Discuss budgets, how you spend, how you budget, your financial goals, and so on. Make it fun by serving green food or playing a round of Monopoly. Ask each guest to bring at least one financial tip, piece of advice, or resource to the party.

2. Open a savings account that collects interest. Even if you put only ten dollars a month into it, you are at least taking a step in the right direction.

3. Find a financial advisor at a financial organization or your local bank and set up an informational meeting (at no cost to you). You could also organize a group of women to get together for dinner and ask a financial planner to speak to the group. Usually advisors will do this for free because you and your friends are potential clients.

4. Enroll in a basic financial-planning or investing class at your local community college or learning annex.

5. Talk to a trusted parent, sibling, or friend who knows about money and manages her or his own well.

6. Become well-versed in a few stocks. Pay attention to companies you like. Women are the best consumers,

and we tend to know which companies do well. Looking at stocks is not boring if you are interested in a company and its products.

———∞∞∞———

Learning Smart Financial Habits

Learning and practicing smart spending habits are perhaps the greatest investments we can make in our future. We do not think twice about brushing our teeth at night, because we are in the habit of doing so. Similarly, if we get into the habit of paying attention to our financial future, it will become second nature. In our twenties, it is important to ask ourselves if our spending is in line with our long-term goals and what we want, and whether we are falling into the "not-enoughness" and comparison pitfalls that can make us careless with our

> "In your twenties, take the time to learn what you need to do in order to live the life you desire. Then it's just a matter of learning and disciplining yourself to do those things."
>
> — Anita, sixty

money. Additionally, investing perpetuates another good habit — investing does not always mean we must set money aside; it can also mean purchases that serve our goals. For instance, Regina, a producer and graphic designer, doesn't blow money on things that don't matter. When she makes big purchases, they are for her future. "Any spare money I have, I'll put into an editing system add-on or Web-design software or my house."

When planning our future, our goals will change, and we need to have a secure financial foundation to support those goals. When I asked her what she wanted for her future, Gina, twenty-nine, told me, "I think my goals have changed now that I want children. I used to be more carefree about finances since I didn't know what I wanted or whom I wanted to be or be with. I have to be smarter about my money, and I honestly wish I had gotten into the habit a lot sooner." As what we want becomes clearer, we find that it's easier to get those things if we don't try to build on a weak financial foundation. We also find that our financial security affects our overall security, and thus more secure people are attracted to us.

Granted, this was a rather dry chapter, but financial security is necessary to solidify our foundation as we answer the questions of the twenties triangle. A sense of balance about money sets us on a steady course for the future and the exciting things that lie ahead. But our twenties are also about enjoying our lives and having fun. It is not necessary to become a penny-pincher, piggy-banker, or budget Nazi. Just doing a few little things to create good financial habits can be enough. Please refer to Resources, at the back of the book, for helpful sources of additional information about money and budgeting.

But first, below is a summary of some of the main points of this dense chapter, as well as a few other financial tips.

CREDIT CARDS

Our best friend, our worst enemy...

- Always, always make your minimum required payments on time each month to avoid late fees and to keep your credit cards active.

- A finance charge is always assessed on the remainder of the balance on the card. The only way to avoid this charge is to pay your statement balance in full each month. If you are unable to do so, look for credit cards with low APRs.

- Know your FICO score, which is your credit rating. You can go to www.myfico.com to obtain your credit rating. Any time you apply for a loan, make a big purchase, or sign a lease, your FICO is checked. Not making your payments on time or having lots of outstanding or revolving debt lowers your FICO score.

- If you have credit cards, obtain those with perks. For instance, choose a card that gives you airline miles with each purchase. Be aware, however, that a lot of these cards charge an annual fee to be in their spending/perk programs.

- Focus on padding your wallet with cold, hard cash (and pictures of your loved ones) rather than credit cards from every store out there. The more credit cards you have, the more bills you have. Money management is easier if all your spending is done on one primary card.

- Do not become addicted to credit cards. Cash and debit cards are often a better way to stick to your budget.

OTHER TIPS

- Consistently be a wage earner. Even if you are in a job transition, do something to keep money flowing in.

- Every month, put money into your emergency speed-bump fund, and do not touch it. Open an interest-bearing savings account.

- If you are moving, at least one month beforehand, go to www.usps.com/moversguide/welcome.htm?from=home& page=changeaddress and change your address to avoid falling behind on your bills.

PART 3

Relationships and Career
during Your Quarter-Life

In the previous chapters, we excavated your foundation and began the process of laying a more secure one for the future. However, we cannot just read a few self-help books and reflect on our lives — we have to actually live them. So now it is time to take a deeper look at the "rooms" we are constructing in the house of our lives.

The two concerns that come up most among twenty-something women are relationships and career— as Freud observed, our happiness is defined by our ability to love and work. We feel tremendous pressure, desire, and even obligation to be completely fulfilled in these two areas. Even if we are happy in our careers, we might feel that this is not good enough if we are not in relationships as well. Likewise, those of us in healthy relationships often feel something is missing if we don't have great jobs. We want both fabulous careers we feel passionate about and passionate relationships that feel fabulous. When either is lacking, we tend to suffer from anxiety and disappointment. One reason for this is the proverbial biological clock that many of us hear ticking. To have kids (at least in the old-fashioned way), we need mates. And if we want careers, we had better decide on them and move ahead before we have children, when we'll have to decide whether to return to work, stay home, or juggle the two. We often perceive our twenties as "crunch time": the years in which we *must* get on the family and career track.

However, what happens if our expectations and perceived time constraints are the only motivations for the decisions we make regarding love and work? The answer is that we might never feel content, and we might carry our twenty-something crisis right into midlife crisis. If these key areas in your life are not quite what you want them to be, this does not necessarily mean that anything is wrong. We often just need to look at our relationships and careers from a different angle. That is what this part of the book is all about — reframing how we approach love and work, two very significant parts of our lives. To break down and explore these cumbersome topics, we will revisit the questions of the twenties triangle. We'll explore specifically who we are, what we want, and how to get what we want in our relationships and in our careers.

CHAPTER 7

TWENTY-SOMETHING LOVE

Finding "the one," seeing fireworks, feeling butterflies in your stomach, falling deeply, passionately in love, and then living happily ever after — that is how a relationship should go, right? We are told that the twenties are when we will find the loves of our lives and the fathers of our children (no pressure there). Yet many of us haven't found our soul mates and are questioning whether they exist. In our early twenties, we are under less pressure to settle down, but as the calendar pages turn, many of us find ourselves thinking of wedding bells (or, at the very least, a person to spend Saturday nights with). We wonder how to find "the one" and if we will know for sure that marriage is what we want.

The way women answer "Who am I, what do I want, and how do I get what I want?" in relationships is different from the ways women of previous generations answered these questions. Our grandmothers and most of our mothers had the goal of becoming wives in their twenties — marriage was their job, and many of them stuck with it no matter what. Today many of us choose to postpone marriage, and even relationships. Others find life partners in other women, which is not seen as taboo as it used to be.

Additionally, we as a generation are more vocal about our needs, less willing to compromise, and more satisfied with our independence than women of the past were. Still, many of us yearn for soul mates and the blissful relationships that they supposedly bring (for that idea, you can thank every sappy romantic movie you have seen). Our relationship status occupies a great deal of space in the mental "hot-air balloons" of most female twenty-somethings, whether we're looking for love, fed up with love, recovering from love, or in love. This is okay unless we become so consumed that it distracts us from attaining our self-security. In this chapter, we focus on issues surrounding romantic relationships that color our answers to the questions of the twenties triangle.

WHO AM I IN A RELATIONSHIP?

In chapter 1, exercise 4 asked you to identify who you are in different aspects of your life. Turn back to the page in your journal where you answered the question "Who am I with someone I am dating/in a serious relationship with/married to?" Before delving into this section rewrite your response on a new page, adding any new realizations. Keep this in mind as you continue.

When we fall in love with someone, that person naturally becomes a significant part of our support system. Knowing who we are in relationships is essential, regardless of our current relationship status, because it gives us clues about ways that we might amend our identity in order to be with someone.

A romantic relationship is one of the most rewarding experiences we can have with another human being. And it can also be stressful, confusing, and possibly even unhealthy if we do not stay true to who we are. If our foundation is solid, the intimate relationships we attract will follow suit. If we struggle with insecurity in various aspects of our lives, we could attract rather unstable relationships. That is why we must know who we are and how to take care of ourselves before we get deeply involved with someone else. Forget tips from magazines and dating books. Knowing and loving ourselves before anything and anyone else are always the best aphrodisiacs. Yet so many of us may be more deeply in love with someone else than we are with ourselves. So let's examine some common ways we twenty-something women lose sight of ourselves and make reactionary decisions in relationships.

I Love You, Forget Me

Lynn, twenty-six, is beginning to figure out who she has been in relationships. She met her exboyfriend, Scott, during her senior year in college and was instantly attracted to him. Lynn loved that Scott was ambitious and decisive, especially since she was confused about what she wanted to do with her life. She decided to move to Washington, D.C., where Scott had lined up a job after graduation. Lynn did not know anyone there, and her life became about him and their relationship. He made the decisions, which was comforting and familiar to Lynn. For some reason, she had always loved a "powerful" man — her dad had been that way. When Scott broke up with Lynn because she was "smothering and needy," she was crushed. All this time, she had thought she was being the perfect girlfriend.

When I asked Lynn what she had learned from the heartbreak, she said, "I learned that I didn't like the person I had become, and I learned that it is something I am really going to have to be aware of in the future, because this is the kind of relationship I want. I let it happen; it made me happy to make him happy, which isn't necessarily a bad thing, except that I sacrificed my own identity in the process."

If you relate to Lynn's experience, consider why you are or have been willing to immerse yourself in someone's life at the expense of your own. Of course, it is wonderful to be giving in relationships, but if we give too much, we risk depleting ourselves. Also, we might end up only with takers — individuals who are often selfish and narcissistic. People who love and appreciate us for who we are will support and encourage us to maintain our own identity. If we find ourselves complaining about our singlehood or relationships, we should stop to ask ourselves, "Do I even like myself enough to date or be with?" If we don't, we cannot expect anyone else to love us with honesty, respect, and integrity.

EXERCISE 46

What Sacrifices Do You Make?

As women, appeasing and caring for others seem to come very naturally to us. So naturally, in fact, that we might not be conscious of where to draw the line between healthy compromise and sacrifice. Ponder this while asking yourself whether you've ever sacrificed (even just a little) any of the following things in a relationship:

- Your identity

- A career opportunity

- Your ambition

- Male friends

- Money

- Your independence

- Your hobbies

- Your morals or values

- Time with family or friends
- Your sexual health (for example, you went further sexually than you wanted to, got an STD, or had an unwanted pregnancy)
- Your peace of mind
- Anything else not listed above

After completing this exercise, are you at all surprised by what you have sacrificed in relationships? Notice whether you tend to sacrifice the same things repeatedly or whether you've vowed to never make the same mistake twice. You might feel a little remorseful or perhaps even ashamed, but do not be too hard on yourself. Many of us are willing to sacrifice things for love, and each time we love, we open ourselves up to learn great lessons. A secret to healthy relationships is to recognize unhealthy patterns so we do not have to learn the same lessons over and over again.

Philipa, a twenty-four-year-old from London, checked off more than one item on the list above. "I have compromised my sanity on many occasions, ranging from stupidly staying with a guy who cheated on me to staying in a four-year relationship because I didn't want to hurt someone." Of hundreds of women who did the "What Sacrifices Do You Make?" exercise, many checked off multiple items on the list. In fact, every single item got at least ten yes answers. 60 percent of the women I surveyed selected "Your identity" and "Your independence" in addition to at least one other item. We need not feel alone or ashamed if we have allowed a relationship to jeopardize one or more of these things — but we do need to be aware of the sacrifice.

"If something you are doing in a relationship doesn't feel right to you on any level, don't do it. Trust your gut instincts and be true to yourself. Nothing in this life is worth sacrificing your personal integrity, and the path of integrity is uphill all the way, so put on your sneakers and get ready for some serious legwork!"

— Margaret, forty-five

After we've examined what we might give up to be in relationships, the next step is to ask ourselves why we do it. I am sure it's not because you answered the question "Who am I?" with "I am someone who sacrifices important things for a relationship."

Shannon, twenty-nine, got married at twenty-five to a man whose race and culture are very different from her own. Her husband is "set in his ways," and while he is tolerant, he will not change many things. Shannon admits, "I have given up many of my ideas of 'equality' and leisure activities so that the relationship can survive. Some of his passions have even replaced my own. At one time, I sacrificed my relationship with my family completely. I stopped college with only one year left in nursing school. I gave up my deeply ingrained ideas about sharing household chores. I could go on and on, but I feel that doing so would be a bit self-righteous and unimportant."

We can be flexible and make adjustments in relationships without sacrificing who we are. But in Shannon's case, she has given up significant things at the core of who she is, such as time with her family, her values, and her education, yet she still feels that these things are "unimportant" to acknowledge. If making a relationship last is more important than tending to the things that make us who we are, we will eventually feel a sense of loss.

EXERCISE 47

Adjustments and Sacrifices

To make sure we keep ourselves in balance when we look for, begin, or continue relationships, we need to identify what we are willing to adjust versus what we are not willing to sacrifice. As you create the lists described below, think about your answers to "Who am I?" to trigger your thought process.

First list those things that you feel you can and are willing to adjust in a relationship. At the top of this list write "Adjustments." Then make a second list of things so inherent to who you are that you are unwilling to change/sacrifice them. At the top of this list write "Sacrifices." For instance, I am a very independent person. I like doing things that I want to do on my schedule. However, I know that to have a healthy relationship, I also have to consider my boyfriend's de-sires. So, in my adjustment list, I wrote, "I am willing to adjust my very rigid and independent schedule." I am also a healthy, active person, and I value my body. I could never be with someone who was a drug addict or who sat on the couch and drank beer all day. So, in my sacrifice list, I wrote, "I will never sacrifice my healthy lifestyle or be in a relationship with someone who does not have one." Now it's your turn.

Staying true to these lists is key to sanity and healthy interaction in a relationship. We might spend our lives answering the question "Who am I?" but

> "Never break a date with your girlfriends to go out with a man, and always continue to do the things you enjoy doing on your own."
>
> — Dawn, fifty-five

by our twenties, we have enough sense of ourselves to recognize essential elements of our identity. Adjustment is different from suffocating parts of who we are. If someone asks you to sacrifice something that is a significant part of your identity, that person is not the best partner for you. Trust that someone will come along and celebrate who you are.

⸎

Who I Am Depends on Who I'm With

In part 1 of this book, we discussed in detail the dangers of looking to things outside ourselves to shape who we are. This concept
can be especially crucial in romantic relationships. Karen, twenty-
eight, just wants to be the "woman behind the man." She is a successful pharmaceutical sales representative but believes that the
void she feels in her life will be filled by a man. "Yes, I have a good
job and a lot of friends, but I do not feel content unless I am in a
relationship. I do not like being alone, and when I am, I feel like
a big loser." Pam is a twenty-six-year-old
working as a waitress. She is a serial dater
and admits she does it because it increases
her confidence. "If I am asked out, I feel
appealing and powerful. If I go a few
weeks without a date, I begin to question
what is wrong with me." Both Karen and
Pam have made a common mistake: they
have confused who they are with who
they are with. The reason I call it a mistake
is that allowing our relationship status to
affect how we think of ourselves weakens our foundation: our self-
worth is defined by someone else.

> "Never feel that there is
> anyone out there who
> can make you feel better
> or more complete. That
> will never come from
> outside yourself. If you
> have a need, there is no
> one out there who can
> fill it other than you."
>
> — Janice, fifty-seven

In chapter 5 we explored why we cannot heal our insecurities
with quick fixes, despite the short-term positive results they might
yield. Our partners or dates might dim our insecurities for a while
with their attention and affection. However, if we do not learn to
establish our own security, a "not so happily ever after" could
result. We might become overly dependent on the relationship. Or
we might sabotage the relationship because it still cannot answer
"Who am I?" for us.

Even worse, our identity might become completely defined by
who we are with. Gabrielle, twenty-six, saved herself from a fairy

tale turned nightmare when she realized that to discover her identity, she needed to experience being alone and single. "Breaking up with my long-term boyfriend was probably the hardest thing I have ever done. I still cared so much for him, but I felt that my life was becoming all about him — I even moved to a city I did not like and left my passion and career behind. I saw myself becoming the housewife of a rich venture capitalist, which is not what I wanted. I knew I would always wonder 'What if?' if I didn't jump off the proverbial cliff and go out in the world to find myself and what makes me truly happy."

Questions about our identity might not begin to surface until we make a serious commitment, such as getting engaged or married. Or these questions might arise out of such decisions as whether we should change our last names after marriage. Aimee, twenty-seven, told me, "It was very hard for me to give up my last name because it was part of who I was for so long. I still feel funny saying my husband's name, because it doesn't belong to me."

Twenty-something married women are often torn between being part of a couple and clinging to their own, separate identities. Commitment can be both comforting and intimidating. This is yet another reason that we need a grounded commitment to ourselves before we commit to another.

> "Being with a man just to avoid being alone is shortsighted, weak, and a waste of time. Get a dog instead."
>
> — Abagail, sixty-one

If we take the time to develop a strong sense of self, committing does not involve a sense of loss of our individuality. Something like a name change becomes simply a different last name rather than an identity change if our foundation is solid.

Intimacy is not something that comes naturally to everyone. Many of us who are now coming into our power and sense of purpose in life are a little scared of losing them in relationships. Balancing our softness and vulnerability as women with our power and values requires a solid foundation and sense of who we are. Mimi, twenty-seven, told me, "I just have decided not to date because I don't want to get into a relationship. I really need to focus on my career right now, and I know if I fall in love, it may slow down my progress or, worst-case scenario, take me off my path. I don't want to risk it. My career is too important to me." Yet Mimi does admit that she wants to be in love and get married.

Mimi's choice to remain single illustrates how fear of losing ourselves can keep us from entering intimate relationships. Her passion for her career does not have to negate her desire to eventually share her life with someone. Being in a relationship and being independent do not have to be mutually exclusive. If we are in healthy, communicative, trusting relationships, we can structure them with our partners so that they suit us — there is no reason our independent lives must stop. If we want a "girls' night out," we can have one. If we need a weekend to work, we can have that as well. If our partners have problems with this, maybe we need to reevaluate why we chose them. As we strengthen our foundation, we become more aware of our choices in relationships and more adept at making them.

If you are dead-set on being single right now, consider whether this is a reactionary or intrinsic decision, as defined in chapter 4. In other words, if you are single because you enjoy it and love who you are as a single person, then that decision is intrinsic: it's in line with who you are right now. On the other hand, if you avoid relationships because you are scared of what you might have to give up, but still feel deep down that you really want to be with someone, your decision to be single could be a reaction to your fear or beliefs. Perhaps your parents' marriage was a disaster, so you don't want a relationship. If you think that you might define who you do or don't want to be in a relationship based on reactions to something from your past, turn back to exercises 8, 9, and 20 to review the beliefs and reactionary decisions you identified there. If you fear losing your identity, consider whether your sense of self might need some reinforcement. Finally, if you are single and searching, continue to look inward and don't doubt that you will meet your match.

WHAT DO I WANT IN A RELATIONSHIP?

In our twenties, as we are discovering who we are and what we want for ourselves, defining what we want and need from another person can be tricky. Joining a convent and spending our lives in self-reflection is not appealing, so we date, have sex, move in together, get engaged, and walk down the aisle. Throughout each relationship stage, evaluating what we want is the first step in securing it. Gaining perspective on this twenties-triangle question is possible regardless of our current relationship status. If we are single, this perspective can help us manifest what we want. If we are with someone, it can help us evaluate whether our current relationship is what we truly want.

EXERCISE 48

Listing What You Want

Let's begin the process by simply answering this question: "What do I want in a relationship?" (Or, if you're already in one: "What do I want in my current relationship?")

If you are in a relationship right now, this is a good question for you and your partner to answer and discuss together. Each of you can list what you want from the relationship to make sure you are on the same page and, quite possibly, to stir up necessary conversation. Often a lot of what we want goes unsaid, which may be problematic in a relationship. For example, if you want to live near your family in Dallas and he wants to live near the beach, it's time for a conversation. Needless to say, ignoring conflicting desires does not increase our odds of getting what we want.

The relationship between twenty-nine-year-old Michaela and her boyfriend started two years ago when they met through mutual friends. They have a lot in common and have a great time together. He is everything that Michaela feels she spent her twenties searching for. He has a good career and a nice family, has always treated her well, is attractive and witty, and has no excessive emotional baggage. Her friends are asking Michaela when he is going to propose, but every time they do, she gets a knot in her stomach. "I know I love Jeff, so I just don't understand why I am not excited about getting engaged or why sometimes I question how deeply I am in love with him. On paper, he really is everything I always wanted. Is he 'the one,' or is there someone else out there? I don't know if I am expecting too much or settling for what just happens to be in front of me right now."

> "As much as we'd love them to, men cannot read our minds, and we should never be afraid to tell them what we want. Communication is the key in maintaining a loving relationship."
>
> — Hannah, fifty

Michaela's questions paint a picture of the two ends of the expectation spectrum. At one end is the belief that our relationships should fulfill everything we have ever wanted or fantasized about. At the other end is the belief that we do not deserve or should not expect too much. Our position on the spectrum is dictated by our experiences, beliefs, and the amount of pressure we feel to be in relationships. As relationships evolve, questions about cohabitation, marriage, and having children arise, which can either clarify things or add more confusion. Can we have lives straight out of a romance novel? Or, if we'd rather live happily ever after on our own, does that mean we are destined to be that old lady down the street with ten cats? The best way to answer these questions is to dissect what we want from relationships and why we want it.

Overcoming Unrealistic Expectations

Remember our discussion in chapter 2 about all the expectations we place on ourselves and others? Well, a lot of what twenty-something women expect from men seems to be based more on romance novels than on reality. We tend to make laundry lists of what we want from romance; in fact, many women in a twenty-something crisis know what they want in only one area: their love lives. We are on the hunt for a soul mate. Our only trouble is finding them.

We begin to create our romantic fantasies before puberty hits, with help from books, movies, and the relationships we observe. (Remember the first movie you saw in which a woman was rescued by her Prince Charming?) Those beliefs and expectations lead many of us into a "wanting it all" mindset in our intimate relationships.

When I asked women to describe their ideal mate, their lists of criteria were long and intricate. However, I noticed that often the women seemed to be describing a character from a romance novel or film. Here is just one example: "I want someone who is self-confident, compassionate, adventurous, attractive and sexy, romantic, inquisitive, intelligent, creative, funny, successful, sweet, good with kids and animals, dependable, willing to be vulnerable, outgoing, supportive, an excellent listener, not too much of a guy's guy (not obsessed with sports or homophobic; groomed yet not too groomed; can hang with the girls), generous sexually, ambitious yet not work-obsessed, has money and a good body, and likes to surprise me." Wow! Does this guy actually exist? If so, how do we bottle him?

We expect a lot from our partners, which puts pressure on both them and us. It is important to maintain our standards and not settle for people who don't make us happy, but if we have an insane checklist of things that constitute the "perfect" man and our guy does not match up completely, should we just kick him to the curb? Furthermore, a lot of us want our boyfriends to be more like our girlfriends. We forget that many men do not verbalize feelings and thoughts the way we do. They will never get us like our girl-friends and sisters do. Most do not talk just to talk; they talk with a solution in mind; they are problem-solvers. They want to fix things and move on, but we might want them to just listen to us. Then we get frustrated and even disappointed. Fortunately, we are blessed with a generation of men who — much more than our fathers — are in touch with their emotions, are good communicators, are willing to do traditionally female tasks, are fairer and more honest in relationships, have a sense of humor, are willing to enter partnerships, and are supportive of women in the working world. Still, our male partners can't be all things to us, and we shouldn't expect them to be.

> "Never wait for a man to fulfill your needs. Learn how to fulfill them yourself and you will be unstoppable, not to mention incredibly alluring."
>
> — Tanya, forty-eight

Of course, we have all encountered losers or jerks along the way, but do we appreciate the opposite sex for what they have to offer? Do we set unrealistic expectations of men? Do we expect them to be both our lovers and our girlfriends? Do we expect our mates to think and operate in the same way that we do? Do we overanalyze and compare a current boyfriend or husband to someone else? When pursuing what we want in relationships, we can't expect to be with Prince Charming, someone else's significant other, our best girlfriend, or someone exactly like ourselves (would you really want to date yourself?).

Another tendency in relationships is the expectation that our mates will embody the characteristics we desire for ourselves. For instance, might we say we want "secure" men because we do not feel confident and hope they will pick up the slack? If we expect our mates to fill our voids, we are abandoning our internal support systems, and we risk being enabled or disappointed by our partners. Of course, some of our differences from our partners can also balance out our relationships. For instance, my boyfriend is a great decision maker. This is great for me, because the planaholic in me loves taking the day off. On the other hand, he is also very focused and driven, and I tend to float a little. I have to watch myself and not expect him to be proactive for the two of us. Balance is integral to a relationship, yet partners still need to flow through life in a similar way — differences should not be too extreme. If you love to socialize, dating a homebody or someone you have to babysit at social functions will eventually become frustrating. Polar opposites might attract, yet they do not necessarily stay together.

Unrealistic expectations regarding time also cause problems when we're living for the future, not the present (see chapter 3's discussion of this mentality). Many of us have a certain timeline in our heads when it comes to our love life. We then expect someone to come along at the right time. If he does not, we grow concerned. This anxiety is heightened if we make frequent trips to comparison land and let our girlfriends' relationship status affect us.

Vanessa, twenty-nine, states, "I have been okay with being single since I have been so content with my career. But last week something awful happened. My last uncommitted girlfriend, who

I always counted on being single for at least as long as I was, told me she is ready to call the guy she is dating her boyfriend. I died inside. If she is now a 'girlfriend,' where does that leave me?" In our twenties, when comparing ourselves with others is a more common habit than biting our nails, we often expect our relationship status to match that of our peers. But, to quote our mothers, if everyone else were jumping off a bridge, would that mean we should, too?

We are in our twenties, not our fifties. There is time to let things evolve in our lives independent of any expectation or comparison.

EXERCISE 49

Fantasy versus Reality

To clarify what we want and need in relationships, we have to check in on our expectations. To find out what they are, list all your expectations of a mate and a relationship, including everything you ever wanted or dreamed of. Be both extreme and realistic. As you make this list, think about what you have learned from past relationships and what each one did or did not have. Also, recall your parents' relationship and what you liked and did not like about it that may have influenced what you expect from a partner.

Next, looking over your expectation/desire list, distinguish those items that are realistic from those that are fantasy. In order to do this, you have to commit to being reasonable rather than romantic. For example, a fantasy expectation is that a man will always know exactly what to say because he is so in tune with your needs. A realistic expectation is that your mate will be open and ask you questions when he does not understand you. Also, anything related to time, such as, "I expect to be married by thirty" belongs in the fantasy list since we have absolutely no control over time. So now make two columns: "Fantasy" and "Reality." Relist each item in the appropriate category.

If it is hard to identify your realistic expectations, talk to a few of your guy friends (choose ones who are fairly self-aware) about whether they think your expectations are realistic. The more firmly we live in reality (leaving fantasyland for occasional visits), the more empowered we will feel, whether we are single or in relationships.

Is What You Want Healthy?

At the other end of the spectrum from waiting until Prince Charming comes along is getting involved with individuals who are not in our best interest. Unfortunately, what we want isn't always good for us. Wouldn't we all rather have chocolate cake than broccoli with dinner? Most of us have met an unattainable yet appealing "bad boy," or a starving artist whose poetry makes our hearts swoon, or a hottie who works out at our gym, or a doctor whom our mother says we should date but who is totally arrogant, or an office flirt who just happens to be married. Deep down, we know our attraction to certain types might be either superficial or unhealthy, but often we are so tempted that we go for it anyway.

Jessica, twenty-three, reports, "I spent a year dating a musician. He was fairly famous in our town, and I loved being his girlfriend. I felt like it gave me status. Forty percent of the time it was great; the other 60 percent I was a basket case. I was always worried he was fooling around or doing some weird kind of drug. Here I was thinking that I had gotten this unattainable catch. Now I realize he was not at all what I wanted. He barely treated me with respect." All of us have a type — the project, the addict, the dreamer, the commitment-phobe, the just-dumped broken-hearted, and so on — that we might need to pursue for a while in order to get it out of our systems, have some fun, or perhaps learn a lesson. If we choose to do this, we need to be conscious that we're doing it and ask ourselves, "Do I really want this?" It could be better to steer clear altogether rather than risk getting caught up with people who definitely are not right for us. Additionally, when we are in love, or when we want to be in love, we sometimes see the world through rose-colored glasses and don't spot the red flags.

EXERCISE 50

Identifying Red-Flag Men

To lighten the hue of those rose-colored glasses, here is a list to help you identify "red-flag men" who are more likely to become learning experiences than lifetime partners:

- Mr. "I'm Not Ready" or the commitment-phobe

- The undercover asshole (really nice on the outside but a snake on the inside)

- The "yes" man (you can walk all over him, and he does whatever you say)

- The palette cleansers, or FIBS ("fill in the blanks"): simply rebound men who we like because they are there

- The "wounded bird" (he just got his heart broken and thinks you will be the one to heal it)

- The really rich guy without a lot of depth
- The guy who will sleep with you but considers *love* a four-letter word
- The older (as in old enough to be your dad) man
- The married or very recently divorced man
- A guy who reminds you too much of your father or the kind of guy you wish were your father
- The project (a guy you are convinced you can improve)
- The mama's boy
- The guy whose baggage shares cargo space with yours (he has all your issues)
- The "you'll never do better than me" guy
- The addict, the heavy drinker, or the party guy
- The text-messaging-emailing-but-never-calling guy
- The friend who wants more but to whom you are not attracted
- The friend you want but who is not attracted to you
- The guy who would rather get you into bed than take you out to dinner
- The guy who *always* says all the right things (that could mean you are not the only one he says them to)
- The "good on paper" guy (the one your parents like more than you do)
- Mr. Chronically Unemployed
- The dreamer (all talk, no action)
- Anyone who carries a man purse
- Grown men who still live at home for no good reason

Now that you have come clean with yourself about the kinds of guys who you are attracted to and/or attract, don't waste much of your energy on those you know deep down are just not worth it. Although these types might be appealing for a variety of reasons, they very rarely, if ever, morph into what we *really* want. Why not invest that energy in your education, health, friendships, or career while making room for the guy who is a healthy match?

> "If you think they are bad for you, they probably are. If you are afraid you are going to get hurt, you probably will."
>
> — Loretta, forty-nine

Do You Want to Say "I Do"?

As we think about what we want, the importance of deciding whether to include marriage on the list can't be overstated.

Avery married her college sweetheart at twenty-one, the summer after college graduation. She knew her parents loved him, and she saw how relieved her dad was that she would be taken care of. Avery loved the idea of being a wife and could not imagine being alone after graduation. She had doubts on her wedding day but attributed them to cold feet — and she feared disappointing her parents if she shared any second thoughts. A year into her marriage, Avery was miserable. She found herself changing and did not look at her husband in the same way. Avery realized that she had been naïve to decide who she would spend the rest of her life with at age twenty-one. She felt completely ashamed and suffered in a miserable marriage for a year. She did not have enough confidence to make it on her own. Eventually she could not take it anymore and left her husband. Divorced one week before her twenty-third birthday, she felt relieved, ashamed, and incredibly regretful. Now twenty-five, she is scared to date again. "I dread having to tell any-one that I am divorced — I feel like it just conveys the message that I am a failure at relationships." Avery thinks she wants to get married again, but she is deeply afraid of making the same mistake.

Finding a husband is no longer number one on the postcollege to-do list, as it was for our mothers; however, some of us (like Avery) feel that it is something we *should* do or want. Although most of us don't end up married at twenty-one, as Avery did, many of us, especially those of us in our late twenties, have felt urgency to find a husband. Some of us do not want to be alone and look at marriage as a logical first step into adulthood. Reports Julia, twenty-two, "I have always known I want to get married, so I'd like to do it soon so I can start building a foundation with someone." Wait a second, what about building your own foundation first?

We often have very romantic notions about marriage. Yes, we are smart and don't have to be dependent on a man . . . but it sure would be nice to have one around the house. After all, the "real world" is a lot less daunting with someone by our side. Marriage can become yet another expectation we place on ourselves in our twenties, and longing for it creates restlessness as we wait impatiently for "the one" to arrive. Twenty-nine-year-old Janet says, "I guess I am relatively happy, but I still feel like something is missing. I just know that once I find my soul mate and get married, then I will be truly happy."

Some of us also might feel urgency about marriage because of our age and desire to have families. Says Anna, twenty-nine: "I don't feel pressure to marry from anyone but me! I want a life partner, and I also want a family, and I'd like to start by the time I'm thirty-three. I don't want to be an older mom." If we hear the tick of our biological clock, our desire to get married might be less about romance and more about timing. We feel that we must complete so many tasks in our twenties that many of us think that the sooner we can check off marriage, the better. Mary, twenty-six, reports, "I am really getting concerned that I am not in a serious relationship right now. I feel like I need at least one year to date, one year of engagement, and one year of marriage before I start having children, which puts me at thirty. Time is running out, and I can't afford to date men who aren't serious candidates for marriage."

Yet not all quarter-lifers feel this urgency. In fact, many don't even place much importance on the concept of marriage. Gone are the days when walking down the aisle was a given. With the divorce rate as high as it is, we are hesitant to rush off to the chapel. Living with someone first is often a lot less complicated and entails less finality. Joan, twenty-nine, told me, "Marriage doesn't really mean much to me one way or the other. What matters is how committed you act toward each other. . . . Legal promises and expensive ceremonies don't really make a person act committed, so who cares about that superfluous stuff?" We often look at friends and parents in miserable or broken marriages and think, "No thanks!" Sure, getting married once and having it last forever sounds great, but how do we know that *our* marriages will last?

Claire, twenty-eight, admits, "I don't know if I want to get married. I'd love to be in love, but I have so many doubts about marriage, and so far I have not met anyone I can imagine feeling that sure about. Plus, my parents said they were so in love when they got married, but twenty years later they hated each other."

Marriage and even dating can simply seem to get in the way of many twenty-something women's ambitions, too. We have a lot of things on our minds, and a ring might not be one of them. If we place most of our emphasis on career and self-development, we might not have the time or desire to date.

We might also fear that a husband would be jealous of or competitive toward our success, or even want us to make our careers less of a priority. Melissa, twenty-seven, is a chef. "I feel like saying to guys I date: 'Get between me and my career, and you are toast!' My career is a priority right now; plus, I never want to be dependent on a man. I just feel like marriage is not a necessity for me." Melissa is similar to many women who don't think marriage fits into their current plans. Many of us observed our mothers disappearing into the shadows of our career-driven fathers and don't want the same thing for ourselves. But despite these empowering feelings, underneath we might still fear that not getting married will sentence us to becoming old ladies who play bridge and knit sweaters for our poodles.

All the above stories affirm that the question "Do I want to get married?" can be paramount in our twenties. So, what now? Those of us who know for sure that we want marriage just have to find the guy (we'll delve into this topic a bit later). Those of us who are ambivalent about marriage might feel pressured to come to a decision. Natalie, twenty-eight, says, "I really do not know if I want to get married, but it seems to be such a topic of conversation among women my age. Biologically and by society's standards, I feel the pressure to start a family, but if that pressure weren't there, I think I would be content just being single." Haddie, twenty-six, says, "I am not sure about marriage because I like my space and I haven't found someone who I would even consider marrying. I like my alone time. Marriage is just not on the top of the list of things I want to do in my life."

We do not all have to desire marriage, despite pressure from our friends, parents, biological clocks, or society. Taking the spiritual and legal vows of marriage is appropriate only when it is an intrinsic decision. Furthermore, walking down the aisle while unsure about the person at the other end can be a mistake that is painful to undo. For me, trying on wedding dresses for the first time was my initial glimpse of the fact that my decision to marry had been somewhat reactionary. I loved him, we were best friends, and we were at the right age. However, when I walked out of the dressing room to show my friend that big white gown without an ounce of enthusiasm on my face, I wondered, "Why am I not more excited about this? I have been dreaming about my wedding since I was three." Fortunately for me, my fiancé had the guts to call off the marriage because he knew deep down it was not what either of us intrinsically wanted. However, the idea of the wedding, the party, and calling someone a "husband" can so consume many twenty-something women that we ignore gut uncertainties about whether marriage is what we want.

> "Marriage is supposed to last a lifetime, which is hard to comprehend in your twenties. Give some serious thought to who you are going to be waking up next to when you are eighty before you get caught up in rings, dresses, and floral arrangements."
>
> — Fran, forty-six

EXERCISE 51

Do You or Don't You?

Whether you are considering marriage as an option or feeling unsure about it, the following questions will help you decide. Even if you're about to walk or have walked down the proverbial aisle, read through these questions to see how many you have asked of yourself.

1. Do you feel that marriage will provide you a sense of security and stability that you do not feel you could achieve on your own?

2. Do you think marriage will diminish your identity?

3. Do you fear that if you get married, you will have to sacrifice something very important to you, such as your career or time with your friends?

4. Do you feel that marriage will finally make you feel happy and complete?

5. Are you in a hurry to get married? Do you feel that you are racing against the biological clock?

6. Do you think you can change someone after you get married?

7. Do you think you have to change in some way before someone will want to marry you?

8. How was your parents' marriage or relationship? Might anything from your past cause a reactionary view of marriage? For instance, if your parents' marriage was full of anger, do you fear having the same experience?

9. Do you feel that you should get hitched because all your friends are doing it or because you are approaching a certain age?

10. Do you think after you are married, something that is bothering you about your relationship will change for the better?

I now pronounce you ready to answer the questions "Do I want to get married?" and "What do/did I want from my marriage?" As you answer these questions, also write down any thoughts, fears, dreams, and expectations about marriage. Putting them on paper will remind you of who you are and what you want when you're making a decision that is intended to last forever.

"I got married too soon and was not clear about whether it was what I wanted — I just thought it was the right thing to do. After my divorce at age twenty-seven, I was able to learn and know what my needs and desires truly are. I just wish I would have done it before I walked down the aisle."

— Ellen, forty-five

Looking at our goals in relationships from a rational rather than a fantastical viewpoint is not very romantic, but it can save us a lot of heartache. We need to be aware of unrealistic expectations while listening to our inner voice that tells us what we really want and need. Trust me, our inner wisdom is there, and learning to acknowledge it is part of building a secure foundation on which a healthy relationship can thrive.

After my breakup with my fiancé, I did an extremely powerful thing: I wrote out a list of everything I wanted from a relationship and all the characteristics I wanted in a partner. I was emotionally raw and willing to look at both my unrealistic expectations and the ways in which I had sacrificed or suffocated parts of who I was. The list I made was long and specific. I included everything from "good oral hygiene" to "accepts my quirks and does not try to change me" to "calls me out when I am being a brat" and "always communicates when something is bothering him." When I finished, I tucked the list under my mattress and mostly forgot about it. Two months into dating my current boyfriend, I pulled out the list just for kicks. I was amazed. He is the list. All the things that I intrinsically wanted and knew I valued actually exist in human form. I joke now that I "manifested" him, as he does indeed embody what I intrinsically want.

EXERCISE 52

Making Your Wish List

Now it is your turn to do a little manifesting. List all the characteristics you want in a partner — no matter how much of a long shot some of the items might seem. Do not write about what you do *not* want; keep everything positive. Once you finish it, fold it up, put it in an envelope, and tuck it away somewhere (under your mattress is a good place). Resist the urge to add to it — be satisfied with the list as it is.

This exercise is a great way to really focus on what we want in a mate. However, just listing what we want is no guarantee that Prince Charming will knock on our front door. Bottom line: No one will ride in on a white horse and give us everything we want — except the women we see in our mirrors every morning. *No one* is perfect, and there is no such thing as one predestined soul mate for everyone. However, if we have a healthy and balanced sense of self and a vision of our desires in a relationship, we are more likely to attract a person who is our match.

HOW DO I GET THE RELATIONSHIP I WANT?

Now that we have thought about what we want in a relationship, how do we get it? First, we have to find the person we want to be in the relationship with, which to some of us might feel about as easy as finding a comfortable pair of heels. We might have to try on many pairs and endure a lot of blisters along the way.

Just as with other topics addressed in this book, a whole book could be dedicated to how to get what we want in relationships. But for our purposes, let's divide a relationship into three stages — pursuing a relationship, being in a relationship, and ending and moving on from a relationship — and then explore how we can get what we want in each stage.

Most quarter-lifers have been through at least one (if not all) of these stages. If we are consistently unhappy or unsatisfied at any stage, the feelings generated by a twenty-something crisis will be magnified. Before reading on, first ask yourself the question "How have I gone about getting what I want in a relationship?"

Pursuing a Relationship

Devin is an attractive twenty-six-year-old receptionist at a large telecommunications company. An extrovert, she has never had problems making friends. In fact, just three years after moving to a big city, she has a large group of close friends. But Devin has always been single. She's been on dates, but no one has earned the title of "boyfriend." Someone is always trying to set her up, but Devin is finished with blind dates. "So much buildup comes with a blind date, and on most occasions I am pretty disappointed. Where are all the good guys? The men I find myself sitting across from are egomaniacs, ambitionless, mama's boys, unattractive, possessive, unintelligent, drink too much, lack values, or are just downright boring!" Because she has never had a serious relationship, Devin is starting to think that maybe she is too picky or that there is something wrong with her.

Since most of us do not live in cultures where marriages are arranged, dating is a necessary step toward getting what we want in relationships. By the time we reach our mid- to late twenties, the novelty of dating is wearing off, and we are more selective. After all, in high school, we might have considered wine coolers sophisticated, but our palates changed with age and we now crave the 1978 French Bordeaux. Many of us find the process of dating extremely frustrating. Either we are not asked out on dates or we don't like those who ask.

The process of getting what we want in relationships is further complicated by the fact that the fine art of dating seems to be disappearing. Holly, twenty-seven, explains: "It seems like no one courts or asks you out properly anymore. People just tend to hook up at parties or bars or through friends." Just as women's roles have become less clear, the rules of dating have also blurred. Do men still pay? Who calls whom? Is it okay if he doesn't open our door, and do we even want him to? Where do we draw the line between being "slutty" and "hard to get" when it comes to sex? The questions we ask about dating are endless and often go unanswered. We practically need a dating manual to understand all the game playing that goes on.

EXERCISE 53

Making Your Own Dating Rulebook

Having said that, I actually want you to forget any rule-book or dating guide you might have read. It is time to make your own rules. To get what we want in relationships, we should date in a way that is in balance with what we want. Who cares what others do or what they think men expect? If we look at dating like a sport, we can be our own referees.

Come up with at least ten rules, using the following criteria: You should be able to play by them, and they should be in balance with who you are and what you want. Here are a few of mine: "Always meet a guy on a first date, because I don't want him to know where I live. Use a valet whenever possible so there is a sense of urgency at the end of the date to avoid that awkward 'Do we kiss or not?' moment. Never pay on a first date [sorry, I'm old-fashioned that way]. Be open to meeting and going out with anyone at least once, because you never know. Never do anything I am not 100 percent comfortable doing, no matter how persuasive he may be — rejection is easier to get over than regret."

Okay, now it's your turn. Make a list of *your* rules in your notebook or journal.

Coming up with our own dating rules might help us to create a sense of both lightness and empowerment about dating, which many of us desperately need. If we do not date according to our standards and values, we will fall into dating traps and possibly even get hurt. We need to really know how we tick before we venture out there. Attempting to secure a relationship without a secure sense of self can perpetuate the unsettling feelings of a twenty-something crisis.

———— ✑ ————

Missy, twenty-six, feels a tremendous amount of pressure to get married, especially from her mother, to whom she has always been very close. Dating has become Missy's number-one priority, yet she admits that the men she dates rarely have husband potential, which her mother is always on her case about. "My mom has always been really involved in my dating life. I think it's because her marriage was pretty unfulfilling, so she feels the need to make sure I choose correctly. She says I date too many dreamers, but I like them because they are so carefree. She is always encouraging me to do things where I can meet good men — like joining an upscale health club." Is Missy playing by her mother's rules or her own?

Jackie, twenty-eight, refuses to go out socially unless there is an opportunity to meet men. Getting into a serious relationship is a high priority, and dating has become a second job. She is constantly on the hunt. She has done online dating and three-minute dates, has used professional matchmakers, and often just hangs out in places she has been told she might meet someone, such as the grocery store. "I am almost thirty years old, and I am still single. I am not embarrassed to say that I have tried and will try every resource. Online dating is really not that different from meeting someone at a bar — sometimes you stay for the second drink, and other times you excuse yourself to the bathroom as soon as possible. I just want to find someone soon so I don't have to worry about being alone anymore." Does Jackie's dating regime come from a solid sense of self or a fear of being single longer than she'd like to be?

Missy's and Jackie's stories are just two examples of the problems that dating without a secure foundation can manifest in our lives. Others include moving too quickly, allowing dating to totally consume our thoughts, not being honest and up front about who we are and what we want, and dating just because we feel like we should. Like Jackie, many of us have a "doing, doing, doing" approach (discussed in chapter 3) to relationships. We make dating a profession, always searching for Mr. Right rather than getting to know ourselves better. Dating becomes yet another thing we put on our to-do lists and try to control so that one day we'll be able to say we have it all.

Dating distress is also caused by expectations. If we bring all our fantasy expectations of "the one" into the dating world, we'll hunt for him for a long time. And that hunt makes it impossible for us to ease into relationships with people who might appear less than perfect but may just be a match for us. If we approach dating with too much judgment and attitude, we are less likely to stick around for a few dates or relax enough to see the good parts of a person.

A case in point: At the very first moment I met my boyfriend, I did not think I liked him. But he pursued me, and I eventually agreed to have dinner with him on a Monday night (he was not overly thrilled about being Mr. Monday). But about one minute into our date, I was completely enamored. Eventually I realized that I was in a funk on the initial night I met him, which impacted my reaction to him. Thank goodness I had the self-imposed dating rule to be open and give anyone a chance, or I might have missed out on the love of my life.

Another experience common to twenty-something women is the postdate expectation hangover. Briana, twenty-five, explains: "I was psyched about my date with this guy because we really clicked on the phone. I bought a new outfit, wore new perfume, and told all my best stories that made him laugh — we even shared a very innocent good-night kiss. I expected him to call the next day, but he didn't. He never called — I was totally distracted and upset for weeks. I analyzed the date with my girlfriends. Since then, I've felt totally down in the dumps. I was so excited about this guy, and it turned out to be a bust. Dating sucks." Briana probably would have been better off just going out with her girlfriends for margaritas and enduring a tequila hangover rather than the nasty expectation hangover she could not shake.

The more we psych ourselves up and the more we try to control how we get into relationships, the less likely we are to date with ease and the more hangovers we will face. As I've stressed, we need to follow our own dating rules, but our rules cannot be so rigid that we leave no room for fate to intervene. We have all experienced the annoying phenomenon of shopping for something very specific, such as a purple candle, and being unable to find it anywhere. However, when we are just out looking and don't plan to buy anything, there seem to be purple candles everywhere. The same can be true in dating.

The best dating tips I can give you are to have faith and to approach getting what you want in a relationship with a clear sense of your identity and goals. If we believe that guys are jerks, that dating sucks, and that only girls who look like models get the good men, then we will be spending a lot of time with our girlfriends watching *Sex and the City* reruns. Also keep in mind that there are many joys to singlehood. There is no one to answer to, no one to stress out about, no one to analyze with our girlfriends, and there are lots of cute people to flirt with. Being single affords us time to be selfish while developing a solid sense of self. Of course, relationships look fun, and we long for a companion when we see a cute couple nuzzling over a shared dessert, but being single is also fun (and very valuable). When we are older and married, we might look back on our time as single people and remember it fondly.

> "Although it was rather 'taboo' for my time, I feel so blessed that I was single for my entire twenties, because I wouldn't be the person I am or have had the experiences I had without the freedom to choose, explore, dream, and make mistakes on my own."
>
> — Fawn, sixty

EXERCISE 54

The Relationship Affirmation

Our approach to pursuing a relationship is very important. Writing an affirmation can be very powerful: it communicates your hopes and faith to the universe, to the powers that be, to God, or to whoever/whatever else is appropriate for you. In your journal, write your affirmation for dating. Keep it simple and realistic (no names of celebrities, please). For instance, mine was "I believe that there are great men in Los Angeles and that I will find a sweet one who is a great fit for me and accepts who I am." Sure, it might sound cheesy, but I am sure that you have endured much cheesier pickup lines at bars! Recite your affirmation to yourself, either aloud or in your head, at least twice a day.

If and when we do find someone to date, a different kind of anxiety can emerge. First there is the phase of wondering, "How does he really feel about me?" Then comes another question: "Where is this headed?" Dating is the warm-up to one of the biggest decisions a woman in her twenties can make (marriage), so it can be stressful. The more we stay in the present, remove expectations, play by our own rules, and do our best to avoid getting sucked into timelines and comparisons, the more we will enjoy the hunt and ease into being in a relationship.

Being in a Relationship

As if dating were not hard enough, once we're with someone, we have to deal with all those anxieties, issues, and awkward "getting to know each other" moments. The "honeymoon" period fades, and the real person starts to emerge. Things such as differing religions, old baggage, unlikable behaviors, family issues, morals and values, and hygienic habits begin to rear their heads. Finally comes the ultimate question: "Is this the person I want to spend my life with?" Falling in love and becoming romantically intertwined with a person make thinking rationally difficult — our hormones often take over. Twenty-something women spend so much time thinking about and discussing their relationships that I was tempted to call this section "Analyzing Our Relationships" rather than "Being in a Relationship." So how do we reach the point in our relationships where we feel secure enough to just "be"? The first step is to look at how we are, or have been, in relationships.

Nedra, twenty-eight, describes herself as a "serial monogamist." When she met her most recent boyfriend, Sam, she had been out of her last relationship for only about two months and was not really looking for another one, but he came into her life and they fell in love. "At first our relationship was long distance, which was great because I was able to do my own thing (that's code for me not feeling guilty about getting into another relationship without giving myself time to be alone)." Now that Nedra and Sam live in the same city, she noticed that she has become anxious and annoyed with him a lot. She is starting to have doubts. She thinks she should know if he is "the one." "There is nothing wrong with the relationship, but I am restless. I think I may be ignoring the funkier, experimental part of me, and I want to be with someone who can at least relate to it. I don't know why I am staying with someone when I know I want something different eventually... but it's a very caring, comfortable relationship. He is my best friend. I guess I am not ready to give that up to go in search of myself and whatever else my life could bring." Nedra also admits that her fear of not finding anyone else keeps her in the relationship.

Randi, twenty-nine, has been on and off with her boyfriend, Justin, for four years. They fight passionately but make up with even more heat. They share a deep love, but Randi feels as though he is distant from her. She often wishes her relationship were more like those of her girlfriends, who spend a lot more time with their significant others. "I know he has issues from his past that make it challenging for him to open up to me... but I feel in my heart that he will change, especially after he knows I am not going anywhere." Justin never discusses marriage with Randi, which hurts, but she never articulates that to him. "I know he just needs to feel more stable in his career before he can think about marriage, so I am giving him time." Randi also hates the fact that Justin works most nights and she rarely sees him. Despite her doubts and anxiety, she sticks it out because she feels so much passion toward him and believes he will change.

The issues that perpetuate our twenty-something crisis and cloud the answers to the questions of the twenties triangle (discussed in previous chapters) can show up in our relationships. For instance, the general doubts and shoulds we feel in our twenties can emerge in relationships, as they have in Nedra's case. Or our insecurities, anxieties, and comparisons can trickle in and out of our relationships, as in Randi's case. Many of us repeatedly do things in relationships that don't match our vision of the relationships we want. Or we do things that aren't in our best interest, and then wonder why we feel so unsettled. Maybe a question many of us need to ask first is "Am I settling?"

The Pitfalls of Settling

Some quarter-lifers find themselves several years into relationships and still unhappy — or they keep getting involved with the same type of people, who are not truly what they want. We might be treated poorly but are scared to leave because we are paralyzed by the thought of being alone and back out in the dating world. We might be girlfriends, fiancées, or wives on the outside, but on the inside we might feel sad, lonely, and even a little bitter. Yet we hang in there, hoping the situation will change. Says Diana, twenty-four, "If my current relationship continues to drive me crazy and my boyfriend continues to be insensitive and self-absorbed, I'll think about moving to Texas and starting a business with my sister. There I could do something that would let me earn money doing something I love. I just am not ready to throw in the towel." My question to Diana was "Why the heck are you not ending it right now? Why settle for insensitive and self-absorbed?"

Alyssa, twenty-eight, is concerned that her boyfriend has a drinking problem. "He always seems to find a reason to drink and always wants me to join him. Lately, I have just gotten sick of it and have cut back, but he hasn't. He drinks more days than he doesn't, and when he gets drunk, his behavior is often unpredictable — and kind of mean." Alyssa wants to stay with her boyfriend despite her concerns because she says he's smart, makes her laugh, and is really sweet to her. She is afraid he will fall apart if she leaves — he needs her. Alyssa feels that she can help him and eventually get him to drink less. She has invested two years in her relationship, and the thought of walking away is "nauseating." But still more nauseating is staying with someone who has a major flaw that we choose to ignore, think we can change, or tolerate to avoid being alone or having to say goodbye to someone we love but who keeps us from fully loving ourselves.

Settling does not have to be so extreme. Take Catie, twenty-seven, for instance. She has been with her boyfriend for about two years and reports they are very happy and in love. "He's ambitious, but often he gets overwhelmed and then lazy. This is frustrating to me because I want to feel that he will be able to provide and that we will be financially stable. I will not always be able to contribute once we start a family. I want him to feel serious about building a life together, just as I do." If a family and a husband with drive and financial security are of high value to Catie, why is she with him? We need to be clear about whether our partners can walk beside us on the path toward what we want, and we should know that they will not hold us back from getting it.

Brooke, twenty-nine, has felt rather "blah" about her relationship but cannot decide if she should end it. "We are always fighting and trying to one-up each other. He says I am too controlling, but I am not comfortable with certain things he does. I don't know if it is just not working or something is wrong with me. To be honest, I do not really love being in a relationship, because I have to give up too much control."

Like Catie and Brooke, many of us stay in relationships with people who do not embody what we want. If we knew a car was broken beyond repair, would we still try to drive it? Or if we really wanted a car, would we settle for a scooter? If a relationship is not working and has not worked for a long time, we need to move on.

The twenty-something crisis is hard enough without the

added anxiety of settling in a relationship. The saying "Love is blind" is popular for good reason. Loving someone does not ensure that we will get what we want out of relationships. Of the women I interviewed, at least 75 percent of those in romantic relationships with men they love mentioned feeling unhappy about how much time their mates spend without them, bemoaned their partners' lack of ambition and drive, talked about problems with their partners' families, reported feeling jealous, or said that money and/or sex had become issues. Of course, no relationship is a bowlful of cherries, and conflicts will arise; but distinguishing between healthy compromises and settling is essential to getting what we want in relationships.

EXERCISE 55

Are You Settling?

Sometimes we're not even aware of when we settle. If you are unsure whether you are (or have been) settling or whether you're in a relationship in which both individuals make healthy compromises, this exercise will bring you some clarity. A good way to tell if we're getting what we want in relationships is to look at issues that stress us out or consume us. If you are now in an exclusive relationship, focus on it as you answer these questions, but reflect on any previous relationships as well. If you are single, just think back to former relationships. The past always gives us insight into our present choices and patterns.

1. Identify and write down any sources of angst in your relationship. For instance: "I hate the way he

looks at other women whenever we go out." When you look at what you wrote, do you think you are settling in any way? If you are unsure of your answer, refer back to exercise 47 and your list of things you're not willing to sacrifice in a relationship. If you are sacrificing a lot, rather than making fair adjustments and compromises, then you might indeed be settling.

2. Are you afraid to bring up certain topics with your mate because it might start a fight or make you uncomfortable?

3. If you are not getting what you want in your relationship, why are you still in it?

4. Look at your answer to question 3. Is this reason compelling enough to give up pursuing things you want?

5. Do you believe that you can have and actually deserve what you want in a relationship?

> "Don't stay in a situation if you are not happy, thinking it's all right for now or that it will get better. You never know what's around the corner, or what you could have had if you had just opened yourself up to it sooner."
>
> — Pauline, fifty-eight

If we do not believe that what we want (our realistic, not our fantasy, desires) does exist and that we deserve it, we will never find it. Our beliefs play a large role in shaping our lives, as discussed in chapter 2. If you feel that you might be settling, your first tasks are to believe that you do not have to settle and to refuse to do so. Hey, leave the settling up to the Pilgrims. Let's go after what we want.

⸺∞⸺

Relating in Our Relationships

The intensity of a romantic relationship can be so consuming that it affects other areas of our lives. This is often a positive thing. When we are in love, we feel confident, giddy, and possibly even more productive. On the other hand, being obsessively consumed with a relationship can be dangerous. Take Tara, for instance. She is twenty-six and has made worrying about her relationship a full-time job. After dating her guy for a year, she is still unsure of where she stands, and she is frustrated with his laissez-faire attitude about the future. "I know the amount of time and energy I invest in analyzing my relationship is probably not good — I think about it incessantly. I waste time at work instant-messaging my girlfriends, trying to figure out what his most recent comment or behavior really meant. Pathetically, I don't make plans for the weekend, hoping he'll ask me out.... I just wish I knew what he was thinking and that I could talk to him without getting emotional."

Matters of the heart involve a great deal of time and thought, but where is the line between caring and obsessing? Once we give up too much or let the relationship dictate our mood, schedule, and decisions, as it has for Tara, we cross the line into unhealthy obsession. Yet even if we lose ourselves, we can reempower ourselves by shifting our focus back to our own lives — even if doing that requires leaving the relationship. Although we might love someone, if the relationship requires us to be constantly anxious and/or selfless, it is time to get out.

One way to stop obsessing and to alleviate some anxiety is to talk to others and express our feelings about what's happening in our relationships. Not doing so can affect our well-being. Take Arie, twenty-seven, for example. "I used to be more open with friends about problems in my relationships. Due to my current boyfriend's wishes that I keep our issues private, I hold things inside more. It is tough, and sometimes I feel it affecting my health

— I have headaches, I can't sleep, and my stomach is a mess." Keeping things inside and turning away from our external support systems place too much strain on our foundation, and that can have long-term effects. If we do not articulate our feelings, they lurk around in other areas of our lives, such as our health. Like Arie, we might think we can handle things on our own, but we forget the importance of interdependence. "I don't like to talk about relationship issues because I don't want my friends to dislike my boyfriend," Arie says. Yet withdrawing from our support systems out of concern about what others will think is isolating, and we miss out on the wisdom and understanding others have to offer. Furthermore, feeling afraid to discuss parts of our lives with people who love us is a big red flag indicating that something is wrong with either the issue we are hiding or the support system we have chosen (or both).

If our relationships become the cement in our foundation, we risk becoming overly dependent on them. Remember the distinction made in chapter 4 between enabling and supporting? Relationships can be great sources of support; however, they become enabling if we are overly reliant on our significant others. Cheryl, twenty-five, says, "I moved out to Los Angeles with my boyfriend so he could pursue his dream of writing. He is the only person I know here, and my world kind of revolves around him. I feel uncomfortable going out and doing things without him. Plus, since he is the one with a job, I feel like I shouldn't be doing things for me." Cheryl's dependence on her boyfriend enables her to not go out and create her own life. And her desire to appease him might keep her from discovering what brings her joy. If we constantly put the other person before ourselves, we will be unable to know if we're truly getting what we want. We'll be too busy worrying about our partners.

> "You can be in love without having a stomach-ache all the time."
>
> — Claudine, fifty-four

On the other hand, we can also be too self-centered or needy in our relationships. Selfishness in an intimate partnership usually derives from a set of expectations. What we expect from people we date often pales in comparison to the expectations we have in serious relationships. Many of us believe we should find our soul mates and that if we do, they must love us unconditionally and understand us completely and that there will always be passion. Explains Amber, twenty-six: "I wish my fiancé was more romantic. He never plans any surprises or does anything really creative. Sometimes he brings me flowers, but how original is that? I mean, he knows me well enough by now to know that I need to be romanced." Maybe Amber should marry Fabio instead. Her expectations of her fiancé blind her from seeing his great qualities.

Additionally, it is unfair to expect our mates to always know what we want and feel. It is our responsibility to communicate those things. Feelings in relationships are more complex than a parent's unconditional love for a child. No one, even those we think are soul mates, is perfect. As independent women in relationships, we can create what we want if we are realistic and articulate. For example, if we want more romance in our relationships, what stops us from lighting a few candles and throwing Barry White in the CD player?

Negative expectations and beliefs also affect how we approach our relationships. Kathy, twenty-six, is currently questioning her relationship. "I've been with a guy for six months now, and it's going okay. I am trying not to be vulnerable or too attached because I don't want to get hurt. I keep getting into relationships that don't work out, and I just keep thinking, 'Maybe the next one will be the right one.' If I am prepared to get hurt, then it won't be such a blow when it happens." Negative expectations disguised as self-protection are lethal. They set up little hurts along the way to avoid a big one down the line and keep us from really connecting to anyone. If we believe we will be rejected, we create a self-fulfilling prophecy: its probability increases dramatically.

When I asked women the question "Which of the following issue(s) stresses you out or consumes you during romantic relationships?" the number-one answer was the inevitable conversation about where the relationship was headed. We have an idea of when we want to hear things such as "I love you. Do you want to meet my parents? Do you want a drawer at my place? Will you move in with me, and will you marry me?" If we relate our relationships to time, rather than focus on their quality in the present, we will consistently find ourselves unsettled and racing against some imaginary clock. Liza, twenty-eight, says: "I've been with my boyfriend over two years, and it's time to get engaged. I don't know what he is waiting for and if it doesn't happen in the next year or so, I'll probably start getting worried. Actually, I am already worried that he does not even hint at it. It is really frustrating." When our romantic partners are not adhering to our timeline, we fear that something could be wrong with either ourselves or with the relationship. This pattern is consistent with our feelings of pressure and our urgency to complete our quarter-life checklists. If our priority is to check off items on our lists, we might end up micromanaging our lives and thus miss enjoying the unique evolution of our relationships. Timelines might also tempt us to make choices before we have given ourselves enough time to mull them over. Over 50 percent of the women I interviewed said they slept with men after four or five dates, even if they were not really ready, because they wanted to move the relationship along. Expectation timelines can cause us to try to control relationships, feel insecure, or rush into things too soon. All that being said, if taking your relationship to the next level of commitment is something you really want because you are truly ready and your man *still* is not stepping up to the plate, it may be time to call in another batter.

As we discussed in chapter 5, too many trips to comparison land can be fatal to our happiness, including happiness in our relationships. Holly, twenty-three, says, "My roommate and her boyfriend are always doing stuff together; they share lots of hobbies and seem so happy. I love my boyfriend, but I wish he would share some of my hobbies with me. I worry that my relationship isn't as solid as hers because we don't spend as much time together." Every relationship is different, and we will be much more content in our own if we investigate our relationships rather than comparing them to others. We investigate by asking ourselves questions such as "Is this working for me? Do I communicate my needs? Am I being realistic? Might I be ignoring any red flags or gut feelings?" and so on. Asking ourselves questions is a much better way to measure a relationship's health than playing the comparison game.

Another way that our perspectives can become skewed is by the very popular belief that we can change our partners. Lori, twenty-six, says, "I really wish my boyfriend was more sensitive, but he has been hurt a lot in the past, so he has been hardened. After he has been with me for a while, I know he will soften up. I have even gotten him some books to read. In the meantime, I just drop a lot of subtle hints about how I'd like him to be." Like Lori, many of us are under the misconception that we have magical tools in our toolboxes that can change guys into what we want them to be, or that they'll change once they see how much we love them. It is no wonder we get frustrated — we're trying to build a foundation for a relationship when the necessary tool does not exist! Let's face it: people do not change just because we want them to. Of course, a little "man-scaping" is always possible, such as getting rid of those dreadful pleated khakis and the TV trays he calls a dining room table. But if our mates have a lot of inherent traits that we cannot stand but think we will be able to change, we might as well put curing cancer on our to-do list alongside changing our partners.

A tool that we *do* possess and that we must employ in relationships is our ability to make intrinsic decisions. The decision to live together provides a good example. Whether to sign a lease with our significant other before we sign a marriage contract is a decision many quarter-lifers face. Despite our mothers' warnings that "he will never buy the cow if he can get the milk for free," many of us feel that living together is a logical step between dating and marriage. Although it is no longer widely viewed as "living in sin," cohabitation is still a serious choice. Anne, twenty-eight, says, "It was a huge adjustment when I moved in with my boyfriend after two years of dating. I really wanted to get engaged first, but he was not on the same page. A lot of my friends were moving in with their guys, and most of them got married, so I figured it was just the logical next step. It's been over a year now, and we started to feel like we were on some kind of timeline — he felt pressure; I felt expectation. Neither of us was happy. I recently decided I am going to move out." Anne's story is an example of a reactionary decision that was made in order to secure a relationship but actually ended up jeopardizing it. Once Anne realized she could not get the level of commitment she wanted, she made the intrinsic decision to move out. As a result, she now feels a lot less "stuck."

> "People really don't change that much, so you have to be very open to seeing who it is you are dating. And if you don't like what you see pretty much right away, then get out. You can chew up a lot of years trying to fix someone and getting them to fit you."
>
> — Judy, fifty-nine

Jennifer, twenty-six, once said she wouldn't live with anyone until she was married. "But when I realized that that was really my parents talking and not me, I moved in with my boyfriend. It was what I really wanted, and it just makes sense economically and geographically. Plus, I do not even know if I want to get married. It's the path my mom took, but marriage does not necessarily guarantee a relationship's longevity." Jennifer initially made a decision that was right for her; she did not simply react to her mother's values and beliefs. She loves living with her boyfriend and hopes her parents eventually come to accept it.

Cohabitation is just one example of the many decisions that we make in relationships. Checking in with ourselves to ensure we're making decisions that are in line with what we want is a great habit to implement. It allows us to avoid a lot of the drama and regret that can result from reactionary decisions, as well as the angst or apathy caused by making decisions about our relationships that contradict what we want in the long run. Relationships should not be so hard — good ones have an ease and flow to them. Similarly, if we have a relationship goal that our partner doesn't share (such as marriage or children), we need to really look at why we choose to stay. Breaking away from relationships that don't align with what we want is empowering and opens us up to find the things we do want in life.

> "If there is so much to work on in the relationship that you'd have to change into different people to get what you want out of each other, then go be with different people."
>
> — Dorothy, fifty

EXERCISE 56

Checking in with Yourself

To truly have the relationship we want, we need to frequently ask ourselves about our behavior and decisions in our relationships. The following exercise pinpoints several check-in questions drawn from the stories you just read. Answer each question and for each question you answer "yes" to, consider what that behavior costs you and write it down. For example, if you are overly dependent on your mate for a social life, that costs you a strong external support system of your own. In your journal, record these costs next to your answers.

1. Do you obsess about your relationship? Cost:

2. Are you afraid to bring up certain topics in your relationship? Cost:

3. Have you sacrificed in your relationship (remember that sacrifices are different from adjustments and compromises)? Cost:

4. Do you keep things that trouble you about your relationship to yourself? Cost:

5. Are you extremely concerned about what other people think of your relationship? Cost:

6. Are you overly reliant on your mate? Cost:

7. Do you consistently put pleasing your mate before taking care of yourself? Cost:

8. Are you selfish in your relationship? Do you have unrealistic expectations? Cost:

9. Do you put your relationship on a timeline? Cost:

10. Do you compare your relationship to those of others? Cost:

11. Do you think you can change the person you are with? Cost:

12. Are your decisions about your relationship more reactionary than intrinsic? Cost:

The fact is that being in a relationship, even a great one, can be harder than we expect. Relationships involve putting our hearts on the line, and sometimes we get hurt. But when we enter relationships that reflect who we are and what we want, they're more than worth it. If we are willing to grow, learn, and be present in relationships while keeping ourselves our number-one priority, we will be in good shape. Women today are much more in touch with their needs and much less willing to compromise them than women were in our moms' and grandmothers' generations. And that's a good thing. Remember, loving who we are is the best aphrodisiac on the market.

Ending and Moving on from a Relationship

As many twenty-something women know all too well, not every relationship ends happily ever after. If you have never had your heart broken or suffered through a difficult, emotional breakup, I encourage you to buy lottery tickets, because you are one of the lucky ones.

Wendy, twenty-seven, went through a fairly traumatic breakup about a year ago. She and her boyfriend had been together almost two years, and while at a wedding they had a big fight about where the relationship was going. "He dropped the bomb that he had just been stringing me along until he found the right time to tell me that he was no longer in love with me and didn't see himself spending his life with me." Wendy was, of course, crushed, and she did not date for a while. Now she is finally out there again, but she never ventures beyond very superficial dating since she is still too scared of getting hurt again.

Breakups are never enjoyable. There is no easy cure, quick fix, or pill you can take to heal faster; we all just have to go through the pain. No matter who initiates the breakup or what the reasons for it might be, it is followed by a mourning and transition process.

It can be just as hard to break up with someone as it is to be dumped. Heather, twenty-five, would concur. "Breaking up with Brad was something that I'd been turning over in my head for a while. He was still the same wonderful person he had been before, but I'd changed, and what I wanted had changed, and I had to acknowledge that to myself. I knew it would hurt him, and that killed me because I loved him so much. When we broke up, I still wanted to call him every day to see how he was doing or share something with him. I felt really alone and scared — I think I cried more than he did."

Breakups present an opportunity to learn and heal. In our twenties, the peak of the dating years for most of us, we might go through several relationships (and perhaps revisit the same relationship over and over again). We might find ourselves in the breakup or transition phase more often than we would like or expect. Who we are, what we do, and how we behave in this phase can dramatically influence our next relationship, and whether we're even willing to have one. For some, the period after a breakup is pretty dark and might involve shock, disappointment, extreme hurt, betrayal, anger, and lots of ice cream. On the other hand, sometimes a breakup can be a relief, freeing, or more painful for the other person than it is for us. Keep in mind, though, that any type of breakup is a change and that any change is stressful, even if we view it as positive. Our behavior and the decisions we make during this change offer additional insight into how we can find the relationships we want.

In chapter 4, we discussed the ABCs of securing our independence and talked about the necessary adjustment period. To secure our emotional sanity, we also need to give ourselves time to adjust after breakups. When my fiancé and I separated, the breakup was an incredible change in my life — it was like someone had died. Because I had shared my home, bed, thoughts, dreams, and family with him for years, his absence made me extremely aware of being alone. Not only being lonely, but literally being alone. I had trouble sleeping, I kept Kleenex in business, I lost weight, and I was scared by the abrupt change in my life's direction. I had gone from knowing who I would spend the rest of my life with to not knowing where I would live next month. Yet I did know that my feelings were completely natural and that I had no choice but to feel them.

Feeling terrible is just plain terrible, and quick fixes that promise to numb the pain and make us feel better can be tempting. We might want to go out, overeat, drink, find another person to date, have a random hookup, or perhaps even seek revenge on an ex. If we are not overly excited about being single, we might jump into something rather than enjoy our freedom. But, as discussed earlier, all quick fixes are Band-Aids rather than cures and in the long run may do us more harm than good.

> "I have had a lot of experience of living, and I know for sure that losses will fade away, new good things will come, and you can love someone more than you do right now."
>
> — Gloria, sixty-two

For example, after breaking up with her boyfriend of a year, Beth, twenty-eight, immediately started to date. "Even though I was the one who ended the relationship because I felt like it was going nowhere, I hated being alone. So I started going out with a couple of guys. Yet after each date, I would feel even lonelier. It eventually made me more depressed, miss my boyfriend more, and doubt my decision. Dating just made everything more confusing." Although Beth might not have been heartbroken by her breakup, she still did not allow herself the necessary time to adjust and to take stock of the relationship she had just ended. If you broke your leg, would you expect to walk on it the next day? Of course not. You cannot expect to heal from a breakup without going through all the feelings that come with it. If we mask, medicate, or deny them, we are likely to get into another relationship that will probably result in another breakup.

EXERCISE 57

Taking a Breakup Inventory

The adjustment phase after a breakup is a great time to take stock of the relationship. Think back to all your breakups, focusing on the most recent, and answer the questions below. (This is important even if you're already in a new relationship.)

1. Why did the relationship end?
2. What would or did your ex say was the reason for the breakup?
3. If a totally objective person knew everything about your relationship, what would he or she say was the reason it ended?

Are the answers to questions 1 to 3 different? If no, at least you are clear about why it ended. If yes, you might still be confused or in denial about why the relationship ended. Coming to peace with the reasons it ended (which often can be as simple as "We just were not right for each other") will alleviate some of the adjustment phase's turmoil. Working to deepen our understanding of what happened is more useful than pushing away feelings or pining over someone.

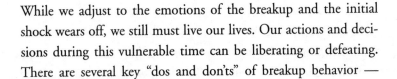

While we adjust to the emotions of the breakup and the initial shock wears off, we still must live our lives. Our actions and decisions during this vulnerable time can be liberating or defeating. There are several key "dos and don'ts" of breakup behavior —

things we should do or should avoid — and they will influence how we secure the next relationship. The most common "don't" of breakups: not truly separating from an ex. It is difficult to let go of relationships, and we seem to find excuses to talk to or see our exes. However, the harder we try to hang on to something that is over, the harder we make things for ourselves. Why fight for someone who does not want us? Why interact with a person we chose to leave? The up-and-down feelings that emerge after a breakup are unavoidable; however, communicating with an ex too soon can interfere with the recovery process, pulling both people backward.

Patricia, twenty-seven, says, "My ex called me two months after he broke up with me without giving me a reason, and he wanted to meet. I was skeptical because I was just starting to really function again, and I was afraid seeing him would set me back, but I wanted to see if he would finally explain himself. He didn't; he let me down again, and it sent me backward. It put me back on an emotional roller coaster." Seeing her ex gave Patricia an opportunity to react to the pain and loss of the breakup, rather than to reflect on it.

Another "don't": obsessing over what our ex is thinking, feeling, and doing, or worrying about whether he is okay. This might sound harsh, but an ex is not our responsibility anymore, and trying to get into his head is just a way to stay out of our own. Worrying about him and beating ourselves up are not self-nurturing behaviors. Our thoughts, positive and negative, are extremely powerful and can influence our moods, productivity, and even our overall health. We need to be kind to ourselves after breakups.

Another unhealthy "don't": keeping the fantasy of the relationship alive. Vicky, twenty-four, told me, "I thought he was the one; I thought we were going to get married. It was great and he was great. He was sweet and romantic, and we had a blast together." I then reminded Vicky that she had told me five minutes earlier that two days before he broke it off, she had told him she was unhappy and wanted to work on things. Like Vicky, we often tend to torture ourselves during breakups by remembering all the good stuff and none of the bad about the person or relationship. Why do we do this? Neither living in fantasyland nor the flip side, demonizing an ex, allows us to get over him. Instead, we need to reflect on the truth of the relationship, ourselves, and our former partner. We can then process the breakup and behave in ways that are balanced and realistic.

The next "don't" is all too common: believing we need closure with our exes before we can move forward. Closure is something we can do on our own and for ourselves. If we yearn for closure and rely on another to get it, we perpetuate a bad habit: needing someone other than ourselves to get what we want. Instead, we can reframe closure as "letting go." When we love someone, that love is hard to just shut off. We do not need to cut them out of our hearts completely, but we can choose to let our exes go by releasing them from our everyday thoughts. Another misconception is that we can be friends with an ex immediately after a breakup. In some rare best-case-scenario breakups, this might be possible, yet most of us need time to recover on our own. The transition from lover to friend can be a messy one, and keeping relationships with blurry lines in our lives can hinder our ability to move forward. A breakup is a *break*, which means "to separate." Spending a year (or at the very least nine months) without any contact gives us an opportunity to feel free from old attachments, to learn how to heal and process on our own, and to become open to attracting the relationships we want when we are ready for them.

EXERCISE 58

Breakup Dos and Don'ts

Below is a checklist summarizing all the dos and don'ts of breakups that we've discussed, as well as some additional ones. Read through the list, thinking about your past breakups, and check off the ones in each category that apply to you.

Dos

1. I did not talk to my ex for a significant period of time after our breakup.

2. I made every effort to get out of his head and into mine. (For example, I wore a rubber band around my wrist and each time I started thinking about or long- ing for my ex, I gave it a little snap to pull myself back into the present.)

3. When reflecting on the relationship, I tried to sepa- rate fantasy from reality. I did not torture myself by only thinking about the good. Instead, I reminded myself of the ways it was not what I wanted.

4. I continued to do the things that bring me joy, even if memories of the relationship were attached to them. (For example, when I split from my ex, I strayed from yoga, which I love and which we had shared. As part of my "return-to-living" program, I returned to one of my favorite classes. When I walked in, the familiarity of the place was comforting at a time when I felt that everything in my life was changing.)

5. I began something new on my own, such as a class, a creative project, or redecorating a room.

6. I put all pictures, letters, cards, and so forth from the past relationship in a box in storage. (I stored mine in a friend's garage, which in itself was healing.)

7. When I ran into people who asked how my "honey" was, and then witnessed their look of shock and pity when I told them it was over, I resisted acting like a

victim or bad-mouthing my ex. (People said to me, "Wow, I never would have dreamed you two wouldn't last. You were perfect." Yeah, that was not helpful in getting over him, but I made it easier on myself by switching the topic and reminding myself that what others said did not matter.)

8. I turned to and strengthened my external support system. I made plans with friends and reached out to people for support and companionship.

9. No matter how depressed I got, I tried to maintain a positive attitude.

10. I gave myself the necessary transition period but eventually made every conscious effort to move on with my life.

Don'ts

1. I continued to talk to, see, or email my ex.

2. I always wondered what he was doing or thinking.

3. I followed him, called him and hung up, and/or drove by his house.

4. I found excuses to contact him.

5. I stopped doing a lot of the things I love to do.

6. I did not take care of my body (for example, I under- or overate, drank too much, or didn't exercise).

7. I thought I couldn't move on until I had closure with him.

8. I am looking (or did look) to get into a new relationship ASAP to have something to be excited about and to feel attractive.

9. I asked people questions about him and talked about him a lot.

10. I did not want him to be happy.

11. I beat myself up constantly and thought of things I could or should have done differently to salvage the relationship.

12. I bad-mouthed him.

If your "don'ts" outnumber your "dos," your behavior might hinder your ability to get what you want. Look more closely at the "dos" and find new behaviors to replace the "don'ts." Behaviors that encourage our growth rather than weighing us down are the secret to getting what we want in future relationships.

Having said all this, I want to emphasize that these are all suggestions, not rules. Every breakup is unique, and each of us must behave in the ways that are most true to who we are.

Eventually, at some point after a breakup, we might want to begin a new relationship. Let's return to our house analogy. If we were building a new home, we would want clear ground to build on, right? Similarly, before we go out and try to create a new relationship, we need to excavate as much of the previous relationship as possible. Otherwise, we could end up dating the same type of person over and over again.

First, we should ask ourselves if we are focusing on fantasies of past or future relationships or focusing on reality. Living in our fantasies not only makes evaluating and eventually letting go of relationships difficult, but it also creates an opportunity for us to compare. If we cling too tightly to the past or harbor expectations and fears about the future, we will not be able to create something truly original and new. Letting go of such habits is difficult but extremely empowering.

Karen, twenty-seven, says, "It is so hard for me to not always be worried about finding someone, because I do want to get married. I don't know where the distinction is between believing that fate will deliver my true love and actively trying to pursue a mate!" *Fate* is a term that quarter-lifers use a lot when talking about relationships. Many of us find solace in the belief that fate rules and that our soul mates will appear when they are supposed to; however, we still would like that to happen on our timeline.

We cannot rely on or control fate, yet one thing that we *can* count on and influence is our beliefs. We can choose to discard beliefs that do not support the creation of the relationship we want, such as "All men are jerks, and the good ones don't want me." And we need to emphasize beliefs such as "My last relationship did not work out, but a future one might work." Good relationships all boil down to awareness and choice. As we become aware of our past relationship patterns and choose to modify them, we open ourselves up to attracting the people who suit us best.

> "Learn from your relationships rather than pining for them. You will be better equipped to know what your needs and desires are. Most importantly, know that you are worthy of asking for what you want — you don't have to settle for any less."
>
> — Vivian, fifty-seven

CHAPTER 8

TWENTY-SOMETHING WORK

Along with relationships, our careers are often in the forefront of our twenty-something crisis. The heat is on in our twenties in terms of earning a living and establishing ourselves in the working world. Those of us who want or are considering children feel added pressure to advance our careers to a certain point before we take on the additional title of "Mom." The ambitions that characterize our generation are inspiring — there are no limits to what we have accomplished and will accomplish. Our careers give us a sense of success, independence, and maturity. However, many of us are in quite a quandary about how to find careers that we enjoy and that give us the financial security and freedom we crave.

A lot of twenty-something women are still waiting to hear that voice from above that will tell them, "This is what you were born to do." Even being armed with an education, a loaded resume, and drive does not protect us from unexpected roadblocks in our career paths, such as not knowing what we want to do, not liking what we do, not making a living at what we want to do, or not doing anything at all. Unlike a relationship, where at least another person is involved, our careers are our individual responsibility. If only it were as simple as it was when we were little. One day we could play teacher; the next, we could be a cop and then maybe a mom; and when we felt really smart and got hold of a calculator, we could play bank. But now, as grown-ups, how do we decide on a direction?

Those of you who are unhappy with your current jobs (or lack thereof) are not alone. Ninety percent of the women I surveyed said their careers topped the list of their biggest concerns. To get some clarity, let's begin by answering a familiar trio of questions:

1. Who am I in my career?

2. What do I want in my career? (Or: What career do I want?)

3. How do I get what I want in a career?

If you already have a great job that completely satisfies you, this chapter is not designed for you (but it still offers the opportunity to discover other things you might like to do). Most women in their twenties don't fit into that category and are stressed out by questions about occupations. Unfortunately, no one magical solution can pull us out of job discontent. Yet we can reach a more understanding place within ourselves so that our motivations for choosing a career path and then working toward it will be more authentic.

WHO AM I IN MY CAREER?

Madison, a twenty-four-year-old administrative assistant, describes her career: "I am making it my job to figure out what I want to do.

So far, I've fired myself four times." Madison graduated with a communications degree and, without a clear sense of what she wanted to do, moved to San Francisco with her college roommate. She had a resume full of intern experience, and she is cute and personable — how hard could finding a good job be? After being out of work for four months, she finally called a temp agency. "I had to settle for a job at a publishing firm that I don't like. I am not using my full potential, and there is little interpersonal contact. Honestly, I feel like I was more successful when I was sixteen." Madison does not understand how people can go to work every day and hate it; she does not want to be one of those people. She is convinced that something is wrong with her because she doesn't know what she wants. "If I knew what I was passionate about, it would not be so hard for me to find a job I like."

Like Madison, many of us still find ourselves asking the question "What do I want to be when I grow up?" We hope to get some clue in college. We go through four years (give or take a few, depending on how much we enjoy ourselves) of all-nighters, parties, football games, community bathrooms, hooking up with upperclassmen, disgusting dorm food, and, oh yeah, figuring out what we want to do with the rest of our lives. A lot of us decided on our majors or supposed life paths when we were just teenagers. Few of us were encouraged, especially by our parents, to take time to travel, work odd jobs, or discover what we wanted. Now, in our twenties, at the same time that we are told, "You're young and have your whole life ahead of you, so enjoy it" we are also told, "You better decide what you want to do with your life." So are we supposed to be young and carefree or serious about our grown-up future? With all the contradictory input we receive, it is no wonder that many of us are confused.

College was a layover between high school and the real world more than it was an actual preparation for adult life. Decisions carried less weight because, hey, it was college — the time of independence and few responsibilities. Most of us spent so much time cramming to get grades and fulfill credits that we rarely took classes just because they interested us. As graduation drew closer, the pressure to embark on a career path intensified. Without a lot of professional or even life experience under our belts, we chose the best paths we could, all the while feeling that our life callings were missing in action. Often our career choices were based on things we liked at the time, what our friends were doing, what our parents wanted us to do, what would make us a lot of money, or what looked interesting when we flipped through the career books at college orientation programs. Few of us stopped to ask ourselves, "Who am I?" because we were too busy securing our first jobs.

Finding Your Identity on the Career Path

Logically, figuring out who we are should precede deciding what we want to do, yet that isn't usually what happens. In our early twenties, without any significant experience of being on our own, our identity is still defined by being a daughter, a student, and a friend. So here we are, still in the adjustment phase of our independence, trying to decide what we want to spend the majority of our days doing. If we haven't decided, we fear something might be wrong with us, and our self-esteem often suffers. Laura, twenty-two, says, "The week of college graduation was the worst of my life. I couldn't sleep. I was around people who were reinforcing the idea that I should know what I want, and I felt like a big loser for not knowing. It is a vicious circle, and it has really shaken me up, especially my self-confidence — how can I believe in myself when I don't know what I am supposed to believe in?"

Like Laura, many of us suffer a postcollege identity crisis. That sounds serious, but it simply means that we panic when we don't know what we want to do. If we do not have great jobs or some master plan, we tend to focus on what we lack and forget about who we are as individuals. Not knowing what we want to do is quite normal; we have just been conditioned to believe otherwise. As in so many other parts of our lives, we need an adjustment phase when making decisions about our career path. There is a reason we did not learn calculus in kindergarten: our brains could not comprehend it then. Similarly, we need time and experience in the real world before we are adequately prepared to know what we want to do. Rarely does college actually prepare us for the jobs we end up doing. Think about it, those of you in your mid- to late twenties: Did college train you for the work you do now?

Imagine if we were brought up expecting to focus on who we are, what makes us tick, and our unique characteristics and skills in our early twenties. Unfortunately, most of us weren't. We are asked the question "What do you do?" much more often than we are asked, "Who are you?" Yet discovering who we are and how we relate to the world around us as we embark on womanhood is more exciting than any job. In my research, I found that women who took time to do things other than starting careers (such as traveling, living in another country, volunteering, being part of a big project, working odd jobs that just sounded interesting, and pursuing a hobby) did not relate to the type of identity crisis suffered by women who went straight into careers or grad school after college. The time they spent on themselves was well worth any delay in starting a career because it helped them to formulate their own identities, separate from what they were doing. Even those of us who cannot afford to *not* work can take a vacation from the pressure to find careers — we can simply get jobs that pay the bills but invest our extracurricular time in self-exploration. To feel content in a career, as in a relationship, we must first arm ourselves with a good sense of self.

EXERCISE 59

Discovering Who You Are on the Career Path

Before starting this exercise, review your original answers to the general question "Who am I?" (see part 1). Keep them in mind as you answer the following questions, without thinking about exactly what job description you want. That is not important right now (but don't worry — we'll get to it!).

1. Who am I as an employee?
2. Who am I when I am faced with something that I do not know how to do?
3. Who am I as a student (not just in school, but whenever I have an opportunity to learn something)?
4. Who am I when I am faced with a decision that is not black and white?
5. Who am I when I am outside my comfort zone?
6. Who am I when I have to speak in front of people?
7. Who am I in a social situation where I do not know anyone?
8. Who am I to strangers who I come in contact with daily?
9. Who am I when I am in front of someone I respect and admire?
10. Who am I in an interview?
11. Who am I when I talk about myself?
12. Who am I when I work with other people?
13. Who am I when I have a lot of things on my mind?

14. Who am I when I have to work under pressure?

15. Who am I when I have to delegate to others?

16. Who am I when I have to take direction from other people?

17. Who am I when I have little time to do things I really enjoy?

18. Who am I when I have to convince someone to do or buy something?

19. Who am I when I sit behind a desk all day?

20. Who am I when I am in a competitive or stressful environment?

How many of these questions have you been asked before? How many have you even considered? Gaining perspective on our identity in various situations is helpful because it shows us whether who we are accords with certain types of jobs. For instance, if we are nervous and restless outside our comfort zone, picking a job that involves extensive travel is probably not wise. This is why discovering who we are, especially in various contexts, ought to be the first stop on our career path. You might need a variety of experiences and jobs before you can answer all these questions about your identity in the working world, but trust that you eventually *will* find the answers.

—∞∞∞—

Separation Anxiety

Who we are is not what we do. What we do is not who we are. (Read those two sentences again a few times — they are the keys to finding peace along your career path.) Confusing what we do with who we are can affect our self-perception. If we are unhappy with our careers, we are often unhappy with ourselves. I asked the women I interviewed, "On a scale of 1 to 10, how much does career shape your identity (1 means it has nothing to do with who you are, and 10 means it is how you define yourself)?" The average answer was between 7 and 8. Thus, for most women, our careers play an extremely significant role in our self-perception. Is that an empowering perspective?

If we do not separate what we do from who we are, our identity will always be dictated by something external — our jobs — and that can significantly weaken our foundation. Chantal, twenty-five, works for her father's company. "It is definitely not what I want to be doing, and I am not proud of it because I am basically a sales assistant/secretary, and I don't feel that title measures up to what my friends do. Since I am working for my dad, my job is like a continuation of my childhood, which makes me feel like a failure." Chantal has confused who she is with what she is doing. Why do we feel so unsure of ourselves when we are not where we think we should be in our careers? Just as our relationships cannot meet all our needs, no job can fill a void or complete us. We cannot wait for perfect jobs to come along and make us happy — we might as well stand on the corner where the knights on white horses are riding by.

Greta, twenty-seven, just had a beautiful wedding to the man of her dreams but is still miserable because she does not have a big career. Every day she wakes up irritable and frustrated next to her incredibly cute, sweet husband. She is highly educated and intelligent and works as a tutor while she figures out what she *really* wants to do. "My job gives me something to do and some income, but it is not stimulating. I am actually jealous that my husband goes off every day to a job in a big corporation where he is around other interesting people all day. I am happy that the man I love has a great job, but I want that sense of accomplishment and purpose, too." When asked if helping kids do better in school and feel better about themselves gives her some satisfaction, Greta shrugged her shoulders and said, "I know it should give me tons of gratification, but I just want more. Once I find the perfect career, I will stop feeling so incomplete."

EXERCISE 60

Disentangling Who You Are from What You Do

Do you relate to Chantal or Greta? If you are having a career crisis, it could be the result of entangling who you are with what you do. Here are questions to help you determine how tangled those knots are.

1. Do you think a job can make you feel better about yourself? Will it (or does it) validate you?

2. Do you think you must have a career in order to be successful?

3. Do you feel embarrassed when someone asks you what you do for a living? Are you ashamed of what you do?

4. Do you think people would think more of you if you had a better job?

5. Do you think your life would be better if you had a job you loved?

6. Do you ever feel worthless because you do not think you are doing something important?

If you answered yes to one or more of these questions, your identity and your vocation are like conjoined twins and need to be separated. To begin to pry them apart, start to shift your thinking. Bringing our focus onto who we are, not what we do, takes practice. Here are two suggestions to get you started. First, write, "Who I am is not what I do" on a sheet of paper and tape it to your mirror. Second, do at least one thing each week that reflects who you are. For example, if you love to be with your friends, plan an evening with a group of them. Caring for who we are is just as much a responsibility of adulthood as generating an income.

WHAT DO I WANT IN MY CAREER?

Now on to the question that resonates with almost all quarter-life women: "What the heck do I want to do with my life?!" But before going any further, answer the following questions:

1. Do you know what your "passion" is?

2. Are you currently doing something you are passionate about and making money at it?

If you answered yes to both questions, you are among a small and fortunate group. The rest of us search for our passions and, if and when we find them, struggle over how to translate them into actual jobs.

The most popular career advice we get is "Follow your passion and you will be happy and successful." Yeah, right! Most of us do not even know what our passions are, and so we feel that something is wrong with us. The concept that each of us is born with a fire burning in her belly that will drive a career has spread like a bad flu. *Passion* has become a buzzword, although many of us don't even know what it really means. The dictionary actually defines *passion* as "suffering." Yes, suffering! As a generation, we have become obsessed with finding our passions, and a lot of us have found suffering instead.

Well, now, isn't it clear why? We are told to "make money doing what you love." That misleads us because it also implies that we should be unhappy at any job that we aren't totally passionate about. Many of us have jobs that are perfectly suitable for us, but we doubt them because we don't love them. Lexie, twenty-six, says, "I have no idea if I am currently doing what I am passionate about, but I am giving it a go. Maybe I am incapable of sustaining a feeling of passion. This concept frightens me and causes me a lot of anxiety at work."

The first step in figuring out what we want from our careers is to get this whole idea of passion, also known as suffering, out of our heads. True, some people have what I call the Mozart gene. Rarely, individuals are born with so strong a love for art or work that it drives them straight to the top. We are continuously exposed to those people, since many of them become famous. But a far more common approach to discovering what we want is to follow the natural progression of events. Without any experience in the fields of our so-called passions, it is hard to know for sure that we would even want or be able to make careers out of them.

Monika, twenty-nine, found her passion through trial and error; she didn't spring from her mother's womb knowing what it was. She always thought she would be a doctor but now works as a very successful editor for one of the most prestigious companies in the world. "I was surprised and devastated after doing poorly on the med school entrance exam. It forced me to reevaluate my entire life dream. Because I did not know what to do, I went into production simply because an opportunity was presented to me. With some reservation, I interviewed for a job at an animation company. As an artist, I do have a creative side. One thing led to another, and I found myself loving editing. I never in a million years thought this is what I'd be doing, but I really like it."

For some of us, our jobs fulfill our purpose. But our purpose does not have to align with our careers. Our purpose might be giving back to the world, having a family, or making beautiful jewelry. We put a tremendous amount of pressure on ourselves to first realize our purpose (which society brands as "passion") and then to immediately generate careers that serve it. One reason that previous generations did not complain about a twenty-something crisis is that they weren't consumed by this passion-finding trend. People placed more emphasis on working to support lifestyles that made them happy. Recall from the Introduction that one of the ways *crisis* is defined is as "an unstable or crucial time or state of affairs in which a decisive change is impending." We make our career decisions with so much urgency and finality that many of us get sidetracked and do not follow the flow of our lives or our purpose (and thus we sense an absence of passion).

If you have no clue about what your purpose is or even what you like, and if this causes you grave concern, you are a victim of the passion craze. Since it is a word that has infiltrated our culture, I asked women the same questions I asked you: "Do you know what your 'passion' is? Are you currently doing something you are passionate about and making money at it?" Eighty percent said that they were not doing something they felt passionate about, and 90 percent of those women also reported that they did not know what their passions were. Especially interesting to me was that every woman who did not know what her passion was had no problem listing a very specific dream job. Women mentioned everything from being a social worker in foster care and adoption to shooting covers for *Vanity Fair* to producing a movie to being a high school teacher to being a mommy/homemaker.

So how can we have dream jobs in mind but still be confused about what we want to do right now? It is because we are still figuring ourselves out and learning how to meet our goals. We allow ourselves to dream but aren't likely to go all out to realize those dreams. If our dream jobs are outside what we perceive as our realm of possibility, we might never consider them to be realistic pursuits.

Some dream jobs probably are best left to our imaginations. I'd love to be a rock star, but I cannot even sing "Happy Birthday." Yet sometimes we miss the link between our dream jobs and our purpose. Our thinking is often myopic. We labor under the misconception that we should decide upon our ultimate career goals and then follow a certain progression to achieve them. That type of thinking serves some women. If you know for sure that you want to be a gynecologist, there is a specific sequence of steps to follow. But what about those of us who do not know exactly what we want and have only far-fetched dream jobs in our heads? We have to look at the dream jobs, determine which of their elements we can attain, and then try our hand at those.

For instance, if I think about why I would want to be a rock star, one of the main reasons is that I like being in front of a crowd. But being a rock star is not the only profession that could fulfill this dream. I can think a little outside the box and consider other possibilities that would put me in front of people (to see if I really liked it or if it was just a fantasy). Becoming a group exercise instructor, the membership director of an organization, and writing this book have all fulfilled this dream of mine, as each has put me in front of people.

EXERCISE 61

Identifying Your Purpose

The following exercises are intended to clarify the question "What do I want in my career?" I hope that you feel slightly relieved to know that even if you don't have a specific passion, you still have a purpose in life (although discovering it might take a while). One strategy for discovering our purpose is to translate very broad ideas and desires into specific activities or jobs that fulfill them. If you already think you know what your purpose is, complete the following exercise anyway, since you might gain additional insight.

The discovery of our purpose can be a lengthy journey, and the rather long exercise below reflects that fact. Before you begin, make sure you have the time to complete it. First, completely clear your mind of any kind of practical thinking. Answer each question using the carefree, little-girl, creative, "I can do anything I want" part of your brain.

Part 1

1. What games did you play when you were little?

2. When you were a small child and a teenager, what types of things did you just love to do?

3. What kind of events or activities have you looked forward to throughout your life and never wanted to end?

4. Call your parents, siblings, and other family members and ask them what you were really excited about as a kid. What did they tell you?

Review your answers to see if you can pick out any common themes that reveal what you have enjoyed in your life. Perhaps you noticed you enjoyed creative things like arts and crafts projects or educational activities like reading. Record those themes in your journal. Notice if any of the things you listed are actually things that you do in your job or anticipate doing in a career you are working towards.

Part 2

Now answer the next set of questions:

1. When you were younger, what did you want to be when you grew up?

2. If you could have any job in the world, what would it be? In other words, what is your absolute, pie-in-the-sky dream job?

3. If you were independently wealthy and did not have to work, what would you do in your spare time?

Review your answers to see which activities would be part of your daily life in each of these scenarios. Your answers for 1–3 may be the same or very similar, or they may be completely different. Record the characteristics involved in each of those activities/jobs. For instance, if you wanted to be a nurse when you grew up, interacting with people would be an example of a daily activity. If your dream job is to be a surgeon, healing would be part of your daily life. If you didn't have to work and you spend your time volunteering, then helping people would be part of your life. A common theme in these examples is working with and helping people. Notice what common themes are evident in your answers. Do not be concerned if they are not as obvious as in these examples; just make general observations.

Part 3

Now let's move on to the "whys." Fill in the blanks to complete the following statements (rewrite each complete phrase in your journal).

1. I wanted to be a _____ when I was little because:

2. My dream job is _____ because:

3. If I did not have to work, I would _____ because:

Now you are ready for the final part of this exercise.

Part 4

1. Summarize what you have learned about what you like or want to do.

2. Brainstorm a list of jobs or activities that might include some of the things you like. Do not worry about being overly specific or even about how you could get those jobs (we'll get to that part later).

3. How many job tasks or activities in your current reality line up with what you think you want or match what you think your purpose might be?

Before doing this exercise, did you know that you actually already knew a lot about what you like to do? When you have thought about your career in the past, you might have thought only about what job you could get. By reframing "What do I want to do?" in terms of your dreams and hobbies, perhaps you will start to discover another approach to answering this question.

> "Do what delights you... more important, figure out what delights you."
>
> — Carin, fifty-three

Your Quality of Life

As we think about what we want to do to support ourselves, it's important to remain aware of our quality of life (QOL). Our QOL reveals how much we enjoy our lives. Our careers can determine our QOL through factors such as these:

- our working environment
- how we get along with our colleagues
- the amount of free time we have to enjoy hobbies or be with friends or family
- the amount of disposable income we can spend on vacations, social activities, and material goods
- how much debt/financial burden we have
- our overall stress level
- our intellectual, interpersonal, or creative stimulation
- the pride we take in what we do
- our job stability

Based on these elements, on a scale of 1 to 10, what would you say that your QOL quotient is?

Our quality of life has more effect on our overall well-being than what is written on our business cards does. Focusing on raising our QOL quotient is a lot easier than waiting for passion to knock on our doors. Even little things, such as putting flowers on our desks or saving twenty bucks a week for a weekend getaway, can increase our QOL. Most of the women I spoke to who were trying to pursue their passions at any cost, rather than taking steps to improve their overall quality of life, were suffering. Many of us who repeat the mantra "I will make this happen no matter what because I believe in it, it's what I want, and it will give me the life I want" are burnt out and unfulfilled in other areas of our lives. One woman confessed, "I recently had to take Xanax to get through a difficult work time. I didn't tell anyone, and I cannot believe I did it, but it did make things there so much easier to handle. I am in the midst of trying to wean myself off it now."

If our jobs are driving us to prescription drugs, it is time to reevaluate the cost of our ambitions. Of course, a lot of career paths do require sacrifices, and some are stressful at times (law school, med school, being a starving artist, working as an assistant in a grueling industry, and so on). This is why we need to be clear about whether a certain career is what we want, as we've investigated in the exercises so far.

An enjoyable job that affords us a good QOL can, for the most part, be enough. So what if we do not go to work with fire in our eyes? It is actually okay to not *love* what we do, because it is not who we are. There are many other things in life to love, such as our families, our friends, our mates, our hobbies, chocolate, nature, children, and animals. The American ideal preaches that we must love what we do to be successful. Yet if what we do combines a few of our skills and a few of the things we like — *that* is success!

Is This Really What I Want?

Imagine this analogy: For a year, you have planned and saved for a great vacation. All your life you have wanted to go on a cruise, and finally you are going. The cruise line is the best, you will visit spectacular cities you have only dreamed about, and you are full of anticipation. But once you get on the boat, you realize the accommodations are uncomfortable, the food is terrible, the itinerary is not what was promised, and the other passengers are boring. On top of that, you get seasick! You are furious; this is not what you expected. But unless you want to drown, jumping ship is not an option. Plus, you have been talking this trip up to your friends and family for months. It's your first solo excursion; you cannot run home. You are disappointed, confused, and questioning where you went wrong in this decision.

Many of us question whether we picked the best career ship to sail in. We jumped the first hurdle — choosing the direction of our careers — but now we face an even bigger one: we don't like them. We begin to realize just how naïve we were in college, when we actually thought we knew what we wanted. Outgrowing our previous career choices makes us think it is time for a change, yet we struggle with giving up an identity that we immersed ourselves in for years. And is there even time to go back and start over, or will that screw up our life plans? Panic hits, and, boom, we are in a career crisis.

EXERCISE 62

Why Are You Doing What You're Doing?

Making changes is not easy. We have invested time, sleepless nights, hard work, money, and to some extent our sense of self in our careers. We feel obligated to stick with them; we don't want to deal with the guilt of having made the wrong decision. To calm our panic and avoid staying in the wrong career too long or jumping ship too soon, we need to reevaluate what propelled us into our current profession and why we've chosen to stay there. Start by answering the following questions in your journal:

1. What qualities do you like about your current job?
2. What qualities do you dislike about your current job?
3. What qualities would you like to have in your current job?

———∞———

Discovering that the careers we have chosen do not have many qualities we actually like can be very disconcerting, especially when we planned great careers in order to avoid a career crisis. A self-proclaimed "planaholic" and "control freak," Abi, twenty-eight, always knew she'd be either a doctor or a lawyer because those were the career paths for intelligent people with a clear-cut direction. Abi hates taking risks and always has felt that she needs to know what is ahead. She decided to pursue the lawyer route and followed a well-laid-out plan: she got good grades, went to college, conquered the LSAT, got into a great law school, kicked ass there, interviewed with top firms, interned during the summer, and signed with a top firm, making six figures a year upon graduating from law school.

Currently, two years into her meticulously executed career, she finds herself commuting two hours a day and stressed out by demanding deadlines and excessive hours. "My career crisis moment hit me when I was sitting in bumper-to-bumper traffic laying on my horn at a mom in a minivan who cut me off. I was becoming a mean, crabby, unhappy robot: get up, work out, get ready, eat a Powerbar in the car, sit in traffic, park, walk into the office, grab a cup of coffee, say 'Good morning' to my stressed-out coworkers, and go through paperwork. I am not enjoying what I am doing, and I have no life — I do not even know what my hobbies are."

So why doesn't Abi just quit? Well, because of her success, she has a hard time facing the fact that she does not like being a lawyer. "I am in a bad mood all the time except with people I want to impress, who I fake being nice to. The more approval I receive and the more money I make as a lawyer, the more convinced I am that I should stick with it. I am good at it, which makes me think it is my purpose." The external validation feeds Abi's ego, but inside she feels the truth of her situation. However, when she entertains thoughts of quitting, she immediately feels guilty. Abi admits that many of her career decisions were motivated by her desire to do the right, honorable, impressive thing. "I had my career all planned out to avoid the kind of turmoil I am feeling right now — I am worried that I may have made a big mistake."

Abi's story has several themes that are typical of those questioning and reevaluating their current situations: a very specific and demanding profession that limits the opportunity to pursue hobbies or other interests; repetitive outside reinforcement and praise about a job; and feelings of guilt and obligation. Unexpected questions, thoughts, behaviors, and feelings begin to surface for quarter-life professionals if we discover that our framed degrees just don't fulfill us. We are torn because we have schooling and achievement behind us and opportunities for even greater success ahead of us. To keep our familiar title as "smart" women, we believe we need that power job with its power salary. We begin to doubt ourselves, and our heads cycle through questions such as "Is it really the job, or is it me? Would another type of job in the same field be better? Will I like the job more as I move up the ladder?" And then comes the scariest question of them all: "Did I make the wrong decision?"

The comfort of having a plan has worn off, and we find ourselves at a crossroads. Disliking our carefully executed career path

was not part of that plan. We feel frozen in place and force ourselves to suck it up, but this is not our only option. If we really
inspect the foundation we have been building, we might discover
insight that will help us decide how to move forward. The first step
in determining whether you are on the right path is to examine
what drove you to choose your career. The more we understand
about why we are where we are, the less overwhelming the present
becomes. In Abi's case, much of the reason she chose to become a
lawyer is that she knew she could control her destiny. Plus, being
a lawyer is prestigious, which is important to Abi. Her identity is
wrapped up in being an overachiever. But as intelligent as Abi is,
she admits that she never took the time to discover if she even
found law interesting.

Abi's story reminded me of my own career crisis. For years, I
had known deep down that I did not like my chosen career path,
but I stayed because I kept getting positive reinforcement, promotions, and ego feeding — it was addictive. I felt obligated to stay
in the field I chose at age seventeen since I'd told myself and everyone around me that it was my passion. By twenty-five, proving
myself had become a habit. I prided myself on my achievements to
the point that I became attached to them. Without my title and
accomplishments, what would my identity be? Moreover, what in
the world would I do instead? If I had dealt with and acknowledged my insecurities rather than building a career around them, I
probably would have chosen a path of self-discovery a lot sooner.
However, often it takes an "ah-ha!" moment to get us to finally recognize what was behind our career decisions.

The "Ah-Ha!" Moment

An "ah-ha!" moment is simply an acknowledgment that a career is
not in line with our purpose (even if we do not yet know exactly
what that purpose is) and that it brings down our QOL quotient.

Ever since Melanie, twenty-six, was a little girl, her mother has always told her, "Mel, you are going to be somebody." So Melanie began to pay attention to the types of people her mom referred to as "somebodies." She grew up believing that she had to do something above average in order to be somebody. Naturally, Melanie went to a top-ten school. She continued on the "somebody" path by going to grad school to get her master's in business. By twenty-five, Melanie was working at one of the top consulting companies in Chicago. "Whenever I spoke to my mom about the things I was doing in my job, she would just gush with pride. I could never tell her how stressed-out I was and how dreadful I found consulting. Sure, I had a great expense account to entertain clients, but most of them were a complete drag! Plus, I was gaining weight from all the late-night dinners, and I had no time to do anything for myself." Melanie was indeed a somebody, but that role came with late nights, caffeine replacing vegetables as a food group, egomaniacal clients she had to hustle to keep happy, and wearing a suit every day ("And I hate pantyhose!"). She yearned to be more active, to work with her hands, and to have more "silliness" in her day. She did not like what she was doing and tried to figure out why.

Melanie's "ah-ha!" moment came after a conversation with her mother. "She said to me, 'Oh, Mel, I sure wish I had some big career like yours to talk about.' After I hung up the phone, it dawned on me: I was living my mother's fantasy — she is the one who wanted to be somebody, not me. I finally stopped myself and asked if I was doing anything I really wanted to do, and the answer was a very clear no." Embarking on a career path that someone else paved does not make Melanie a weak person. Many of us look to people we trust, such as our parents, teachers, or mentors, for instruction and advice during times when we feel tremendous pressure to decide something. Our "ah-ha!" moment might come later, when our foundation is strong enough that we're able to separate others' belief systems and expectations from our own.

After her senior year of college, during which she experienced many downs, Hannah, now twenty-four, needed a fresh start. "I had no idea what I really wanted to do, but I knew I had to get out of my college town, so I moved to the most exciting city I could think of where no one knew me — New York." Hannah struggled for months to find a job that fit into the new, exciting life she wanted to create. She works for a film executive and sits at a desk all day while her boss barks orders at her. Recently, her boss slapped her hand as she reached for a brownie and said, "You don't really need that; you are getting pudgy." That was Hannah's "ah-ha!" moment. "I went home that night and cried. I have been justifying being in a city I do not really like, working in an industry I do not even want to pursue, and tolerating being treated like crap on a daily basis, all because I thought the change would make me forget about my past. I got here because I wanted to escape my past, and now I want to run again ... but I have no clue where to."

The moment of epiphany can be a bit of a double-edged sword. It can be very liberating, but feelings of disappointment, regret, and confusion about what to do next also emerge. Before making any drastic actions after an "ah-ha!" career moment, we need to excavate the foundations we built our careers upon to ensure we're making intrinsic, not reactionary, decisions.

EXERCISE 63

Uncovering the "Ah-Ha!"

If we feel that our current career is not the right fit, the first question to ask ourselves is how much influence we actually had on our career path. Were our decisions extrinsically or intrinsically motivated? The questions in this exercise are intended to help you uncover an "ah-ha!" moment about your current career choice.

1. As you were growing up, who talked to you most about your future career, and what was said?

2. What did your parents/teachers/others tell you they thought you would be?

3. If you knew what you wanted to be as you grew up, what made you arrive at that decision?

4. Did you ever think about whether you would like the tasks involved in your future career? Moreover, did you even know what they were?

5. Are you in a specific career because people always told you that you were good at the skills it involves?

6. Do you feel obligated to stay in your current career even though you do not like it?

7. Have you done "safe" things or chosen a safe career although in your heart you wanted to do something different?

8. Is there someone in your life whose opinion about what you did came before your own?

Write down any "ah-ha!"–type thoughts that you had when answering the questions above. Do not worry if they were not mind-blowing, because often little insights can provide understanding and ease the angst we might feel.

After an "ah-ha!" moment, our natural response is to want to change our situation. However, it is not always in our best interests to just abandon our jobs on a whim, strap on a backpack, and go to India to "find ourselves." It is also not wise to immediately jump onto another career track, because that decision could be just a reaction. Instead, we can compromise and balance our obligations with our desire for change.

> "Don't wait until you've followed what your parents want you to do for a career (as that is really for them and not for you). You will waste a lot of time and money, and eventually it will lead you down an unsatisfying path."
>
> — Elisa, forty-eight

First, we need to make the most out of the situation we are in and use it as a growing and learning experience. Embracing our "ah-ha!" moment provides us with an opportunity to discover truths about ourselves. The more we know about our decision-making past, the better we'll be able to approach future decisions with heightened self-awareness. Returning to the cruise analogy, we need to accept that we're on the cruise that we are on, reevaluate what put us there, and then perhaps make logical arrangements to leave the ship the next time it docks.

HOW DO I GET WHAT I WANT IN A CAREER?

Wherever we fall on the knowing-what-we-want spectrum, from having no clue to being absolutely sure, the question on our minds is how to attain it. Our whole lives might be spent in pursuit of this question. To simplify the process: Getting the career we want is no different from getting what we want for dinner. It involves preparation, tuning in to our inner cravings, evaluating what is in our best physical and financial interest, and then being satisfied with our choice. So why has the career path become so treacherous? The overemphasis on passion and the pressure we feel to do and have it all propels us into one of two states: either we put our-selves on an accomplishment timeline, or we waver because we don't know what we want. As much as we want to figure out what to do so we can start doing it, not knowing is part of the process of ultimately discovering our purpose.

Following the Flow

Grace, twenty-six, had no idea what she wanted to do with her life but always had loved helping people. When the time came to choose a career, Grace knew she wanted to do something that would make a difference — she decided that would be her pur-pose. The world of nonprofit organizations had always appealed to her because it combined her desire to work in business with her love of helping people. She got a job as the PR director for a small Catholic youth organization. "I thought it was my dream job. I was so excited!" Day after day went by, and her dream job turned into a nightmare. Grace loved the concept of working for a non-profit, but in reality it was a drag. "The long hours, low pay, and constant fight for a bigger cause became exhausting."

During the first year at her job, Grace got engaged, so any spare time she had went toward planning her wedding. She adored every step of the planning, even the tiny details that most people agonize over. Her wedding was perfect, and everyone told her what a wonderful job she had done. After her wedding, she went through such severe wedding-planning withdrawal that she offered to help a girlfriend with her wedding. "I thought I wouldn't be as into helping my friend as I was into my own wedding, but I loved it even more." At work, Grace found herself surfing the Net for the latest dress styles, locations, photographers, bands, and anything else that had to do with weddings.

Thoughts such as "Maybe this is what I really should be

doing" would enter Grace's head, but she quickly dismissed them. "I thought becoming a wedding planner would be such a frivolous thing to do, and it really didn't fit into my plan of making a difference. I mean, the amount of money that is wasted on weddings could cut a big chunk out of world hunger." Still, Grace continued to daydream about having her own wedding planning business, setting her own hours, and getting up every day looking forward to work rather than dreading it. But she had doubts about whether she would be a good wedding planner, whether she could handle it and get enough clients. These types of concerns did not arise in her nonprofit career. Starting her own business offered no guarantees.

After a referral following a friend's wedding, Grace was able to see new possibilities. It was not just an accident that she stumbled into wedding planning. She decided she could take a risk and leave her job to pursue it. "I started very slowly. On weekends, I went into stationery stores to see if I could get a job working in an invitations department. On weeknights, I met with friends who were getting married to help them plan. Once I lined up a stationery store job that would be a reliable source of income and had signed up a couple as my first paying clients, I took a risk and quit my job, which was my security blanket. I cannot believe it has come together the way it has. It's been stressful, but I am on the right path."

Maintaining enough faith to follow the flow of our lives is not as easy for all of us as it was for Grace. On the one hand, we cannot control everything, but on the other, we cannot sit around and wait for something to happen. Basically, we need to start by making an intrinsic decision but then not attach too many expectations to it. We need to ask ourselves if we are following the flow of our lives or digging ditches to redirect the water. Being open to exploration and the possibility of change while fulfilling our responsibilities is how we can flow without drowning. We can reassure ourselves to trust the flow by realizing that our lives have always involved sequences, with one thing leading to another.

EXERCISE 64

Making a Career Timeline

At any point along our career paths, turning around to look at what has gotten us there is valuable. In this exercise, make a career timeline, starting from your current employment situation and working backward. You can go all the way back to your first job, such as babysitting. Turn to a completely blank page in your journal and begin to chart your course. Your timeline should include things such as:

- specific things you have done and decisions you have made (e.g., "I went to grad school because I wanted a specific career")

- things you did that led you to your career (e.g., classes, job fairs, internships)

- interaction with people who influenced your career or played major roles in helping you to attain jobs (e.g., "My best friend's father was the general manager of the hotel chain I work at")

- things that just happened, which you did not expect or control (e.g., "A family member got sick and I had to take a leave of absence")

- crisis moments (e.g., "I got fired" or "I did not pass the bar")

Now look at your timeline and think about the course of your career thus far. Evaluate how much you flow and how much you control. Which approach yielded more positive results?

---⊶⊷---

Investigating and Preparing for Your Path

Career contentment is a journey. It might take several jobs and life experiences before we eventually find jobs that give us the quality of life we desire. But it is not a journey we must take blindly. Just as we have to be open to following the flow, we should do certain things to prepare for the journey. Recall the concept of investigative versus comparative living discussed in chapter 5? Many of us are guilty of determining where we are based on the careers of others. We look at our peers or higher-ups and think "I want that job" without taking time to truly investigate the job. We want to know our destiny and we buy books on astrology or go to psychics, but do we place equal importance on actually investigating the path we choose? If not, we might be in for a rude awakening.

Through investigative living, Sonya, twenty-nine, was able to save herself from a path to career misery. "I was premed in college because I was going to become an ophthalmologist. A lot of my family members were doctors of some sort, and my grandma was blind, and I grew up telling her I was going to fix her eyes. I wasn't as fired up about medical school as I thought I would be, and I started to have doubts. That summer, instead of going on a big trip to Europe with my friends, I decided to intern at an eye clinic." Her experience surprised her. "I did not enjoy the daily activities and saw a future I did not want: doctors in the same grind every day while competing for business. Missing Europe that summer was totally worth it: I saved myself years, money, and craziness." Sonya did not pursue med school; she moved to a resort town, spent time investigating various types of jobs, and is now the catering director at a top hotel in Los Angeles.

EXERCISE 65

Skills and Dreams

An excellent companion to your career journey is to make a "skills and dreams" list. We all have skills and we all have dreams (if you cannot think of any, go back and reread the discussion of self-security in chapter 5, because you are selling yourself short). This, combined with your career timeline, is your road map for your career journey. Turn to a fresh page in your journal to do this exercise.

1. Divide the paper into two columns and label them "Skills" (the things you are capable of) and "Dreams" (the things you would like to do).

2. Look over your lists and draw lines between dreams and skills you have that match. For example, if speaking a foreign language is a skill and a job in international travel is a dream, draw a line connecting the two. You might draw multiple lines from and to various skills and dreams.

3. Of the things on your dream list that you lack the necessary skills for, consider whether you could attain them. Focusing on building objective skills is more realistic than focusing on subjective ones. For instance, if you want to be a graphic designer and have artistic ability but no proper computer programming training, you could take a class to gain this skill (it is objective). On the other hand, if one of your dreams is to be a famous actress but you never have performed, acting is not a skill you can just pick up; success in this career depends on the opinion of others (it is subjective).

4. Write down any ideas about how your current skills or skills you are willing to acquire might translate into a job or perhaps even a career path.

5. Think of ways you can investigate jobs or career paths that you believe suit your skills and dreams. List people to interview and internships to pursue.

Once we have an idea (even a small one) of the direction we want to pursue, we can take steps to get there. Doing so requires that we have a realistic and optimistic outlook, do our homework, and are willing to take intelligent risks. A secure financial foundation comes in handy here, too, since many skills we decide we want to acquire, such as furthering our education, require money. Doing the work in chapter 6 will make acquiring the skills that further our dreams more financially realistic. Even if attaining those skills requires a loan, it is an investment in our future. Such debt, when it furthers our goals, is favorable debt (unlike debt incurred to buy things such as a fabulous pair of Manolo Blahnik shoes).

Recall Melanie, the consultant who realized she was really working to achieve her mother's dream? "I took a big step back from my situation and evaluated what I needed to do to make it better, while thinking about what I wanted to do instead. I started doing yoga once a week; I cut back on client entertaining; and I even went out of my way to be nicer to my colleagues." Melanie wrote down her dreams, and none of them included martinis, Palm Pilots, or business cards. A skill that truly stood out on her list was that she was good with children. As a child, she always had played teacher, but teachers were never described to her as "somebodies," so Melanie never thought she could be one. Finally, at age twenty-seven, Melanie gave herself permission to switch paths. A teaching degree was something she could attain by working at her consulting firm for six more months in order to save money for a year of schooling.

Anticipating a sharp income drop, she replaced her gym membership with running, scaled back on her social outings, cut up her department store credit cards, and created and lived by a budget. "The process was a bit scary because I was not 100 percent positive that I wanted to be a teacher, but I was 100 percent positive that I did not want to be where I was." By age twenty-eight, Melanie was writing her name on the chalkboard of her fourth-grade class. "I finally enjoy what I do — it is a blend of what I love and what I am good at. I still have my bad days, but I don't have knots in my stomach anymore. Being a teacher fits." Oh, and Melanie's mom? Well, she is excited about the day that Melanie will become a bigtime college professor. Melanie, on the other hand, prefers the nine-year-olds.

Another thing to keep in mind as we evaluate our skills: Being good at something does not necessarily mean we should design a career around it. If we did well in math, that does not mean we must become accountants. Furthermore, we do not have to stick with jobs simply because we have the skills they require (remember Abi, the unhappy lawyer). It is useful to gain perspective on the skills that might come easily to us and then determine which ones we actually enjoy using on a daily basis.

Taking Intelligent Risks

The thought of changing directions is incredibly seductive, but how do we know if it is the right thing to do? Many of us have changes of heart about our careers but worry about the practicality of drastically shifting gears. Yet sometimes we reach a point where we have to go for it. Heidi, twenty-nine, took the biggest risk of her life when she quit her job to realign her outlook on office work and the climb up the corporate ladder. "I felt like my life had become entirely about work. I had nothing but soy sauce packets in my refrigerator. I felt burnt out and confused about my choices within the company when I suddenly realized I didn't even want the next promotion. To prove that I could choose any path at any time, I quit. I took a year off and got my priorities back in order. It was the best thing I ever could have done. Granted, I am working in an office again, but my mindset has changed, and now I live according to me — even my fridge is well stocked."

> "No matter what you decide to do, always prepare to be responsible for your actions."
>
> — Betty, fifty-six

It is always possible to change our situation, but that does take willingness to be uncomfortable. If we are risk-averse and crave security, can we leave a career or a job without entirely freaking out? On the other hand, if we crave drastic change and are ready to take a leap of faith, can we determine if we are being foolish? The answer to both questions is yes — if we take well-thought-out and intelligent risks.

EXERCISE 66

Taking the Right Risks

If you are considering or know you want a change in your career path, process this choice so that any action you take will be in your best interest. If we approach change blindfolded, our increased stress level will feel even worse than our discontentment with our jobs. This detailed exercise will assist you in dissecting your decision by asking you to evaluate the level of risk you might incur.

Part 1: Why Leave?

These questions are designed to help you gain additional perspective on why you want to leave your current job.

1. Do you tend not to stick with something (such as a job or project) for a long period? Do you crave frequent changes?

2. Do you blame any unhappiness, frustration, or lack of fulfillment on your job?

3. Have you avoided making changes in your attitude or work behavior at your current job to improve your situation as much as possible?

4. Do you compare your job to your friends' careers?

5. Do you want to do something else simply because you want more fun, money, and/or free time?

6. Do you expect a job to be fun and rewarding every day?

If you answered yes to one or more of these questions, you might want to reevaluate your desire to leave your current job. Our expectations, work ethic, and overall unhappiness often contribute more to our angst than our actual jobs do. If this is true of you, you might not need to change paths — your discontentment would only follow you to the next job. Instead, brainstorm ideas to make your *current* situation better. Small changes, such as putting up pictures, making a new office buddy, or taking a ten-minute walk during the workday can improve our QOL at work. On the other hand, if nothing helps and we are convinced that our jobs, not ourselves, are making us miserable, then moving on might be an intelligent risk to take.

If you answered no to most of the above questions or already know that your current job is dramatically lowering your QOL, then you are sure that a job/career change is an intrinsically motivated desire. Consider whether it's time to take a few risks, and move on to part 2.

Part 2: Risk Reality List

When we get excited about change, we commonly fantasize about how much better our new situation will be and forget about the ugly stuff, just as when we don those rose-colored glasses in our relationships. To stay out of fantasyland, make a realistic list of *everything* you would have to do to change your career or leave your job. For instance: "Save money, temporarily move home, move to a new city, quit getting facials, study a lot, make a nonlateral move (such as going from being an executive in one field to being an assistant in another), cancel a trip to Europe..." You get the idea. It is also a good idea to talk to people who have made career changes and ask them what they had to do. Of course, you cannot anticipate everything, but do your best.

Part 3: Pondering the Results of Risk

The final part of this exercise is intended simply to help you hypothesize about your future. Answer the following questions:

1. What is the worst thing that could happen if I quit my job and/or pursued something new?

2. What is the best thing that could happen if I quit my job and/or pursued something new?

Now that you have completed this exercise and are aware of the risks (and rewards) ahead, it is time to take action. It might seem to be intimidating, scary, or too much work, but consider your other option: staying on a path that does not align with your purpose or afford you a satisfying quality of life.

———✦———

Adjustments and Sacrifices

Getting what we want takes realistic planning, commitment, and honesty with ourselves about what will be involved. There will be bumps and rough times. It is important to note here that some sacrifice might be necessary along a career path, as long as it is temporary and an investment in a future desired result. If we decide we want to be doctors, we will have to deal with years of little sleep or money. If we want to be actresses, we might need to wait tables and deal with consistent rejection. Our quality of life could suffer while we pursue what we want, so we need to be clear about whether it's worth it. We have to be willing to stretch beyond our comfort zones, but not so far that we snap.

> "Get your dreams on paper, in words or pictures, and just go for it. Someone once said to me: Aim for the sun, and if you fall among the stars, so what?"
>
> — Madge, fifty-one

Grace, the nonprofit worker turned wedding planner, admits that working at the stationery store has been very humbling for her. She is used to being a professional, not a service employee who answers to a twenty-seven-year-old boss. The hours are long, and she is often bored, but she knows it is temporary. She is simply adjusting her quality of life. On the other hand, Hannah, the film industry assistant, continues to suffer through a job that is downright abusive. "I have been working so intensely that I think I will be viewed as a failure if I walk away... so I put my head down and try." Hannah's internal struggle has given her an ulcer. She is sacrificing her physical and emotional well-being for an industry she does not even want to work in.

Those of us who have always known what we want to do might have trouble with the *how*. Nicolette, twenty-seven, has always known she wants to be a writer. She is extremely devoted to what she calls her passion, but she has been unable to make a living at it. "I feel like one of those hamsters on a wheel in a cage — exerting all the effort but getting nowhere. To feel like you have every talent and have paid your dues and you still cannot break in is maddening. I keep the vigil of hope that this year will be my year, but doubts seep in every so often and I wonder, 'What if it never is?' But, having chosen this career, I also have the advantage that no one can take the process away from me."

Many can relate to Nicolette's struggle, especially those pursuing creative passions, such as acting, writing, entrepreneurial endeavors, music, and art, in which results depend on subjective opinions and, quite frankly, luck. There is no direct path toward success, and we ask ourselves, "Am I really good enough at this, or is it just a fantasy?" The *how* of pursuing what we feel to be our purpose involves necessary sacrifices and ultimately feeling okay with what we give up for the result we want. Nicolette, a Berkeley honors grad, "sucked it up" and went to work at Starbucks so she could have flexible hours and a steady paycheck and remain focused enough to write. The pursuit of our purpose takes compromise and commitment.

A lot of us think we have a passion about something but,

when it comes down to it, are unwilling to make the necessary sacrifices to do it. Toni, twenty-seven, graduated with a photojournalism degree and says that photography is what she is meant to do. When she moved to Atlanta, she was unsuccessful at finding a job in the photography business, so she started working for a title company. "My job is really stressful, and I don't really like the people I work with. I want to be doing photography, but I need to pay my bills." I asked Toni when she practiced her art, and she said, "I do not have time — I have not picked up my camera in months. A friend knew a photographer who needed some free help with weekend weddings, but I need my weekends to relax and see my friends." Maybe Toni is not as passionate about photography as she thinks. If she were, she would jump at the chance to get some experience under her belt rather than make excuses to avoid it. If we are truly passionate about something, we look forward to doing it and are willing to not only adjust, but often to sacrifice.

At twenty-seven, Savoy finally had enough of her career in sales and pursued a career as a yoga teacher. She always thought her true passion was in health and spirituality and could not wait to leave the deadline-driven, rigid, unevolved world of business. "I had a rude awakening when, six months into my new career, I found that I did not love what I was doing. I thought I would be able to sacrifice the constant stimulation of the corporate world, but it turned out I was quite bored teaching yoga every day. I am beginning to realize that maybe yoga was just a hobby of mine, rather than something I should be doing as a career. Sure, I am less stressed, but I still feel lost." If we are pursuing or getting ready to pursue a so-called passion, we had better be sure we are 100 percent aware of and committed to the sacrifices it will take. Just as in relationships, often what we think we want is not really what we want at all.

EXERCISE 67

What Adjustments and Sacrifices Will You Make?

Checking in with ourselves to see if we are acting in ways that are harmful or helpful to our overall QOL is an important life skill. In chapter 7, you made a list of what you consider to be adjustments and sacrifices in a relationship. Now do the same thing in terms of a career. For instance, spending an extra hour on your commute might be something you could adjust to; however, earning minimum wage might not be a sacrifice you want to make. Write the following column headings in your journal, and complete the statements:

Adjustments: Sacrifices:
"I am willing to…"   "I am not willing to…"

Upping Your QOL without Quitting Your Job

Some of us who are not ready to make a career change still feel that our jobs are affecting our overall quality of life. It is possible to get a quality-of-life pickup without resigning. Michelle, twenty-seven, is a FedEx employee who was feeling rather bored with her career. "I have never really been one of those people with huge career ambitions. A decent salary and a good working environment are the most important things to me. When I started to get kind of down, someone suggested I needed a job I was more 'passionate' about, but I could not really think of anything else I wanted to do. Plus, my job was pretty good."

Michelle started to think about what she had always loved in life, and immediately "playing the piano" popped into her head.

She saved her money, bought a piano, and looks forward to coming home and playing it every day. Having music in her life made her a happier person all around, and she became more pleasant at work. She even started teaching little kids piano on the weekends just for fun (she puts no pressure on herself to make money as a musician). Although Michelle does not feel passionate about her job, she is glad she did not quit. It affords her great benefits, decent pay, nice people, and the freedom to play piano. Michelle allows her passion to be pure pleasure, which has upped her overall quality of life.

As discussed earlier in this chapter, our purpose (or passion, if you want to call it that) can actually just be a hobby; it does not have to be a career. The answer to a twenty-something crisis is not always a job change. We can do many things to improve our situation. We can find hobbies that bring more joy to our lives; we can stand up for ourselves and demand to be treated with respect in our workplaces; we can approach our bosses about more money, fewer hours, or increased benefits. And, most of all, because our thoughts have a tremendous impact on our quality of life, we can change our attitude and realize that work is work!

EXERCISE 68

QOL "Uppers"

If you feel that you are in a vocational rut, brainstorm ways to raise your quality-of-life quotient. List things you can do right now that will bring you more joy, excitement, and contentment and improve your overall well-being. If we are happier internally, we will carry that happiness into our workplaces.

Speed Bumps and Roadblocks

Our twenties are indeed the time to pursue our dreams without compromising our sanity, credit rating, or quality of life. On the road to getting what we want, we will encounter many roadblocks and speed bumps, which crop up any time we follow a dream. Our old friend expectation tends to lurk behind a lot of our working woes. If we expect our job to fulfill us, if we expect to not have to work that hard, if we expect our dream jobs to just fall into our lap, if we expect others to treat us a certain way in our workplaces, we will constantly have expectation hangovers. As a generalization, women invest more emotion in our jobs than men do. A man's expectations of his job are often more realistic. Men perceive work as a means to an end, while many women, by contrast, want a job to yield "warm fuzzies." If we expect to jump out of our beds every morning bursting with excitement about going to work, we are kidding ourselves. Sure, some people look forward to work every morning, but not everyone, and not every day.

Our judgments and fears are another speed bump that slows our pursuit of what we really want. Becca, twenty-eight, says, "I have always wanted to be a nurse, but I feel like it would be a waste of my undergraduate years." Charly, twenty-nine, always wanted to be an actress, but she never pursued it because she thought she was not beautiful enough. "It was and still is my first love, but I took the 'safe' route and got a real job instead. I feel like acting would have been silly or not responsible enough for a smart but not pretty girl like me to do." Molly, twenty-six, has been working at an advertising firm for a year and is too intimidated to speak up or ask questions. "It is totally a boys' club, and I am afraid I will be perceived as the dumb, emotional girl if I say what is really on my mind." Saharah, twenty-seven, wants to quit her intense job at an investment firm and just work in retail until she gets pregnant. "I don't want and don't need to work, but I am scared to give up my prestigious job because people will treat me differently if I am just a 'housewife.'"

If we are authentically clear about what we want, and it is only our judgments and fears that stop us, we might someday look back and think, "I wonder if...?" Our twenties are quite possibly the only time we can do the things that we are curious about. It is also the time when we have to get in the habit of conquering our fears and insecurities in the workplace. Sometimes risking feeling stupid is often the smartest thing we can do. As long as the risks do not overshadow the potential rewards, we should listen to our inner desires and allow them to have a voice.

In pursuit of our purpose, we might also find excellent opportunities to practice getting around the roadblocks of life. We might get laid off, we might need to move home, or we might need to take a job we do not like just to support ourselves. Yet if we come upon one of these roadblocks unprepared, we might get derailed. Lila, twenty-six, quit her job in PR to pursue her dream of being a designer. Two years ago, her parents let her move home to save money. "Since I've lived at home, I have regressed — I completely reverted to my high school ways. I gained ten pounds, got lazy, and became too dependent on my parents. Now I know I need to get out, but I am so depressed that it is hard to motivate myself."

Lila's case is an example of a derailment that has become a train wreck. Although moving home can be a helpful and smart choice during a period of transition, it can also become a crutch. Other crutches include remaining financially dependent on our parents, sticking with jobs just because they are easy and we are too lazy to look for new ones, allowing boyfriends to support us, and letting ourselves forget about our own ambitions and sense of responsibility. Furthermore, if we do let a career speed bump or roadblock diminish our positive self-image, we might get permanently off track. If our confidence suffers, we cannot really expect to be very hirable or productive. A positive way to get beyond the bumps and blocks in our career path is to visualize the road ahead.

EXERCISE 69

Road-Mapping Your Career Path

Since I love to eat, let's return to the analogy of determining your career path being like choosing a meal. Well, this exercise is your dessert. You have acknowledged your inner cravings, evaluated what is in your best interest, and brainstormed ways to prepare. Now it is time to indulge. In exercise 64, you made your way backward along your job timeline, and in exercise 65 you created your skills and dreams lists. Now you can bring together all the information you have gathered about your career path by road-mapping your career path for the future.

Draw another timeline on a fresh blank sheet of paper. Grab some crayons, colored paper, and maybe even stickers — use your creativity to make a timeline that is appealing to both your mind and your senses. At the very end of the timeline, draw a circle, and within it write your ultimate dream job: the one that is most grounded in reality, based on the information you have gathered about your skills, desires, experiences, and perhaps purpose in life. Don't underestimate yourself by picking the "safe" dream job (this is dessert — you get to treat yourself). Working backward or forward, write down all the things along your path you think must happen to get you there.

After road-mapping your career path, do you find that tasks look a lot less overwhelming and more possible when clearly plotted out? With a clear picture of the actions we need to take along our career path, movement seems less overwhelming. As we move along our path, we keep the ultimate goal in mind but do not become attached to it. Instead, we follow the flow and deal with roadblocks and speed bumps as they emerge. Step by step, we move along our path, always open to change and new direction. Even though we might begin a meal thinking we want the crème brûlée, we might see an incredible chocolate soufflé and decide to choose it instead.

We answer the questions "Who am I, what do I want, and how do I get what I want?" throughout our careers and our lives. Loving ourselves through this process and maintaining our quality of life are critical to our foundation. We might not always do or get what we want, but we cannot let that affect our sense of self. Our road will always look different than someone else's, so we cannot set a standard that is based on factors beyond our own skills and experience. Along our career paths, we might ruffle feathers and make mistakes. This is not easy to always accept, as our egos and pride are often fragile.

Our generation is often guilty of a sense of entitlement. We want the easy road to the dream job and forget that we have to work to get it. But we *are* entitled to a positive vision of success, whatever our personal definition of success might be. We can create that vision and hold it in our heads every day while still having full permission to amend it as we want. Our career choices are not engraved in stone, and our answers to the twenties-triangle questions will evolve over time. If we reassess rather than obsess, we just might discover our purpose.

CONCLUSION

TWENTY-SOMETHING CAN BE EVERYTHING

Each of us has felt pressured to make our twenty-something years our twenty-everything years. We all have moments when we struggle with the questions "Who am I, what do I want, and how do I get what I want?" If a twenty-something crisis is going to happen to you, it will. There is no way to avoid it. We simply have to go through it; the more we try to go around, over, or beneath it, the more persistent it will become. But you know what? It's worth it! A crisis can be one of the most enlightening periods of our lives. It is a time when we can roll up our sleeves and really investigate the questions of the twenties triangle. A twenty-something crisis can make us more certain than we dreamed possible of who we are, what we want, and how to get it.

My own crisis first hit my career, then my sense of identity, then my finances, then my body image, then my health, then my family, and finally my romantic relationship. And it took *all* of that to finally wake me up. Needless to say, I was resistant. But the universe has a funny way of putting things in our lives for a reason.

Right in the middle of my twenty-something crisis: boom! I got a book deal. I had no choice but to continue to examine the topic of quarter-life issues (including my own) under a microscope. Now here I am, exactly one year later, and the only thing that remains the same in my life is the laptop I am writing on. Everything else has changed — most of all me.

Discovering and pursuing what I feel to be my purpose in life became possible when I finally got passionate about *me*. Meeting the man of my dreams and falling in love were effortless after I had become my own soul mate. For years I had searched for fulfillment but instead encountered all kinds of obstacles that blocked the easy flow of my life — and the biggest one was myself. As soon as I began to clear my foundation and get to the root of my own twenties triangle, I was able to remove those obstacles, stop squeezing myself into situations that did not feel right, and learn how to let go. Now that my crisis is over, I feel more connected, balanced, and directed than I have ever felt before. I love my boyfriend, my job, my clients, and my amazingly supportive family and friends — I love my life.

I was inspired to write this book because I wanted other women to love their lives as well. Through sharing my own experiences and those of other women, I have tried to support you in becoming a twenty-something crisis survivor and in viewing your journey with as much gratitude as I have mine. I hope that the exercises in this book have helped you to build a deeper and more loving understanding of yourself. Do not worry if you spend years feeling that you are in a crisis; there is a lot to learn. The only thing that can stop you from loving your life is yourself.

If you have already gotten in your own way, give yourself a break. It takes courage to look deep within ourselves and break down and reconstruct the foundations we have stood on for decades. We tend to become immersed in the areas in our lives that work and to ignore the areas that do not. We become addicted to the parts of our lives that feel good; we would rather not go to the unknown frontier where we might find answers to the questions that linger in the backs of our minds. Feeling uncomfortable is lonely, but we must be willing to let go of things that do not work and to face ourselves in scary, lonely places. And in truth, we are never really alone. We always have ourselves.

Sometimes we allow a sense of entitlement to become a rock in the stream of our lives. We want things to come to us, or we want others to change, but that approach doesn't allow for self-growth. Apathy, too, can be an obstacle, and it's often caused by being too focused on ourselves. (Millions of us are not even registered to vote, which is a terrible disgrace to the women who made it pos-sible for us.) Self-improvement is fabulous, and I honor you for doing the work in this book, but we also need to care about something bigger than ourselves. Drama and self-indulgence cannot be our extracurricular activities during our quarter-life years.

We women are radiant, intuitive, strong, and capable of doing whatever we set our minds to. We are a powerful force to be reckoned with. Getting too wrapped up in the angst of our lives keeps us from claiming that power. We have to face our lives and be willing to take risks. It's like bungee jumping into life. There is no guarantee that we won't get hurt, but we make sure the safety harness is secure and we take the plunge. After all, there are no real guarantees in life other than death and taxes, so we might as well go after the truth of who we are, what we want, and how we are going to get it.

Finally, I want to share with you this very simple advice: Follow your joy. Life, even during the darkest hours of a twenty-something crisis, always contains room for joy. Just smile, and you'll immediately feel that joy.

RESOURCES

This section lists references and other resources that I accumulated in my own journey and that other women suggested to me. I also invite you to visit my website, www.twentysomethingwoman.com, and subscribe to my monthly newsletter. I welcome your feedback, and please tell me about other resources that you have found helpful in your life.

TWENTIES-TRIANGLE QUESTIONS

The following resources may help you answer the essential questions "Who am I? What do I want? And how do I get it?"

The Artist's Way: A Spiritual Path to Higher Creativity, by Julia Cameron (New York: Penguin Putnam, 1992): A twelve-week program and workbook that can help you tap into your inner "artist."

The Four Agreements: A Practical Guide to Personal Freedom (San Rafael, CA: Amber-Allen, 1997) and *The Mastery of Love: A Practical Guide to the Art of Relationships* (San Rafael, CA: Amber-Allen, 1999), both by Don Miguel Ruiz: These two books, based on ancient Toltec wisdom on how to live and create a fulfilling life and relationships, are good references whenever you feel down or confused.

Living in the Light: A Guide to Personal and Planetary Transformation (Novato, CA: New World Library, 1992), *Living in the Light Workbook* (Novato, CA: New World Library, 1998), and *Creative Visualization* (Novato, CA: New World Library, 2002), all by Shakti Gawain and Laurel King: These are powerful guides and offer advice on getting what you want in every area of your life.

The Power of Now, by Eckhart Tolle (Novato, CA: New World Library, 1999): Mandatory reading for anyone who has trouble staying in the present, who practices "when/then" and "if/then" thinking, or is concerned about the future.

The Princessa: Machiavelli for Women, by Harriet Rubin (New York: Doubleday, 1997): Celebrates the idea that men and women are not equal, and teaches you how to be a strong woman and get what you want while maintaining your femininity and utilizing your intuition and intelligence.

When Things Fall Apart: Heart Advice for Difficult Times, by Pema Chodron (Boston: Shambhala, 1997): On how to find happiness even in the most difficult of times.

Women Who Run with the Wolves, by Clarissa Pinkola Estés, PhD (New York: Ballantine Books, 1992): Discover how to tap into your intuitive and instinctive abilities, cultivate your passion, and celebrate being a woman.

A SECURE FOUNDATION

Independence and Support

The Celestine Prophecy, by James Redfield (New York: Warner Books, 1993): A story of a spiritual journey that helps to explain why we are where we are in life and shows what we have the power to manifest in our lives.

Conversations with God, by Neale Donald Walsch (New York: Penguin Putnam, 1995): Takes a practical approach to spirituality; in this book, a man has a conversation with God and asks many of the questions that seekers face. This is a book for everyone who wants to know more about God, whatever "God" means to them — it does not subscribe to any specific religion.

The Way of the Peaceful Warrior, by Dan Millman (Novato, CA: New World Library, 1980): A journey of self-discovery for all who read it; it's a true eye-opener to your inner power.

Self-Image and Body Image

Women's Bodies, Women's Wisdom, by Dr. Christiane Northrup (New York: Bantam Books, 1994): A groundbreaking book from a very forward-thinking holistic gynecologist that examines women's emotional and physical well-being.

www.4woman.gov/bodyimage/ed.cfm: An informational website devoted to education and support related to eating disorders and body image issues of women. The site even offers information on plastic surgery and healthy eating.

www.guidestar.org/: This national guide to nonprofit organizations will help you get involved in activities that nourish your sense of self.

www.nationaleatingdisorders.org/: The website of the National Eating Disorders Association (NEDA): A nonprofit organization dedicated to expanding public understanding of eating disorders and promoting access to quality treatment for those affected along with support for their families through education, advocacy, and research. Also provides information regarding local events that women can participate in.

Finances and Money Management

Get a Financial Life: Personal Finances in Your Twenties and Thirties, by Beth Kobliner (New York: Fireside, 1996): This great overall guide to getting your financial life in order, even if you don't know where to begin, contains practical advice on how to get out of debt, start saving, and begin investing.

Nine Steps to Financial Freedom: Practical and Spiritual Tips So You Can Stop Worrying, by Suze Orman (New York: Crown, 1997): Great financial advice from a woman who makes a lot of sense. Watch for Suze Orman on CNBC, too.

Simple Abundance: A Daybook of Comfort and Joy (New York: Warner, 1995) and its sister books, by Sarah Ban Breathnach: All offer reminders of what is really important and what you already have.

Smart Women Finish Rich: Nine Steps to Achieving Financial Security and Funding Your Dreams, by David Bach (New York: Broadway Books, 1999): Provides an excellent foundation for women who are starting to get their financial lives in order.

www.about.com/money/: An easy-to-navigate site that provides crucial information on two key financial issues among twenty-something women: money management and investing. Also offers a free newsletter.

www.fool.com/: Provides understandable financial tips for anyone looking to learn about the stock and investment markets.

www.msnbc.msn.com/id/3032258/: This is MSNBC's personal finance page. A good site to check out weekly to increase your financial IQ.

www.nfcc.org/: NFCC is the nation's largest and longest-serving national nonprofit credit counseling network. They offer quality credit counseling, debt reduction services, and education for financial wellness.

LOVE AND WORK

Relationships

Bridget Jones's Diary, by Helen Fielding (London: Picador, 1999): All the Bridget books and movies are guaranteed to remind us to accept who we are rather than trying to become someone else.

He's Just Not That into You: The No-Excuses Truth to Understanding Guys, by Greg Behrendt and Liz Tuccillo (New York: Simon Spotlight Entertainment, 2004): This inside look at what men really think helps women to stop wasting their time and energy on dead-end relationships.

If the Buddha Dated: A Handbook for Finding Love on a Spiritual Path, by Charlotte Kasl (New York: Penguin/Arkana, 1999): Shows you how to find a romantic partner without losing yourself.

Single: The Art of Being Satisfied, Fulfilled, and Independent, by Judy Ford (Avon, MA: Adams Media Corporation, 2004): Full of suggestions on how to appreciate and maximize your single life.

Career

Finding Your True Calling: The Handbook for People Who Still Don't Know What They Want to Be When They Grow Up but Can't Wait to Find Out, by Valerie Young (Amherst, MA: Changing Course, 2002): A good resource for those who desire to find their purpose in life and may feel like they are missing out on their true calling.

I Don't Know What I Want, but I Know It's Not This: A Step-by-Step Guide to Finding Gratifying Work, by Julie Jansen (New York: Penguin Books, 2003): Written by a career coach. Uses career assessment quizzes and personality exercises to help readers understand their present work or career situation, discover the type of work for which they're best suited, and learn how to create the changes they need.

The 100 Simple Secrets of Successful People: What Scientists Have Learned and How You Can Use It, by David Niven (San Francisco: HarperSanFrancisco, 2001): Concrete advice about what to do and not to do in the workplace.

INDEX

ABOUT THE AUTHOR

Christine Hassler is originally from Dallas, Texas, and attended Northwestern University, where she studied television and film, communications, and psychology. Immediately after college, Christine moved to Los Angeles to pursue her childhood dream of working in Hollywood.

Drawing upon both her experience and that of others, Christine now works as a dedicated twenty-something coach. From the sidelines, she supports, shares, and offers suggestions to assist her clients in achieving healthy, happy, and balanced lives. Christine is a motivational public speaker and guides seminars on the twenties-triangle, health, manifesting success, and women's issues. She also is proud to serve on the executive board of the Sirens Society (www.sirenssociety.org) as its membership director.

Christine currently resides in Los Angeles. To contact her or to learn more about Christine's personalized coaching sessions along with other services and resources designed to support women, please visit www.twentysomethingwoman.com.